V. T. Barnwell

Barnwell's Atlanta City Directory, and Strangers' Guide

Also, a general firemen's, church, masonic, and Odd-fellows' record; volume I,

compiled (principally in January) for the year 1867

V. T. Barnwell

Barnwell's Atlanta City Directory, and Strangers' Guide
Also, a general firemen's, church, masonic, and Odd-fellows' record; volume I, compiled (principally in January) for the year 1867

ISBN/EAN: 9783337255053

Printed in Europe, USA, Canada, Australia, Japan

Cover: Foto ©Lupo / pixelio.de

More available books at **www.hansebooks.com**

BARNWELL'S

ATLANTA CITY DIRECTORY,

AND

STRANGERS' GUIDE:

ALSO, A GENERAL FIREMEN'S,

CHURCH, MASONIC, AND ODD-FELLOWS' RECORD.

VOLUME I.

Compiled (Principally in January) for the Year 1867.

BY V. T. BARNWELL.

ATLANTA:
INTELLIGENCER BOOK AND JOB OFFICE.
1867.

CONTENTS.

CONTENTS.

INDEX TO ADVERTISEMENTS.

PREFACE.

That "to the making of books there is no end," we do not pretend to gainsay. It is a fact too patent to admit of controversy. And that some pecuniary or other advantage is to be derived from the reading of books, however unpretending they may be, (so long as they do not tend to pervert the good morals of the reader) is another fact equally well founded. The historian, the poet, the novelist, the journalist, and all other writers, have each for himself, to maintain, defend, and support his own peculiar vocation. It is the duty of the compiler of a work like this to study, and advance, as far as may be, the interests of his patrons. A reciprocity should, and generally does, exist between the compiler and patrons of a Directory — decided opposition and severe criticism rarely coming from such as have the liberality and public spirit to patronize such an enterprise. We do not complain at the patronage we have thus far received, but feel truly thankful for the liberality manifested towards us, and the promptness with which most of our bills for advertising have been cashed. We are proud to state that in this little volume will be found the advertisements of nearly all the best and most substantial business firms in the city.

Should we meet with like success in the sale of the book, we hope one year from date to present to the citizens of Atlanta a much larger, more accurate, and much more handsome edition. But to accomplish this end, it will require the general and united patronage of the citizens, and especially of the business interests of the city.

We offer as an apology for the many typographical errors and other inaccuracies which may possibly occur in the lists of names, etc., the fact that there exists no general and well understood rule for spelling proper names. We have endeavored, as far as practicable, to give the names of individuals according to their own spelling. As to their place of residence, we have endeavored to locate them at such places as they have anticipated occupying for the year.

For our Street Directory, we have culled information from various sources. Maps, city assessors, original property holders, surveys, etc., have been consulted while compiling this department. A few streets never having been legitimately christened, are known by two or three names each: in such cases we have either given the various names, or made a choice from among them, according to the lights before us. We hope, therefore, it will prove as nearly correct as could reasonably have been expected under the circumstances.

We here present our acknowledgments to the gentlemen having charge of the books, for the names of members, and for other information relative to their respective Churches, Masonic and Odd Fellows' Lodges, and Fire Companies herein represented. Our esteemed friend, the accomplished scholar and gentleman, Prof. H. F. Smith, of Newnan, Ga., author of the "Science of Love in Courtship and Marriage," (an advertisement of which may be found on another page) is also entitled to our gratitude for valuable suggestions made in reference to this work.

Finally, we call attention to our "Index to Advertisements," and cheerfully recommend the gentlemen whose names appear therein, as energetic, enterprizing, liberal, and public spirited citizens. We bespeak for them the patronage of a discerning public. May their manly efforts to re-build, and make of Atlanta a great city, be crowned with unbounded success; and may they, themselves, live to reap the greatest reward for their labors.

THE COMPILER.

ATLANTA CITY DIRECTORY,

AND

GENERAL RECORD.

KEY TO ABBREVIATIONS.

Agt, agent.
al, alley
arch, architect.
asst, assistant.
atty, attorney.
auct, auctioneer.
b, between.
bar k, bar keeper.
bdg h, boarding house
bds, boards.
bk, book, or brick.
b k, book keeper.
bk m, brick mason.
bkr, broker.
bk slr, book seller.
bldg, building.
bldr, builder.
blk s, blacksmith.
c, or cor, corner.
cab mkr, cabinet maker.
carp, carpenter.
car mkr, carriage maker.
clk, clerk.
com, commission, or commercial.
cond, conductor.
conf, confectioner.
cont, contractor.
dlr, dealer
e, east.

emp, employee.
eng, engineer.
e s, east side.
ex, exchange, or express.
fam gro, family grocer.
ft, freight.
frmn, foreman, or fireman.
fur, furniture.
gdr, gardener.
gro, grocer.
h, house.
insp, inspector.
jn, or junc, junction.
jr, junior
lab, laborer.
m, master, or mason.
mach, machinist.
manuf, manufacturer.
mer, merchant.
mil, milliner, or millinery.
min, mining.
mkr, maker.
mldr, moulder.
n, north.
n e, north-east.
n e c, north-east corner.
n s, north side.

n w, north-west.
n w c, north-west corner.
opp, opposite.
opr, operator.
pat mkr, pattern maker.
pdlr, peddler.
phys, physician.
pro, proprietor.
prov, provision.
ptr, painter, or printer
pub, publisher.
res, residence.
s, south.
s e, south-east.
s e c, south-east corner.
s s, south side.
supt, superintendent.
supv, supervisor.
s w, south-west.
s w c, south-west corner.
tchr, teacher.
telgh opr, telegraph operator.
tr, transfer, or transportation.
undkr, undertaker.
uphol, upholsterer.
yd m, yard master.

STATISTICS.

A Summary Statement of the Census of Atlanta, Ga., taken, under direction of the City Council, in the months of December and January, 1866–'67.

	White Males over 12 years old.	White Males under 12 years old.	White Females over 12 years old.	White Females under 12 years old.	TOTAL WHITES.	Widows of Confederate Soldiers.	Widows other than of Conf. Soldiers.	Orphans of Confederate Soldiers.	Orphans other than of Conf. Soldiers.	Colored Males over 12 years old.	Colored Males under 12 years old.	Col'd Females over 12 years old.	Col'd Females under 12 years old.	TOTAL COLORED.	AGGREGATE.
First Ward.	1084	490	1977	519	3170	42	71	80	92	463	278	601	325	1667	4837
Second Ward.	641	221	463	234	1559	14	24	19	23	363	178	436	213	1190	2749
Third Ward.	358	178	409	205	1150	14	28	29	20	229	165	308	184	886	2036
Fourth Ward.	708	422	757	439	2326	28	45	58	53	764	631	979	689	3063	5389
Fifth Ward.	895	499	857	484	2735	57	60	108	63	623	514	800	545	2482	5217
Total.	3686	1810	3563	1881	10940	155	228	294	251	2442	1766	3124	1956	9288	20288

CONDENSED HISTORY OF ATLANTA.

In presenting to the patrons of this book a chain of historical facts, relative to Atlanta, we cannot conceive a plan we think would meet with more general favor, than that of giving the "Sketch of Atlanta," written for "Williams' Atlanta Directory," for 1859 and 1860, by her highly esteemed citizen, Col. G. B. Haygood, deceased, as the history alluded to, prior to that date, The eloquence, the brevity, the accuracy, and other features displayed therein, commend it as the *desideratum*. Were we the most eminent writer, we should scarcely attempt an improvement. We only regret that Col. Haygood has not survived the years of calamity through which our city has passed since that time, and that a pen so feeble must continue a history so ably began.

In our remarks, which follow the "Sketch," it has been our utmost ambition to deal out truth, without favor or partiality, giving such items as, in our judgment, should be remembered by our citizens, not that we would stimulate or perpetuate feelings of animosity between individuals or sections but that the facts may be culled and weighed in a sober moment—the good emulated, and the like evil avoided in the future.

The following is the "Sketch" above mentioned:

SKETCH OF ATLANTA.

" Atlanta is situated seven miles east south-east ofthe Chattahoochee River, on the dividing ridge between the waters of the Atlantic and the Gulf of Mexico ; on the 34th parallel of north latitude, at an elevation of one thousand and fifty feet above the level of the sea.

" The Ocmulgee River, which flows to the Atlantic, has its source in the central part of the city. The head spring of South River, its principal tributary, being located within the Railroad Reserve, near the present Passenger Depot, its precise spot being now indicated by the large perennial cistern, between the Holland House and the Macon and Western Depot, on the south side of the railroad track; while Walton Spring, an early celebrity of the place, situated a little north of the road, flows into the Chattahoochee, and thence to the Gulf of Mexico; so that here in the heart of the city, the marriage of the waters of the Atlantic and the Gulf might have been celebrated high in air, by our own engine companies, drawing their supplies the while, from the natural fountains, flowing thence to their far distant destinations in the bosom of the Atlantic and the Gulf. But Charleston must needs go to Memphis, that old Ocean, pent up in hoops and staves, may be received into the embraces of his Amazon bride, and the "father of waters" is shorn of his glory, and is changed into a huge "water station" on the road to the West.

"On the 21st of December, 1836, the Legislature of Georgia passed an Act authorizing the construction of a railroad communication by the State, from some point on the Tennessee line, subsequently extended to the Tennessee River, to some point on the south-eastern bank of the Chattahoochee River, which should be most eligible for the extension of branches thence to other important points in Georgia.

"The present site of the public depot was located sometime afterwards, by Wilson Lumpkin, Ex-Governor of the State, upon the recommenation of the Chief Engineer, Mr. C. F. M. Garnett. The station was called "Terminus" prior to December 23d, 1843, when the place was incorporated by the name of Marthasville, in compliment to Miss Martha Lumpkin, daughter of His Excellency, Governor Lumpkin, and whom we thus recognise as the early *matronymic* of the thrifty, bustling village, the embryo city. In the short space of four years the village had outgrown the expectations of its early inhabitants, and had become too fast, too gross, too great, and too pretentious to wear any longer, with maidenly modesty, the name of its fair matro-nymic; a change was demanded, and on the 29th of December, 1847, it was incorporated as a city by the name of Atlanta, a name which is understood to have been proposed by J. Edgar Thompson, at that time Chief Engineer of the Georgia Railroad. The signification of the name, the reasons for its adoption, and the various theories on the subject have now become a theme of inquiry and investigation not without interest. The writer has heard it claimed as due in honor to a mythological goddess, Atalanta, said to have been remarkable for fleet, ness, strength and endurance. It was certainly a *fast town* then and may have been supposed entitled to the honor of a recognition by the goddess, by reason of its early character, and its wonderful achievements. The infant has become a giant, and is rapidly overcoming the obstacles to its growth and prosperity, and making the surrounding country, and neighboring villages, all tributary to its prosperity, permanency and celebrity. The name was for a short time written *Atalanta*, which seems to favor the claims of the goddess. An orator of no mean pretentions, claimed for it the signification of "A city among the hills," while a shrewd writer has declared that it was the opposite of "*rus in erbi*," and proclaimed it "the city in the woods." And its commercial and geographical position has recently procured for it the appellation of "The Gate City."

"And still another theory is set up by some who claim for it an origin more worthy of its present importance as a railroad entrepot and commercial emporium, taken in connection with its future prospects as a great railroad centre and manufacturing city. The great State work, connecting the western waters with the Atlantic, commencing at Chattanooga on the Tennessee River, and terminating at this point, had been nearly completed. The name "Western and Atlantic Railroad" had been given to it by the Legislature of Georgia, and it was not inaptly considered the great connecting artery through which must pass the incalculable mass of produce, manufactures, and commerce from the great valley of the West, and the Atlantic coast, and the imports from abroad passing thence to the far West.

"Atlanta had been permanently fixed as the south-eastern terminus of that great State work, and gave a local idea to its eastern terminus, and that idea represented or qualified by the adjective Atlantic, was incomplete of itself, but clearly pointed to something more definite, and the mind is put upon the inquiry for the thing signified. The connections by rail from Charleston by way of Augusta, and from Savannah by way of Macon, had both been completed to this point. These roads had been gradually ascending the hills from the coast, in search of a "north-west passage," they had searched the hills upon which the city stands, and here they met the Western and Atlantic road, just emerging from the wilds of the north-west, seeking by a sinuous and difficult ascent from the Western Valley, for a highway to the Atlantic. They met together in our streets, they embraced each other upon these headlands of the Atlantic.

"These *Atlantic head-lands*, when embodied in the noun *Atlanta*, to our mind, meets the demand, and represents the ideal of the thing sought after, and the mind rests upon it as the thing signified by the several *indices* pointing to *Atlanta* as the proper name for such a city, in such a place. This we now state to the public as the true derivation, sustained by the facts in the case.

"Atlanta has had a growth unexampled in the history of the South. In 1854, the population had reached 6,025. The increase for several years has averaged 1,000 per annum. On the first of

April, 1859, it is ascertained by the census taken under the State authority, to be 11,500 souls.

" The assessed value of the real estate in the city the present year, 1859, is $2,760,000, and the personality, cash, merchandise, etc., in proportion.

" The number of stores in 1854, was 57, exclusive of drinking saloons. The amount of goods sold in 1853, was $1,017,000, and amount sold in 1858 is not known with accuracy, but is believed to have been about $3,000,000, and is now rapidly increasing. It is now widening and extending the area of its supply on every side. Dry goods are sold to the country for over one hundred miles around, on terms as favorable to purchasers as the retail markets of the great northern cities, New York itself not excepted, and still our merchants are prosperous, thrifty and energetic. No respectable house here had to suspend during the severe crisis in commercial affairs in 1857 and 1858.

" The great secret of the safety, success, and independence of convulsions, is to be found in the fact that sales are made at low rates, almost entirely for cash, and the profits, though small in detail, are often repeated, and amount to a vast sum in the aggregate : a few have fallen by unfortunate speculations.

" The number of stores and other business houses at present is unknown to the writer. Nineteen commodious brick stores were erected in 1858, and as many more are now in progress of erection in 1859, besides a large number of fine dwellings, mostly of brick ; many of the new improvements are imposing structures, and would be creditable in the elegant portions of any of our modern cities.

" There are at present four capacious hotels, now open, and in successful operation, and another still more extensive, is nearly completed, designed, we understand, chiefly for the accommodation of families, hitherto a felt necessity in the city.

" The city now has in successful operation *four* large and flourishing machine shops, two of these are connected with railroad companies, and two belong to private companies, where stationary engines, mill gearing, with almost every variety of castings, and machinery are manufactured at short notice. Two planing mills, and sash and blind factories are also in successful operation, besides there are various smaller manufacturing establishments in the city ; three or four tanneries, one or two shoe manufactories, besides several smaller establishments. The most important establishment in the place is the rolling mill, for the manufacture of railroad iron, which is capable of turning out thirty tons of railroad iron of superior quality.

" The clothing trade has become an item of no inconsiderable importance within the last few years, and presents some new features when contrasted with any other southern cities of equal size and age. The manufacture of clothing in this city is a decided success, and has increased with an unparalleled rapidity for a southern city. In 1854 five hands were employed in the manufacture of clothing, the number now thus employed exceeds seventy-five, the larger portion of whom are females. The clothing made here has been received with favor by the public, and is believed to have attracted much attention to the wholesale trade of the city in that article. In this connection, it may be stated that this is the great southern depot for the sale of the most approved models of sewing machines, the use of which, extensively, has doubtless added greatly to the trade in the clothing department.

"The city was first brilliantly lighted with gas, manufactured from Georgia, Alabama, and Tennessee coal, on the 25th of December, 1855.

"The incorporated shape of the city is a circle two miles in diameter, with a handle of half a mile in length, and six hundred yards wide along the line of the Macon and Western Railroad. It covers a portion of sixteen original land lots, each of which was laid off upon a plan to suit the views of the respective owners, and hence our streets are not all so regular in width and uniform in direction as is desirable—many of them being much too narrow for public convenience.

"The City Hall and County Court House is a convenient, commodious, and handsome structure, erected in 1854 and 1855, at a cost of a little over $30,000. It is 70 by 100 feet in size, two stories high, of fine architectural proportion and design, well adapted to the uses intended, is elegantly finished throughout, surmounted by an imposing dome, and is alike creditable to the city and the artist.

"The Medical College is now in its fifth course of lectures, all delivered in the summer, with a larger class than any former one—numbering one hundred and fifty-six students: has had its day of probation, trial and difficulties; but it is now a decided success, and its enemies and rivals have almost ceased to persecute it. It has an able and efficient faculty, and a very complete chemical aparatus, and is collecting a very respectable museum.

"The geographical position of Atlanta being nearly in the centre of the southern section of the American Union, at the point of the great railroad crossings in a right line from New York to New Orleans, and nearly equi-distant from each; four prominent lines of railroad all centering here, and pouring into the depots and warehouses of the city an amount of trade, and transporting throughit a vast tide of travel: situated, too, just upon the dividing line between the cotton and grain sections of the State, altogether, give to Atlanta facilities for receiving and distributing the productions and the commerce of the country from one section to another, greater than can be claimed for any other inland city in the South. Atlanta is now connected by rail with Chattanooga, Nashville, Memphis, and thence with the Upper Mississippi, also, with London and Knoxville, Tennessee; Lynchburg, Virginia; and thence with the great lines North and east; on the south-west with Montgomery by rail, thence by water with Mobile, New Orleans, and all the Lower Mississippi; also with Columbus and all south-western Georgia, and Savannah, and the Atlantic, through Macon. By the Georgia Railroad with Augusta, Charleston, Columbia, Greenville, most of the prominent places in North and South Carolina, Virginia, and the great Northern cities. Another Railroad is now in projection. and considerable progress made towards its accomplishment, in the direction of Anderson Court House, South Carolina, through the beautiful and productive territory, known as Northeast Georgia; and another, still, has been chartered from this point to the great and inexhaustible coal fields of North-eastern Alabama, destined to supply fuel and motive power to the teaming millions that shall inhabit these lands for untold ages. Forty-four freight and passenger trains arrive and depart daily from the city.

"The city now contains thirteen Christian churches; and one more has been recently projected.

"It is not believed that any other city in the country is blessed with greater or better facilities for procuring building materials, the supply of granite near at hand, of a quality peculiarly adapted to building purposes, is literally inexhaustible; bricks of good quality are made in and around the city on reasonable terms. Lumber of good quality is also obtained at reasonable prices; lime is produced in any desirable quantity near at hand.

"The population of the city is remarkable for its activity and enterprise. Most of the inhabitants came here for the purpose of bettering their fortunes by engaging actively in some kind of business, and this presents the anomaly of having very few aged persons residing in it; and our people show their democratic impulses by each allowing his neighbor to attend to his own business, and our ladies even are allowed to attend to their own domestic and household affairs without being ruled out of respectable society.

"The mechanical element prevails in our city, and the major part of them are enterprising, thrifty and prosperous men, who are rapidly rising in the public esteem.

"The health of the city is almost unprecedented, being entirely exempt from the usual summer and fall fevers, cholera, &c. No epidemic has ever prevailed here, and the bills of mortality show a state of health almost without a parallel.

"The city is chiefly supplied with the very best free stone water, from wells usually from thirty to forty feet deep, though a very great number of excellent springs are found within the city limits. Among these we may not omit to mention the Chalybiate Spring in the western part of the city, which has within a few years attracted the public attention, and now forms one of the inducements for the sojourn in our city of those in search of health.

" The public spirit of some of our citizens has recently projected considerable improvements at this point, whereby its attractions are greatly increased, and it is rapidly becoming a place of public resort. All things considered, we may safely assert the prophecy of that far-seeing statesman, John C. Calhoun, is in process of rapid fulfillment, who predicted, while passing through the place in 1847, that it was destined ultimately to become the largest inland city of the South.

" This hasty sketch has been prepared under very unfavorable circumstances, in the midst of severe family afflictions, and other pressing engagements, and will doubtless be found defective in many particulars, but it was called for in haste, and is given to the public, without further apology for what it is worth.   G. B. H."

It will be seen from the foregoing, that Atlanta has, in the way of improvement, far exceeded the expectations of the most sanguine of its early settlers. In 1843 it was incorporated merely as a village, and in 1847, a lapse of only four years time, it had grown to such an extent as to demand the charter of a city. By the year 1859, twelve years more, she had attained a population of 12,000 ; presenting to the world a scene of unparalleled energy, enterprise, and prosperity. The real estate in the city, as assessed in 1859, amounted to nearly $3,000,000 ; personal property, cash, and other items of value in proportion : including almost every article of wealth known to the world. From the little " Village in the Woods," of a sparce population, supplied with provisions mainly from the countryman's cart, and clothed in the handiwork of our own noble women, Atlanta gradually, but rapidly, sprang up, until in 1860 to 1862, the minor means of transportation had been nearly supplanted by the huge "Iron Horse," bringing inexhaustible supplies of provisions, &c., from more fertile regions, and our fair ladies relieved of the arduous task of manufacturing their own fabrics, by the importation, directly or indirectly, of dry goods, and the various articles of wear, from almost every market in the world.

" But riches make to themselves wings and fly away." Prosperity is alike uncertain to countries, kingdoms, cities, and individuals ; and Atlanta has not proved herself an exception to this general rule. From 1862, with no other apparent reason than the darkening of the political horizon, and the threatening aspect of the clouds of war, improvement in this hitherto enterprising and prosperous city, was considerably checked, except in point of population. About this time, the attention of our best manufacturing establishments was diverted from their legitimate business (that of domestic articles) to the manufacture of the various appliances of war. Would that we could, with propriety, avoid referring to so terrible a calamity. But we must act impartially. We must state the facts, to the best of our knowledge and belief, painting them in no gaudy hues, that each, in its place, may bear the impress of truth.

Atlanta advanced very little, except in population, from 1862 until after its destruction ; but it increased very materially in this respect, reaching, perhaps, 20,000 to 22,000 souls—many of whom were only transient employees and attachees of the Confederate Government, whose business was the manufacture of various articles and implements of war. There were, during the three years, from the commencement of 1862 to the time the city was occupied by the United States Army, manufactured in Atlanta, almost every article known in the annals of American warfare—from field ordnance to a first class revolver. Also, ammunition of every description from the largest shell to percussion caps, balls, &c. Swords, sabres, and in fact, almost every instrument destructive of human life, were made in great variety and abundance. To these manufacturing, war interests, is attributable the large increase of population during the years to which we have above alluded ; and, had not the city been destroyed, there would not have returned to Atlanta, after the surrender of Generals Lee and Johnston, nearly so many as were here prior to the commencement of the siege ; perhaps not more than 18,000 to 20,000. Many good citizens, however, from Tennessee, Kentucky, and other States, have returned, and made Atlanta their permanent home.

This city was kept under strict martial law by the Confederate authorities from April 1862, until occupied by the United States forces.   It was, also, headquarters for Quartermaster and Commissary-stores, hospitals, &c., for the Confederate Army of Tennessee, from March 1862, until they were removed for safety, by order of General Joseph E. Johnston.   During this time, many of the most prominent buildings, public and private, were used —impressed when necessary—for hospitals, Government stores, &c.   Among the buildings thus used, were the Empire House, American Hotel, (then known as Gate City) the Medical College, Female Institute, Kile's Building, Hayden's Hall, and Concert Hall; the Gate City Hotel being latterly used as the Distributing Hospital. There were also established large hospital accommodations at the Fair Ground, and a convalescent camp near Mrs. Ponder's residence, on the W. & A. Railroad.   The Confederate barracks, for this post, was west of Peach-tree street, north of, and not far distant from the Walton Spring.

Atlanta being the great hospital depot for the above mentioned army, during the campaign from Chattanooga to this city, in the Spring and Summer months of 1864, especially, the most intense anxiety and solicitude prevailed among our citizens.   Great numbers of sick and wounded soldiers, daily arriving at the Passenger Depot, were met by the ladies of our first families, with baskets filled with such delicacies, &c., as were most needed by them.   It is estimated that, from time to time, during the war, there were in hospital at this place not less than 80,000 Confederate soldiers, and that of this number about 5,000 died; 4,600 of whom were buried in the City Cemetery.   There were probably 2,500 Federals, also, in hospital at this place, about 150 of whom were buried in the City Cemetery.

Up to this date, the remains of over 1,300 Federal

soldiers, including those buried in the Cemetery, and over 800 from the battle-field of Peachtree Creek, have been exhumed, and removed to the National Cemetery at Marietta, or to their homes.

From the time the contending armies crossed the Chattahoochee river, which was about the 15th of July 1864, a state of panic existed, and the greatest confusion prevailed, until a great many non-combatants had retired from the city. Every available means of conveyance was either impressed by the Confederate authorities, or employed at exhorbitant prices, in removing the effects of such citizens as were able to obtain railroad transportation for the same.

To such as remained, for want of transportion, or for any other reason, until after the bombardment of the city by the United States artillery, had fairly commenced, a scene at once fearful and sublime was presented. Huge bumbs, and smaller shell, presenting, in the darkness of night, the appearance of glaring comets or meteors, flying in every direction, bursting and dealing death and destruction amidst zealous firemen, soldiers, and citizens w'ho were striving to extinguish the fiendish flames of a burning city, and driving, with precipitate movement, our frantic women and children into rude "holes in the ground," hastily prepared for their preservation, is a sketch of the facts—much too feeble and inadequate—of one of a series of evening entertainments given the citzens of Atlanta during the month of August 1864.

Atlanta was bombarded, at intervals, from about the 20th of July 1864, until evacuated by the Confederates. Latteraly, even the women and children became, apparently, regardless of these missiles of death, and children were not debarred of their usual amusements on account of their frequent visits. Comparatively few casualties occurred among the citizens during the contest for Atlanta. Most of the non-combatants were permitted to survive these terrible scenes, and to leave the city before the work of destruction had advanced to its full extent.

During the siege, there were thrown up, by the contending parties, continuous lines of fortifications around the entire city—a distance of at least eight or ten miles—in and near which were fought some of the most sanguinary battles of the war.   In an engagement, near Peachtree Creek, on the 20th of July, the Confederates lost, killed and wounded, not less than 1,500, and the Federals lost, perhaps, as many.   In another battle, extending from the Rolling Mill, on the Georgia Railroad, to Decatur, the Confederates lost about 2,000, and the Federals 3,500.   There were other hotly contested engagements around the city, in which great numbers were killed and wounded on both sides—the final and decisive battles being fought at Jonesboro, August 31st and September 1st, in which the Confederate loss was very heavy, while that of the Federal army was much less. The whole number killed and wounded around Atlanta, from the time the armies crossed the Chattahoochee river until the city was invested by the United States Army, including the Jonesboro battles, is unknown to the writer, but must have been at least 18,000 to 20,000 Confederates, and as many Federals.

How quickly fade from the memory of man impressions made by the contemplation of such a scene! Yet, the citizens of this bustling city, however heedless they may be, sleep nightly in the midst of one vast graveyard.   Friend and foe lie shoulder to shoulder, and will take up arms against each other no more ; but must one day stand together before their Creator. Let us hope they died with such charitable feelings, and with such faith in their Saviour, as shall secure to them the salvation of their immortal spirits.

Before the evacuation of the city by the Confederate General Hood's army, the Rolling Mill, formerly owned by Messrs. Markham & Schofield, on the Georgia Railroad, about one hundred cars, and a great deal of ammunition, and other army supplies, were destroyed, and the railroads torn up to a considerable extent. On the morning,

and until night, of the 1st of September, 1864, Maj.
Gen. Stewart's Corps, Gen. Ferguson's Brigade of Cav-
alry, and the Georgia State Militia, were in the city, and
a corps, under command of Gen. S. D. Lee, came within
six miles of Atlanta, (to Mr. Killis Brown's, on South
river,) in the afternoon. Gen. Slocum's command were at
the Chattahoochee river, eight miles distant. At night,
the Confederate forces were withdrawn from the city,
and the following day, the Hon. J. M. Calhoun, then
Mayor of Atlanta, with a committee of some twelve
citizens, after going more than two miles up the Marietta
road, and first meeting with a Captain Scott, obtained an
interview with Col. John Coburne, of Indianapolis,
Indiana, the substance of which we give below:
· After having been introduced by Capt. Scott, Mayor
Calhoun said : " Col. Coburne, the fortunes of war have
placed Atlanta in your hands. As Mayor of the city, I
come to ask protection for non-combatants and for private property." To this Col. Coburne replied : " We did
not come to make war on non-combatants, nor on private
property : both shall be respected and protected by us."
On this day, also, the command of Gen. Slocum regularly
invested the city, Gen. W. T. Sherman, himself, coming
in September 7th. On the morning of the 3d, the above
remarks, on the part of Mayor Calhoun, were, by
request, reduced to writing, and addressed to Gen. Ward,
instead of Col. Coburne ; but the reply was not reduced
to writing.
  The headquarters of Gen. Sherman was at the residence of Judge R. F. Lyon, corner Mitchell and Washington streets. Gen. Thomas' headquarters was at the
residence of Mr. M. Meyers, on Peachtree street ; Gen.
Geary's at Mr. E. E. Rawson's, on Pryor ; Gen. Stanley's at the residence of Mr. Lewis Scofield, on Peachtree
street ; and Gen. Slocum's at Wm. H. Dabney's, on Washington street. The best store-houses, on the main business streets, the hotels, Medical College, City Hall,
Female Institute, and other houses, were used, in turn,

by the Federal army, as store-houses, hospitals, &c., during their occupancy of the city.

According to orders issued on the subject, soon after the entrance of the United States army into Atlanta, commenced the work of tearing down such houses as were found unoccupied, and not required for hospitals, store-houses, headquarters, or other army purposes, as they stood, and the conversion of the same into small, compact ·cabins—with chimneys and glass windows in many instances—to be used as quarters by the United States soldiery.

About the 10th of September, Gen. Sherman issued an order requiring the evacuation of the city by all citizens, except those who engaged themselves as employees of the United States Government, as mechanics, clerks, watchmen, &c., allowing all to go South who wished to do so, and sending others beyond the Ohio river. This required an armistice of ten days, which was agreed upon by Generals Sherman and Hood. Mr. James M. Ball, and our late lamented fellow-citizen, James R. Crew, acting as a committee, appointed for that purpose by His Honor, Mayor Calhoun, carried the above order, and also a proposition for an armistice, from Gen. Sherman to Gen. Hood, whose headquarters was then one mile below Lovejoy's Station, on the Macon & Western Railroad. It is also due to Mr. Ball, and other gentlemen coöperating, whose names are not known to the writer, as well as to the memory of Mr. Crew, to remark, in this connection, that they rendered assistance eminently valuable to the citizens, in the removal of their effects from the city. Col. LaDuke, Q. M., U. S. Army, from Minnesota, and other officers of the Federal army, rendered every possible assistance. The Federals furnished the citizens transportation to Rough and Ready, on the Macon & Western Railroad, and the Confederates from thence to Macon, and other points. Having only ten days time to complete the evacuation of a city of 20,000 population, and considering the distance, scanty means of transportation, the great excitement and confusion, natural on such an occasion, it is not strange that a great deal of private property, (furniture, &c.,) should be left unprotected. Much of the furniture, according to an arrangement between Gen. Sherman and Mayor Calhoun, was collected and deposited in the Second (Trinity) M. E. Church, and protected by Gen. Sherman, during his occupancy of the city. This Church-full, however, constituted scarcely a tithe of the vast amount of furniture left here by the exiled citizens.

About the 15th of November 1864, Gen. Sherman found it expedient to divide his army, sending a portion of it, under command of Gen. Thomas, up the Western & Atlantic Railroad, and into Tennessee, for the purpose of intercepting and thwarting the designs of Gen. Hood, who had, by this time, instituted a flank movement in that direction, while he, with the remainder of his army, made his way to the sea coast, at Savannah, Georgia.

Before evacuating the Post of Atlanta, it was thought advisable, by officers commanding the United States army, to destroy the city, which was almost completely accomplished. There was scarcely one stone left upon another. Some of the buildings, the Macon & Western Railroad Depot, the Car Shed, or General Passenger Depot, (one of the finest in the United States,) the Georgia Railroad Bank Agency building, the Georgia Railroad Depot and Machine Shop, the Western & Atlantic Railroad Depot and Shops, and other buildings required more powerful agents of destruction than fire, and were either battered down with battering-rams, or blown up with gun-powder. The churches destroyed were Dr. Quintard's Episcopal, corner Bridge and Walton streets; the Protestant Methodist, corner Forsyth and Garnett; Evans Chapel, M. E., on Nelson street; the Christian Church, on Decatur street, and Payne's Chapel, M. E., on Marietta street. The Female College did not escape the flames. All the railroads and shops, and every foundry, machine shop, planing mill, &c., were completely

consumed by fire, or otherwise ingeniously destroyed.
The Atlanta Gas Works, built years ago, at an immense
cost, were also destroyed, as if to make the dismal aspect
more hideous by the darkness of night. In fact, such a
destruction of public and private property has not been
witnessed in any city during the war, except, perhaps,
Columbia, South Carolina.

The Masonic Hall, a fine, three story brick building, on
Decatur street, by the interposition of members of the
fraternity, in the United States army, was preserved.
Several good buildings on Alabama street, east of Pryor,
including the Gate City Hotel, were also saved. To
Maj. Gen. O. O. Howard, is said to be due the preservation of the valuable residences left on Peachtree street.
Through the instrumentality of Father O'Rielly, and
of Gen. Slocum, the Catholic Church, Second Baptist,
Second Methodist, (Trinity,) Second Presbyterian, and
St. Philip's, (Episcopal—much damaged,) together with
the City Hall, and other valuable property in that
vicinity, were preserved. Dr. N. D'Alvigny interceded
for the Medical College, which was, also, spared. Other
persons, not known to the writer, doubtless, saved
valuable property, and should long be remembered as
public benefactors.

By those who returned to Atlanta soon after its destruction, a disgusting and heart-sickening scene was witnessed. Ruin, death, and devastation met the eye on
every hand. The legions of carrion crows and vultures,
whose vocation it might have been to hover over and
pick at the decaying carcasses of animals that lay among
the scarred and broken walls of our ruined city, were
surpassed by the hosts of Georgia's own sons, who might,
otherwise, have been styled our brothers, congregated
here from a distance of fifty miles, in every direction—
not to guard unprotected property—but, many of them,
to steal, and haul away the effects of their absent and
unfortunate countrymen. There were, also, numerous
packs of dogs, that had become wild, on account of the

absence of their masters, attacking citizens, and belching forth their frightful howls, as if to render the scene still more fearful, gloomy, and desolate.

During the months of December and January, after the destruction of the city by the Federals, some of the citizens, who went South, returned home. A few found shelter in their own houses, while the majority of them were compelled to take up their abode in the houses of other parties, or live in tents with their famalies. The destitution consequent upon the scarcity of provisions and fuel, and the utter worthlessness of Confederate currency, during the winter months of 1864 and 1865, produced an amount of suffering beyond the comprehension of most persons who did not witness the facts. For want of teams, some parties were forced to carry their fuel a distance of nearly a mile, and many suffered severely from both hunger and cold. But they managed to survive the winter, and some had, by the spring following, accumulated considerable little stores. On the surrender and parole of Lee's and Johnston's armies, however, as the soldiers were passing through Atlanta, *en route* for their homes, they made free with everything that came in their way, leaving many, again, utterly destitute. So much for war, which, under every circumstance, and for whatever cause, is demoralizing in its tendencies—rendering in some instances, the best men incapable of performing an act of kindness, or even of administering simple justice to his fellow man.

Atlanta, during the year 1865, presented quite a picturesque appearance. There might have been seen small houses, put up in many instances expressly for rent, which presented the appearance of having been built of the remnants of half-a-dozen houses. Calico fences, too, still remain quite fashionable in some localities. But, it is to be hoped that the city will outgrow the effects of the war, and that at an early day her citizens may again become comfortably situated, and that good feelings, and a disposition to encourage and foster each others interests, .

may be cultivated by them. Then may we hope, and expect to see education advanced, fraternity revived, christianity practiced, and society much improved and benefitted.

Atlanta has, already, made rapid strides in the way of improvement. There were licensed by the City Council, during the last six months of the year 1865, about three hundred and thirty-eight business firms, representing various branches of trade—nearly all of whom commenced on very small capital, occupying *shanties* as storehouses. There was very little manufacturing done in Atlanta in 1865. Planing mills, &c., were much needed to assist in the work of rebuilding the city : among the first of such establishments put into operation was that of Hoge, Mills & Co., on Marietta street. Others of a similar character rapidly sprang up The several railroad companies went to work in good earnest, repairing their respective roads, and rebuilding their depots and shops, and at this time, they are all in comparatively good condition. Foundries and machine shops were established ; first-class business houses took the place of the shanty substitutes which had at first been thrown up by the impoverished citizens, and large stocks of goods soon found their way into them.

The city fathers, too, went to work with great energy. Two neat and tastily arranged market houses were soon completed ; the bridge across the Macon & Western and Western & Atlantic Railroads, near the site of the old market house, was rebuilt, and Broad street opened from Alabama to Mitchell, and widened from Alabama to Peachtree street. The City Cemetery received their early attention, and has been re-fenced, enlarged, and otherwise improved. The streets of the city, though filled with huge heaps of rubbish less than two years ago, have been put in a fair condition. The incorporate limits have been extended so as to enclose the area of a circle three miles in diameter, the center of which is still located near the General Passenger Depot. They have also

3

provided a place for the M. & W. R. R. Depot, at the corner of M. & W. Railroad and Mitchell street, for which they have taken in exchange the site on which stood the old Depot, corner Railroad and Whitehall street—making a decided improvement by this transaction. The Gas Works have also again been put into operation; and at this time the city is tolerably well lightged. The Rolling Mill, owned by Messrs. Markham & Schofield during the first years of the war, having been destroyed, has not yet been rebuilt. Another, however, on a very extensive scale, has been erected, and put into operation, on the W. & A. Railroad, near the city, under the firm name of the "Atlanta Rolling Mill & Mining Company, by John D. Gray, A. Alexander, and others. There are, also, in Atlanta, three Iron and Brass Foundries, seven Machine Shops, (including those in connection with Railroads,) and three large Sash, Door, and Blind Manufactories, besides other and smaller manufacturing establishments.

The printing, publishing, and, also, the educational interest of the city deserve notice. We have at this time three daily newspapers, one large weekly literary paper, one monthly Medical Journal, and one large monthly magazine; also, several large job offices, and two bookbinderies. All these establishments seem to be well conducted, and in a prosperous condition. The Medical College has been re-fitted, and will doubtless soon become eminently successful and popular. The cause of education, generally, is attracting attention. We have already several good schools, notwithstanding the absence of appropriate buildings for that purpose, and we hope some practicable system of free school education, both mental and manual, will at an early day, be established, that the poor children who are learning nothing but beggarly and vicious habits on our streets, may be taught that they were created for more noble and glorious purposes.

The number of stores on the business streets will reach

at least two hundred and fifty—mostly brick buildings. The assessed value of the real estate in the city in 1866, was over $7,000,000, and the amount of goods sold is estimated at $4,500,000. The population of the city, as shown by the census just taken, under direction of the City Council, is 10,940 whites, 9,288 blacks, nine hundred and twenty-eight (nearly five per cent. of the whole number) being widows and orphans; four hundred and forty-nine of whom are widows and orphans of Confederate soldiers—the aggregate showing a population of 20,228 souls.

It will be seen that this city, within the past two years, has risen out of her own ashes, to the populous, mercantile, and manufacturing Atlanta of 1861 and 1862. Her future, who can foresee? The tides of immigration and of improvement still continue to flow in her favor. The two new railroads to this city, in contemplation before the war, will probably be completed at an early day. The Georgia Air Line Railroad will, we are advised, be in running order as far as Gainsville, Hall county, within the year 1868. The grading on this road will be commenced, between this point and Gainsville, in March or April next. From the history of the past, we may, with a degree of certainty, anticipate the effects that will be produced on this city by the completion of these roads. On the railroad and manufacturing interest of Atlanta, and the mineral resources of Upper Georgia—which are now rapidly being developed—and not on agriculture, (for the surrounding country is comparatively poor,) must this city base her hopes of prosperity. Success attend them! and may we not again be cursed by the demoralizing and destructive tendencies of war, but continue, as a community, to march onward and upward in every ennobling cause, until Atlanta shall have become one of the great cities of the continent.

CORPORATE LIMITS.

The Incorporation Line of the city of Atlanta, as extended by an Act of the General Assembly of the State of Georgia, approved March 12th, 1866, incloses the area of a perfect circle three miles in diameter, the centre of which is located near the General Passenger Depot.

BOUNDARIES OF WARDS.

Atlanta is laid off into five Wards bounded as follows, to-wit:

FIRST WARD:—On North by W & A R R, East by Whitehall Street, and on the South and West by corporation line.

SECOND WARD:—On North by W & A and Ga Rail Road, East by Calhoun and McDonough Streets, West by Whitehall Street, and South by corporation line.

THIRD WARD:—On North by Ga R R, West by Calhoun and McDonough Streets, and on the South and East by corporate line.

FOURTH WARD:—On South by Ga R R, West by Ivy Street, and on the North and East by corporate line.

FIFTH WARD:—On South by W & A R R, East by Ivy Street, and on the North and West by corporate line.

Note.—In order to reduce the following to practice, when you wish to find a given street, first turn to the street you wish to find, and note the direction in which it runs, then turn to a street with which you are acquainted, and which crosses the given street: follow it from a well known point, observing all the crossings, until you come to the proper street;

Thus, Ellis street runs east and west: Now trace Calhoun north-east from Decatur, crossing Gilmer and Jenkins to Junction of College and Line, thence north, crossing Wheat and Houston, to Ellis, and you are at the corner of Calhoun and Ellis.

ALABAMA.—First South of Passenger Depot, and North of Hunter. From M. & W. R. R, East; crosses Forsyth, Broad, Whitehall, Pryor, and Lloyd, to Washington.

ALEXANDER.—First North of Simpson, and South of Mills. From Peachtree West; crosses Spring, Williams, Orme, Hayden, Hull, and Luckie, to Marietta.

BAKER.—First South of Simpson, and North of Harris. From Luckie, at terminus of Hull, East; crosses Hayden, Orme, Williams, Spring, Peachtree, Ivy, Collins, Calhoun, Butler, Fort, Yonge, and Jackson.

BARTLETT'S ALLEY.—First South of McLin. From Whitehall, at junction of Windsor, West, to M. & W. R. R.

BARTOW.—First West of Spring, and East of Foundry Alley. From W. & A. R. R, North-east; crosses Marietta, Walton, and Luckie, to Cain.

BELL.—First East of Moore, and West of Fort. From Ga. R. R., North; crosses Decatur, Gilmer, Taylor, and Pratt, to Line.

BOOTH ALLEY.—First West of M. & W. R. R. From Peters, North-West, to Walker.

BRIDGE.—See Broad.

BROAD.—First West of Whitehall, and East of Forsyth. From Mitchell, North-East; crosses Hunter, Alabama, R. R. (at Bridge,) Marietta, and Walton, to junction with Peachtree, at Luckie.

BUTLER.—First East of Calhoun, and West of Terry, Pratt, and Fort. From McDonough, North-east; crosses Hunter, Ga. R. R., Decatur, Gilmer, Jenkins, and College, to Line—thence North; crosses Wheat, Houston, Ellis, Cain, Harris, Baker, and Oslin.

CAIN.—First North of Ellis, and South of Harris. From Grubb, (Luckie) runs East; crossing Orme, Williams, Spring, Peachtree, Ivy, Collins, Calhoun, Butler, Fort, Yonge, and Jackson.

CALHOUN.—First East of Collins, and West of Butler. From McDonough, at East corner of City Hall Square, North-east; crossing Ga. R. R., Decatur, Gilmer, and Jenkins, to Junction of College and Line—thence North; crossing Wheat, Houston, Ellis, Cain, Harris, Baker, Oslin, and Currier.

CHEROKEE.—See Line Street.

CHURCH.—First North of Luckie. From Peachtree, at Junction of Forsyth, North-west; crossing junctions of Ellis and Cone, to Spring Street.

CLARK.—First South of Rawson, and North of Fulton. From Windsor East; crossing Cooper, Formwalt, Pryor, Pulliam, Washington, Crew, McDonough, Frazer, Martin, Connelly, and Hill.

COLLEGE.—First South of Line, and North of Jenkins. From angle of Calhoun, (between Jenkins and Wheat) South-east; crossing Butler, to Pratt Street.

COLLINS.—First East of Ivy, and West of Calhoun. From

Ga. R. R., North-east; crosses Decatur, Gilmer, and passes end of Jenkins, to angle between Jenkins and Wheat—thence North; crosses Wheat, Houston, Ellis, Cain, Harris, Baker, Oslin, and Currier.

CONE.—First West of Forsyth, and East of Spring. From Marietta, North-east; crosses Walton and Luckie, to Church Street.

CONNELLY ALLEY.—First West of Fair Ground, and East of King and Martin. From Fair, South; crosses Jones, Rawson, Clark, Fulton, Richardson, and Crumley.

COOPER.—First West of Formwalt, and East of Windsor. From Whitehall, South; crosses Jones, Rawson, Clark, Fulton, and Richardson.

CRAP'S ALLEY.—See Trebursey.

CREW.—First West of McDonough, and East of Washington. From Fair, South; crosses Jones, Rawson, Clark, Fulton, Richardson, and Crumley.

CRUMLEY.—First South of Richardson. From Cooper, East; crosses Formwalt, Pryor, Pulliam, Washington, Crew, McDonough, Fraser, Martin, and Connelly.

CURRIER.—First North of Oslin. From East-Peachtree, East; crosses Collins, Calhoun, Butler, and Fort.

DAVIS.—First South of Stephens. From Walker, West; crosses Race, (now called Green's Ferry Avenue) to corporate line.

DECATUR.—First North of Ga. R. R. Street, and South of Gilmer. From junction of Peachtree and Whitehall, South-east; crosses Pryor, junction of Lloyd and Ivy, Collins, Calhoun, and Butler, to Pratt—thence East; crosses Moore, Bell, Fort, Randolph, Yonge, and Jackson.

DELAY.—See Henry.

DUNCAN.—See Bartow.

ELLIS.—First North of Houston, and South of Cain.

From Church Street, East; crosses Peachtree, Ivy, Collins, Calhoun, Butler, Fort, Yonge, and Jackson.

ELMORE.—West side City Cemetery. From Ga. R. R., South; crosses Fair, to old corporation line.

FAIR.—First North of Jones, and South of Hunter. From Forsyth, East; crosses Whitehall (at junction of Cooper,) Northern terminus of Formwalt, Pryor, Lloyd, and Pulliam, Washington, Crew, South-east end of Peters, McDonough, Frazer, Terry, Martin, King, Connelly, Hill, and to corporation line.

FAITH's ALLEY.—See Rawson Street.

FILMORE.—See Gilmer.

FORMWALT.—First West of Pryor, and East of Cooper. From Fair, South; crosses Jones, Rawson, Clark, Fulton, Richardson, and Crumley.

FORSYTH —First East of Cone and Thompson, and West of Broad and Whitehall. From Peachtree, at Luckie, South; crosses Walton, Marietta, W. & A. and M. & W. R. Roads, Alabama, Hunter, Mitchell, Peters, Garnett, Grenville's Alley, and Fair, to Whitehall, opposite Windsor.

FORSYTH ALLEY.—First East of Pryor, and West of Ivy. From Line Street, North; crosses Wheat and runs into Pryor, near Houston.

FORT.—First East of Butler, and West of Yonge. From Ga. R. R., North; crosses Decatur, Gilmer, Taylor, Pratt, Line, Wheat, Houston, Ellis, Cain, Harris, Baker, and Oslin.

FOUNDRY.—First South of Thurman and North of Magazine. From W. & A. R. R., (South side Winship's Foundry,) West; crosses Fowler, Mangum, and Haynes.

FOUNDRY ALLEY.—First North-west of Bartow, and South-east of Short Street. From W. & A. R. R., North-east; crosses Marietta and Walton, to Luckie.

FOWLER.—First West of Old Monroe Railroad, and East of Mangum. From Mitchell, North; crosses Green, Rhodes, West end of Mechanic, Magazine, Foundry, Thurman, Rock, and Henry.

FRAZER.—First East of McDonough, and West of Terry. From Hunter, South; crosses Fair, Jones, Rawson, Clark, Fulton, Richardson, and Crumley.

FULTON.—First South of Clark, and North of Richardson. From Windsor, East; crosses Cooper, Formwalt, Pryor, Pulliam, Washington, Crew, McDonough, Frazer, Martin, and Connelly.

GARNETT.—First South of Peters and North of Grenville's Alley. From Peters, South-east; crosses Thompson, Forsyth, Whitehall, Pryor, Lloyd, and runs into Fair.

GARTRELL.—See Jackson.

GA. R. R. ST.—From Pryor, East, on North side of Ga. R. R., to A. & W. P. R. R. Depot.

GILMER.—First North of Decatur, and South of Jenkins. From Ivy, South-east; crosses Collins, Calhoun, and Butler, to Pratt—thence, North of Decatur, and South of Taylor, East; crosses Moore, Bell, Fort, Randolph, Yonge, and Jackson.

GREEN.—First North of Mitchell, and South of Rhodes. From Fowler, West; crosses Mangum, Haynes, and another Street, (name not known,) to corporation line.

GRENVILLE'S ALLEY.—First South of Garnett. From Thompson, South-east; crosses Forsyth, Whitehall, and runs into Fair, at Pryor Street.

GRUBB, (LUCKIE.)—First North-east of Marietta, (at junction of Walton.) From Bartow, North-west, to Simpson.

HARRIS.—First North of Cain, and South of Baker. From Luckie, East; crosses Hayden, Orme, Williams, Spring, Peachtree, Ivy, Collins, Calhoun, Butler, Fort, Yonge, and Jackson.

HAYDEN.—First West of Orme, and East of Hull. From Luckie, North; crosses Harris, Baker, Simpson, Alexander, Mills, and Hunnicutt.

HAYNES.—First West of Mangum. From Nelson, North; crosses Rice, Markham, Mitchell, Green, Rhodes, Magazine, Foundry, Thurman, Rock, and Henry.

HENRY.—First North of Rock. From W. & A. R. R., West; crosses Fowler, Mangum, and Haynes.

HENRY ALLEY.—See Richardson Street.

HILL.—East side of Fair Ground. From Ga R R, South; crosses Hunter, Fair, Jones, Rawson, Clark, and Fulton.

HOUSTON.—First North of Wheat and South of Ellis. From Peachtree, East; crosses Pryor, Ivy, Collins, Calhoun, Butler, Fort, Yonge, and Jackson.

HUNNICUTT.—First North of Mills. From West-Peachtree, West; crosses Spring, Williams, Orme, Hayden, Hull, and Luckie, to Marietta.

HUNTER —First South of Alabama, and North of Mitchell. From M & W R R, East; crosses Thompson, Forsyth, Broad, Whitehall, Pryor, Lloyd, Washington, Calhoun, Terry, King, Nursery, and Hill, to city Cemetery.

HULL.—First East of Luckie, and west of Hayden. From Baker, North; crosses Simpson, Alexander, Mills, and Hunnicutt.

IRWIN.—North of Wheat, South of Houston. From Houston, South-east; crosses Fort, Yonge, and Jackson.

IVY.—First East of Pryor, and Peachtree, and West of Collins. From Decatur, North; crosses West end of Gilmer, Wheat, Houston, Ellis, Cain, Harris, and Baker, to junction with East-Peachtree.

JACKSON.—First East of Yonge. From Decatur, North; crosses Gilmer, Taylor, Pratt, Line, Wheat, Irwin, Houston, Ellis, and Cain.

JENKINS.—First North of Gilmer, and South of College. From Collins, South-west; crosses Calhoun and Butler, to Pratt.

JOHN'S ALLEY.—See Fulton Street.

JONES.—First South of Fair, and North of Rawson. From Windsor, East; crosses Formwalt, Pryor, Pulliam, Washington, Crew, McDonough, Frazer, Terry, Martin, Connelly, and Hill.

KING.—First East of Terry, and West of Nursery. From Ga R R, South, across Hunter, to Fair.

LINE.—First North of Decatur. From Peachtree due East; crosses Pryor and South end of Forsyth Alley, and is obstructed from Ivy to Calhoun. Thence, first South of Wheat, crosses Butler, Fort, Yonge, and Jackson.

LLOYD.—First East of Pryor, and West of Washington. From Decatur, South-west; crosses Ga R R, Alabama, Hunter, Mitchell, Peters, and Garnett, to Fair, near Northern terminus of Pulliam.

LUCKIE.—First North of Walton, and South of Church Street. From Peachtree, North-west; crosses Forsyth,

Cone, and Spring—thence West, to Bartow—thence, North-west, to Simpson, and thence North; first West of Hull, crosses Alexander, Mills, and Hunnicutt.

McDANIEL.—From Peters, near South-western corporate line, runs South-east, across M. & W. R. and Whitehall Street.

McDONOUGH.—First East of Crew and West of Frazer. From corner City Hall Square, South; passes South. east end of Mitchell, South-west end of Butler, and crosses Fair, Jones, Rawson, Clark, Fulton, Richardson, and Crumley.

McLIN.—First North of Bartlett's Alley. From Forsyth,

opposite North end of Cooper, West, to M & W Railroad.

MAGAZINE.—First South of Foundry, and North of Mechanic and Rhodes. From old Munroe Railroad, West; crosses Fowler, Mangum and Haynes.

MANGUM.—First West of Fowler, and East of Haynes. From Nelson, at junction of Walker, North; crosses Race, Markham, Mitchell, Green, Rhodes, Magazine, Foundry, Thurman, Rock, and Henry.

MARIETTA.—First North of W & A Railroad, and South of Walton. From junction of Whitehall and Peach-tree, North-west; crosses Broad, Forsyth, South end of Cone, Spring, Bartow, and Foundry Alley, to junction of Walton—thence parrallel with W & A Railroad, to North-east corporate line.

MARKHAM.—First South of Mitchell, and North of Race. From M & W Railroad, West; crosses Fowler, Mangum, and Haynes, to Trebursey.

MARTIN.—First East of Terry, and West of Connelly, From Fair, South; crosses Jones, Rawson, Clark. Fulton, Richardson, and Crumley.

MECHANIC.—First South of Magazine, and North of Rhodes. From Munroe Railroad Street West, to Fowler.

MILLS.—First North of Alexander, and South of Hunni-cutt. From West-Peachtree, West; crosses Spring, Williams, Orme, Hayden, Hull, and Luckie, to Marietta.

MITCHELL.—First North of Peters, and South of Hunter. From McDonough, West; crosses Washington, Lloyd, Pryor, Whitehall, Western Terminus of Broad, Forsyth, and Thompson, to M & W Railroad—thence South of Green, and North of Markham; crosses Fowler, Mangum, and Haynes.

MOBDS ALLEY.—See Crumley Street.

MUNROE RAILROAD STREET.—Rear of W. & A. Railroad Machine Shop, (on South-west.) Runs from said shop, North-east, to Winship's Foundry.

MOORE.—First East of Pratt and West of Bell. From Georgia Railroad, North; crosses Decatur and Gilmer to junction with Pratt, near Jenkins.

NELSON.—First South-east of Race, and North-west of Peters and Walker. From M. & W. Railroad South-west; crosses Mangum and Walker at their junction, and passes South-east ends of Haynes and Trebursey, and runs into Race near Stonewall.

NURSERY.—First East of King. From Georgia Railroad South; crosses Hunter, to Fair.

ORME.—First West of Williams, and East of Hayden. From Cain, North; crosses Harris, Baker, Simpson, Alexander, Mills, and Hunnicutt.

OSLIN —First North of Baker, and South of Currier. From East-Peachtree, East; crosses Collins, Calhoun, and Butler.

OWENS.—First North of McLin. From Forsyth, West, to M. & W. Railroad.

PAYNE.—See Marietta Street, North-east of junction with Walton.

PEACHTREE.—First West of Pryor, and East of Broad, to Ellis—thence first West of Ivy, and East of Spring. From junction of Marietta and Decatur, North; passes Line, Walton, Luckie, Forsyth, Houston, and Church.

Thence crosses Ellis, Cain, Harris, and Baker. Here separates East and West-Peachtree; West-Peachtree being the Eastern terminus of Simpson, Alexander, Mills, and Hunnicutt.

PEACHTREE, (OLD, OR EAST.)—From West-Peachtree, North-east; forms junctions with Ivy, Oslin, and Currier, on East side, and with a continuation of Alexander on the West.

PEARCE.—See Decatur, East of Pratt.

PETERS.—First South of Mitchell, and North of Garnett. From Fair, North-west; crosses Crew, Washington, Lloyd, Pryor, and Whitehall, to Forsyth—thence West, crosses Thompson Street and M. & W. Railroad—thence West of said road, and East of Walker, Southwest, passes Eastern end of Booth Alley, and forms junction with Walker, near old corporate line.

PRATT.—First South-east of Butler, and North-west of Moore. From Decatur, North-east; passes Gilmer, Moore, Jenkins, Taylor, and College, to Bell—thence East, North of Taylor, and South of Line, East; crosses Fort, Randolph, Yonge, and Jackson.

PRYOR.—First East of Peachtree and Whitehall, and West of Ivy and Lloyd. From Peachtree, (between Houston, and Ellis) South-west; crosses Houston, junction of Forsyth Alley, Wheat, Line, Decatur, Georgia Railroad, Alabama, Hunter, Mitchell, Peters' and Garnett, to Fair—thence South, first East of Formwalt, and West of Pulliam; crosses Jones, Rawson, Clark, Fulton, Richardson, and Crumley.

PULLIAM.—First West of Washington, and East of Pryor. From Fair South; crosses, Rawson, Clark, Fulton Richardson, and Crumley.

RACE.—First North of Nelson and South of Markham. From Mangum, South-west; crosses Haynes and Trebursey, and forms junction with Nelson, near Stonewall.

RANDOLPH, (OLD WASHINGTON.)—First East of Fort, and West of Yonge. From Decatur, North; crosses Taylor and Pratt.

RAWSON.—First South of Jones, and North of Clark. From Windsor, East; crosses Cooper, Formwalt,

Pryor, Pulliam, Washington, Crew, McDonough, Frazer, Martin, and Connelly.

REID.—First East of Elmore. From City Cemetery North, to Georgia Railroad.

RICHARDSON.—First South of Fulton, and North of Crumley. From Windsor, East; crosses Cooper, Formwalt, Pryor, Pulliam, Washington, Crew, McDonough, Frazer, Martin, and Connelly.

ROCK.—First South of Henry, and North of Thurman. From W. & A. Railroad, West; crosses Fowler, Mangum, and Haynes.

SHORT.—First North-west of Foundry Alley. From W. & A. Railroad, North-east, to Luckie; crosses Marietta and Walton at their junction.

SIMPSON.—First North of Baker, and South of Alexander. From Peachtree, West; crosses Spring, Williams, Orme, Hayden, Hull, and Luckie to Marietta.

SPRING.—First West of Cone and Peachtree. From W. & A. Railroad, North-east; crosses Marietta, Walton, Luckie, and Church—thence North, crosses Cain, Harris, Baker, Simpson, Alexander, Mills, and Hunnicutt

STEPHENS.—First South of Stonewall, and North of Davis. From Walker, West; crosses Race.

STOCKTON.—See Mitchell, West of M. & W. Railroad.

STONEWALL.—First North of Stephens and South of Trebursey. From Walker, West; crosses Race near junction of Nelson.

TAYLOR.—First North of Gilmer. From Pratt, East; crosses Bell, Fort, Randolph, Yonge, and Jackson.

TERRY.—First East of Butler and Frazer, and West of Martin. From Georgia Railroad, South-west, to Hunter—thence South; crosses Fair and Jones, to Rawson.

THOMPSON.—First West of Forsyth, and East of M. & W. Railroad. From Alabama, South-west; crosses Hunter, Mitchell, Peters, and Garnett, to Grenville's Alley.

THURMAN.—First North of Foundry, and South of Rock. From W. & A. Railroad, West; crosses Fowler, Mangum, and Haynes.

TREBURSEY.—First South-west of Haynes, and North of Stonewall. From Nelson, North-west; crosses Race, Markham, and Mitchell.

WADLEY.—See Forsyth North of W & A Railroad.

WALKER.—First West of Peters, and East of Nelson. From junction with Mangum, at Nelson street, South; passes Booth Alley, Stonewall, Stephens, and Davis, to Peters.

WALTON.—First North of Marietta, and South of Luckie. From Peachtree, North-west; crosses Broad, Forsyth, Cone, Spring, Bartow, and Foundry Alley, to junction with Marietta at Short Street.

WASHINGTON.—First East of Lloyd, and West of McDonough. From Alabama, South-west; crosses Hunter, Mitchell, and Peters, to Fair—thence West of Crew and East of Pulliam, South, crosses Jones, Rawson, Clark, Fulton, Richardson, and Crumley.

WHEAT.—First South of Houston, and North of Line. From Pryor, East; crosses Forsyth Alley, Ivy, Collins, Calhoun, Butler, Fort, Younge, and Jackson.

WHITEHALL.—First East of Broad, and West of Pryor. From junction of Marietta and Decatur, South-west; crosses Railroad, Alabama, Hunter, and Mitchell—thence East of Forsyth and West of Pryor; crosses Peters, Garnett, and Grenvill's Alley, to Fair; passes junctions of Forsyth, Windsor, and Bartlett's Alley—and is crossed near old corporate line by McDaniel Street.

WHITEHALL, (OLD,) see Peters, west of Forsyth.

WINDSOR.—First West of Cooper. From junction of Forsyth and Whitehall, South; crosses Jones, Rawson, Clark, Fulton, Richardson, and Crumley.

YONGE.—First East of Randolph, (old Washington,) and West of Jackson. From Decatur, North; crosses Taylor and Pratt, to Line.

4

CITY GOVERNMENT.

MAYORS OF ATLANTA.

From its Incorporation as a City to the year 1867,

inclusive.

1st Moses W. Formwalt went into office January, 1848.
2d Benjamin F. Bomar went into office January, 1849.
3d Willys Buell went into office January, 1850.
4th Johnathan Norcross went into office Janaury, 1851.
5th Thomas F. Gibbs went into office January, 1852.
6th John F. Mims went into office January, 1853. (Resigned October 29th, 1853.)
6th Wm. Markham went into office November 14, 1853.
7th Wm. M. Butt went into office January, 1854.
8th Allison Nelson went into office January, 1855. (Resigned July 6th, 1855.)
8th John Glenn went into office July 20th, 1855.
9th William Ezzard went into office January, 1856.
10th William Ezzard, re-elected, went into office January, 1857.
11th Luther J. Glenn went into office January, 1858.
12th Luther J. Glenn, re-elected, went into office January, 1859.
13th William Ezzard into office January, 1860.
14th Jared I. Whitaker went into office January, 1861. (Resigned November 25th, 1861.)
14th Thomas F. Lowe went into office December 13th, 1861.
15th James M. Calhoun went into office January, 1862.

16th James M. Calhoun, re-elected, went into office
January, 1863.
17th James M. Calhoun, re-elected, went into office
January, 1864.
18th James M. Calhoun, re-elected, went into office
January, 1865.
19th James E. Williams went into office January, 1866.
20th James E. Williams, re-elected, went into office
January, 1867.

MUNICIPAL GOVERNMENT,

For the Year 1865.

J. M. CALHOUN, Mayor.

S. B. Love, Cl'k of Council. J. T. Porter, Treasurer.
L. P. Thomas, Marshal.   W. P. Lanier, Dpty Marshal.

ALDERMEN.

First Ward.—John Collier, B. N. Williford.
Second Ward.—F. M. Richardson, L. S. Salmons.
Third Ward.—C. F. Wood, George W. Terry.
Fourth Ward.—L. S. Mead, George W. Adair.
Fifth Ward.—E. R. Sasseen, J. N. Simmons.

STANDING COMMITTEES.

On Finance.—John Collier, J. N. Simmons.
On Ordinances.—John Collier, J. N. Simmons.

On Police.—E. R. Sasseen, L. S. Salmons, B. N. Williford.

On Streets, &c.—F. M. Richardson, J. N. Simmons.

On Market.—B. N. Williford, F. M. Richardson, G. W. Terry.

On Fire Department.—G. W. Terry, F. M. Richardson, Geo. W. Adair, John Collier.

On Wells, Pumps, &c.—F. M. Richardson, G. W. Terry, L. S. Mead.

On Public Buildings, Grounds, &c.—L. S. Salmons, John Collier, E. R. Sasseen.

On Relief.—J. N. Simmons, John Collier, F. M. Richardson, L. S. Mead.

On Tax.—John Collier, E. R. Sasseen, J. N. Simmons.

MUNICIPAL GOVERNMENT,

For the Year 1866.

J. E. WILLIAMS, Mayor.

S. B. Love, Cl'k of Council. Joseph T. Porter, Treasurer. G. W. Anderson, Marshal.   W. P. Lanier, Dept Marshal.

ALDERMEN.

First Ward.—A. P. Bell, D. P. Ferguson.
Second Ward.—A. W. Mitchell, F. M. Richardson.
Third Ward.—Robert Crawford, James G. Kelly.
Fourth Ward.—W. T. Mead, R. M. Farrar.
Fifth Ward.—B. D. Smith, Anthony Murphy.

STANDING COMMITTEES.

On Finance.—R. M. Farrar, A. W. Mitchell, A. P. Bell.

On Ordinances.—A. W. Mitchell, B. D. Smith, W. T. Mead.

On Police.—D. P. Ferguson, Robert Crawford, W. T. Mead.

On Streets, &c.—Robert Crawford, F. M. Richardson, Anthony Murphy.

On Market.—B. D. Smith, D. P. Ferguson, R. M. Farrar.

On Fire Department.—A. P. Bell, Anthony Murphy, James G. Kelly.

On Wells, Pumps, &c.—Anthony Murphy, James G. Kelly, F. M. Richardson.

On Public Buildings, Grounds, &c.—W. T. Mead, R. M. Farrar, D. P. Ferguson.

On Lamps, Gas, &c.—F. M. Richardson, W. T. Mead, R. M. Farrar.

On Cemetery.—James G. Kelly, A. W. Mitchell, Robert Crawford.

On Relief.—F. M. Richardson, A. P. Bell, Robert Crawford, W. T. Mead, B. D. Smith.

On Tax.—B. D. Smith, A. P. Bell, A. W. Mitchell.

MUNICIPAL GOVERNMENT,

For the Year 1867—(*See Corrections.*)

J. E. WILLIAMS, Mayor........................$2,000
S. B. Love, Clerk of Council................... 1,500
S. B. Hoyt, City Attorney...................... 800
Robert M. Farrar, City Treasurer.............. 800
R. J. Roach, City Physician................... 1,500

James F. Cooper, City Engineer................ 1,200
Robert Crawford, Commissioner of Public Works. 1,500
George Stewart, Overseer of Streets............ 1,000
Jo. S. Smith, Tax Receiver and Collector........ 800
Pat. Fitzgibbon, Hall-Keeper.... 600

ALDERMEN.

First Ward.—M. T. Castleberry, D. P. Ferguson.
Second Ward.—F. M. Richardson, A. W. Mitchell.
Third Ward.—George W. Terry, W. C. Anderson.
Fourth Ward.—J. E. Gullatt, W. B. Cox.
Fifth Ward.—Anthony Murphy, A. P. Bell.

STANDING COMMITTEES.

On Finance.—W. B. Cox, A. W. Mitchell, A. P. Bell.
On Ordinances.—A. W. Mitchell, W. B. Cox, D. P. Ferguson.
On Streets and Sidewalks.—J. E. Gullatt, F. M. Richardson, Anthony Murphy.
On Wells, Pumps and Cisterns.—Anthony Murphy, W. C. Anderson, M. T. Castleberry.
On Lamps and Gas.—F. M. Richardson, George W. Terry, D. P. Ferguson.
On Relief.—F. M. Richardson, M. T. Castleberry, George W. Terry, J. E. Gullatt, A. P. Bell.
On Market.—D. P. Ferguson, J. E. Gullatt, M. T. Castleberry.
On Fire Department.—A. P. Bell, J. E. Gullatt, Anthony Murphy.
On Police.—M. T. Castleberry, W. B. Cox, W. C. Anderson.
On Cemetery.—George W. Terry, A. W. Mitchell, F. M. Richardson.
On Public Buildings and Grounds.—W. C. Anderson, George W. Terry, D. P. Ferguson.

On Tax.—A. W. Mitchell, A. P. Bell, W. B. Cox.
On Salaries.—W. B. Cox, A. W. Mitchell, F. M. Richardson.

POLICE DEPARTMENT.

L. P. Thomas, Chief Marshal...................$1,500
E. C. Murphy, Deputy Marshal.................. 1,300
J. L. Johnson, 1st Lieutenant of Police........... 1,000
T. C. Murphy, 2d Lieutenant of Police.......... 1,000

POLICEMEN—($2 25 PER DAY.)

I J Cook,	J S Holland,
F J Bomar,	R D Haynes,
D Rogan,	D Queen,
E A Center,	J R Love,
F T Kicklighter,	L Ferguson,
—— Hinton,	R B Hutchins,
J W Stokes,	J M Connally,
J L Crenshaw,	Green Holland,
G W Bowen,	H W Wooding,
C M Barry,	H J Holtzclaw,
A Jarrard,	M W Rasberry,
A P Woodliff,	J F Barnes,
Jasper Groves,	T G McHau,
W H C Cowan,	J A Lanier,
James Campbell,	L W Boon.

Clerk First Market.—Theophilus Harris.
Clerk of Second Market.—Frank T. Ryan.
Sexton.—G. A. Pilgrim.
City Assessors.—R. S. Waters, W. C. Humphries, and C. F. Wood.
Assessors of Land taken for Opening Streets.—Levi C. Wells and F. P. Rice.

FIRE DEPARTMENT.

S. B. SHERWOOD, Chief Engineer.
HENRY GULLATT, First Assistant Engineer
W. G. KNOX, Second Assistant Engineer.

ATLANTA FIRE COMPANY, NO. 1.

(STEAM ENGINE.)

Organized, March 24, 1851.
Incorporated, April 4, 1851.

Meets first Monday night in each Month, at their Engine House,
cor. Broad Street, and M. & W. R. R.

OFFICERS.

JOHN B. NORMAN, President.
CHARLES SCHNATZ, 1st Director.
JOHN BERKELE, 2d Director.
JOHN WILBEY, 3d Director.
SAMUEL WILSON, Secretary.
H. MUHLENBRINK, Treasurer.
JOHN H. ELLSWORTH, Rep. to Fire Dept.
JOHN BRIDWELL, }
M. ROGAN,   } Axe-men.

ACTIVE MEMBERS.—(PRIVATES.)

Alexander, L.
Bell, H. G.
Broxton, H. W.
Cannon, P J
Collier, M L
Collier, John W

Cox, W B
Daly, Pat
Eisenhut, John
Ficken, John
Fleck, Daniel
Galvin, Jhon
Garcia, B
Garvy, P
Grambling, John
Grogan, Z W
Goudy, D H
Haney, Thomas
Haney, Henry
Haverty, M
Henderson, A F
Immel, J
Immel, M J
James, Wm
Jentzer, John
Joyner, H W
Klotz, Jno
Kuhrt, Henry
Klassett, A
Krog, Wm
Kavanaugh, P

Lynch, Peter
Lynch, J
Mann, J E
Mann, James
Mann, John
Mann, Wm J
Mann, Henry
Mason, J P
Mason, Wm. K.
Murrins, L
McGee, John
Nelley, Martin
Olerich, P
Peel, John
Pettis, W P
Roab, George
Ransford, H
Robers, M L
Schoen, J
Spencer, Wm
Sherwood, S B
Weaver, J K
Van Loan, A H
Van Loan, Richard

HONORARY MEMBERS.

Bracken, P J
Daly, Martin
Flynn, John H
Forsyth, Wm
Heinz, Charles
Hunnicutt, C W
Kershaw, John

Kidd, Wm
Kirby, T
Lamb, B T
Lynch, John
Mecaslin, J H
Murphy, T C
Stadelman, J

MECHANIC FIRE COMPANY, NO. 2.

Organized, Dec. 10, 1856.

Meets First Friday night in each month, at their Hall over Engine House, Corner Washington street and Ga. R. R.

OFFICERS.

J. E. GULLATT, President.
JAMES G. KELLY, Vice President.
W. D. LUCKIE, Jr., Secretary.
O. H. JONES, Treasurer.
E. BUICE, First Director.
C. BEERMANN, Second Director.
W. G. MIDDLETON, Chief Engineer.
JOEL KELSEY, 1st Ass't Engineer.
G. W. TERRY, 2d Assistant Engineer.
JAS. DANIELS, 3d Ass't Engineer.
G. T. ANDERSON, } Pipemen.
W. F. WOODS, }
J. M. BUICE, } Axe-men.
JOSEPH WILEY, }
M. L. LICHTENSTADT, Rep. to Fire Dep't.
JAS. ALEXANDER, M. D., Surgeon.

MEMBERS.

Buice, C W	Krogg, Fred
Buice, J D	Langford, W Y
Bellingrath, H	Lyons, J L
Bradbury, T W	Manning, W H
Bannan, W J	Middleton, M J
Campbell, J T	Moore, B F
Crenshaw, J L	O'Connor, Thomas
Darby, Arch	Read, Thomas
Dewberry, J R	Rogers, J C
Doby, J B	Rodes, C C
Harmsen, Carl	Rosenfeld, S

Rote, M
Schramm, P
Shlotfeldt, George
Spillman, Joshua

Steinheimer, D
Steinheimer, I
Williams, J E
Wilson, Hue

TALLULAH FIRE COMPANY, N.O 3.

ORGANIZED FEBRUARY 22, 1859.

Meets First Wednesday night in each Month, at their Hall in Engine House, on Broad, between Marietta and Walton Sts.

OFFICERS.—[See Corrections.]

E. C. MURPHY, President.
S. W. GRUBB, Vice President.
W. C. SHEARER, 1st Director.
JESSE SMITH, 2d Director.
F. M. QUEEN, Hose Director.
J. N. WILLIAMS Secretary.
L. H. CLARKE, Treasurer.
H. S. ORME, Surgeon.
A. P. BELL, Rep. to Fire Department.
E. MERCER, Foreman 1st Squad.
L. B. SCUDDER, Foreman 2d Squad.
W. R. BIGGERS, Foreman Hose Squad.
DAVID BUICE,
B. KANE, } Axe-men.

ACTIVE MEMBERS.

Bohnefeld, Carl
Bohnefeld, Herman
Bohnefeld, Richard
Center, E A
Christopher, Frank
Clarke, Wm F

Crew, B B
Clarke, John D
Deringer, J A
Fife, R A
Fitts, Robert C
Groves, J B

Haralson, A J	Smith, J B
Hill, John A	Starnes, J M
Holland, J S	Steadman, Charles
Henson, F	Stokes, J W
Jack, G W	Smith, C D
Johnson, C A	Theme, A
Judson, W N	Thompson, George
Love, J R	Thrower, C A
Mead, W T	Valentino, Gabe
Mobley, E L D	Valentino, John
Mullin, J E	Warwick, E A
Parks, John R	Warwick, T F
Queen, B C	Wells, J Y
Rogers, J J	Whaley, J R
Robinson, R A	Williams, Isaac

ATLANTA HOOK & LADDER CO. NO. 1.

ORGANIZED NOVEMBER 28, 1859.

Meets First Saturday night in each Month, at their Truck House east side of Pryor, between Alabama and Hunter sts.

OFFICERS.

J. L. QUEEN, Foreman.
C. F. S. D'ALVIGNY, Ass't Foreman.
J. S. YARBROUGH, Secretary.
GEORGE JOHNSON, Treasurer.
ED. HOLLAND, Rep. to Fire Dep't.

ACTIVE MEMBERS.

Bockout, J M
Bradburn, A B
Bryant, W M
Buckhardt, G A
Burr, George
Erginzingar, A
Forsyth, C A
Franklin, George
Hartman, M
Holley, C W
James, J H
Johnston, F M
Lowry, R J
Lumpkin, W J

McDade, W C
*McWaters, A
Morris, L G
Parrott, G W
Peters, W G
Queen, D M
Rakestraw, George
Reeves, J W
Richardson, F M
Smith, E C
Wilson, Henry
Young, John

HONORARY MEMBERS,

*Edwards, George
*Fowler, N R
*Love, S B

Morrison, John
*Peck, J C
Scrutchen, Thomas

*Charter Members.

CHURCH RECORD.

WESLEY CHAPEL, M. E.

East Side Peachtree, near junction of Broad Street.

(AGGREGATE MEMBERSHIP 337.)

Church Meetings 3rd Sabbath in each Month.
Communion 1st Sabbath in each Month.
Services every Sabbath at 10½, A. M., and at Night.

WM. P. HARRISON, *Pastor.*

PETER G. BESSENT, *Secretary Church Meeting.*

STEWARDS.

E. R. Sasseen,
Er Lawshe,
Willis Peck,
J. C. Davis,

William Ezzard,
J. N. Simmons,
S. T. Atkin.

TRUSTEES.

William Ezzard,
Lewis Lawshe,
S. T. Atkin,
N. J. Hammond,

J. C. Davis,
John L. Hopkins.
Joseph Winship.

COMMUNICANTS.

Adams, Benson W
Adams, mrs L
Adamson, miss Nellie
Atkin. S T

Atkin, mrs N E
Atkin, miss Emma
Atkin, miss Lizzie
Barnes, mrs Amanda

Farnes, mrs H J
Farnwell, V T
Farnwell, mrs L A
Farrett, W J
Farratt, mrs Anna
Bass, mrs M E
Bass, mrs Margaret
Beauchamp, mrs E J
Belding, James
Bell, M R
Benton, mits Mary
Berry, mrs Harriet
Berry, miss Carrie
Bessent, Peter G
Bessent, mrs V F
Bessent, miss Anna
Bleckley, L E
Bleckley, mrs Carrie
Boring, Dr J M
Boring, Mrs Irene P
Boyd, Augustine W
Boyd, mrs Nancy A
Boyd, miss Mary
Boutell, John
-Boutell, mrs M E
Boutell, mrs Hannah
Bridwell. John
Bridwell, mrs Elizbaeth
Bridwell, mrs Harriet
Bridwell, miss Ella
Bridwell, miss M E
Brown, mrs Georgia
Brown, J W
Burnam, E B
Burnam, Wareham
Burnam, mrs Mary
Burnam, A
Burnam, miss Emma

Burnam, miss Martha
Busby, W T
Busby, mrs Eliza
Butler, Thomas
Butler, mrs Elizabeth
Butler, miss Emma
Butler, miss Ellen
Crussell, Thomas
Crussell, mrs Thomas
Calhoun, mrs Amelia
Carmichael, mrs Eliza-
  beth
Carmichael, miss C E
Carmichael, miss Mary A
Center, miss Julia
Champ, mrs T C
Chandler, mrs Julia
Chandler, mrs E A
Cohron, Joseph
Cohron, mrs Irene
Clardy, P E J
Clarchy, mrs T J
Clarke, Lewis H
Clower, mrs Nancy H
Clower, mrs Sarah E
Cofer, Merritt J
Collins, mrs Cynthia
Cook, Geo W D
Cook, mrs Mary
Corley, mrs Ella
Corron, miss Parrie
Cox, Wm B
Cox, mrs Kate H
Cozart, mrs Ann M
Cozart, miss Lou C
Cozart, miss Anna M
Cozart, miss Susie
Cozart, miss Sallie

Cozart, miss Ella
Crouse, Harry
Craven, mrs Mary
Davis, J C
Davis, mrs Mary A C
Davis, Webster
Davis, C C
Davis, mrs C C
Davis, miss Mary
Dean, miss Georgia
DeFoor, mrs L M
Delpey, mrs Emily
Dorsey, miss Mary
Ducker, Wm N
Ducker, mrs Mary
Dunn, mrs M C
Edmondson, miss Mary
Elyea, mrs Ann Eliza
Ezzard, Wm
Ezzard, mrs Sarah S
Ezzard, mrs Fannie R
Fambrough, W E
Fambrough, mrs M F
Flannegan, mrs Matilda
Foreacre, mrs Delia
Fowler, mrs Flora
Freeman, W K
Freeman, mrs Julia
Gartrell, L J
Gartrell, mrs Anna
Garwood, Johnson
Garwood, mrs Harriet
Gay, A O M
Gay, mrs Z E
Gilmore, Almer
Gilmore, mrs Eleanor
Gilmore, Harman

Gilmore, mrs Lucy
Godfrey, Rev Jas E
Godfrey, mrs Agnes
Godfrey, miss Anna B
Goode, Hamilton
Goode, mrs A E
Gyrdon, Daniel L
Gordon, mrs Nancy M
Griffin, J D
Griffin, mrs J C
Grist, B A
Grist, mrs A J
Grist, mrs Elizabeth
Grubbs, mrs Sarah
Godfrey, miss Rachael A
Hairston, mrs N A
Hammond, N N
Hammond, A W
Hammond, mrs Mary A
Hammond, George
Hammond, N J
Hammond, mrs L F
Hammond, miss Lula
Hammond, miss Ella
Hammond, Wm P
Hammond, miss Mary
Haney, Joanna
Haralson, mrs Mira
Harrison, mrs C A
Harrison, mrs E J
Harrison, John W
Harrison, George W
Hays, I N
Hays, mrs Sarah
Hearn, miss Emily
Henderson, mrs Mary
Hendrix, J C

Hendrix, mrs M E
Hinton, miss Sallie
Hill, miss Melissa
Holmes, Mathew
Holmes, Mrs M
Holmes, W C
Holmes, mrs W C
Hopkins, John L
Hopkins, mrs Mary E
Horton, mrs Carrie E
Howard, R A
Howard, mrs T C
Howard, mrs E V
Hoyle, Wm E
Hoyle, mrs M A
Hunnicutt, C W
Hunnicutt, mrs Letitia
Jenkins, miss Sarah A E
Jenkins, J J
Jenkins, mrs E A
Jenkins, miss Amanda J
Jenkins, G W
Joiner, H
Joiner, mrs Mary
Johnson, Jacob
Johnson, mrs Mary
Johnson, miss Lizzie
Kelly, David
Kelly, mrs Lucy
Kile, mrs Mary
Kile, miss Josephine
King, Rev H K
King, mrs M C
Knox, E P
Lackie, mrs Eugenia
Landrum, L L
Lane, mrs Margaret E
Lawshe, Rev Lewis

Lawshe, mrs Louisa
Lawshe, miss Lou
Lawshe, Er
Lawshe, mrs Sallie
Lester, mrs Sarah
Lester, miss Hattie
Lester, miss Eva
Lester, miss Mattie
Lester, miss Ella
Lester, Wm
Lovejoy, mrs Martha
Lumpkin, miss Clementine
Maddox, mrs Anna
Maffit, mrs Carrie
Martin, Ganaway
Mayson, Rev J R
Mayson, miss Fannie J
McAffee, W W
McAffee, mrs A L
McConnell, mrs Wm
McConnell, miss Leona
McFail, mrs V E
McLendon, Capell
McLendon, mrs Ruth
McLin, J G
McLin, mrs M
McLin, miss Mary
Mell, W H
Mell, mrs Sarah E
Mell, miss M A
Miller, mrs Nancy
Miller, miss Mary
Mills, J M
Mills, mrs Joseph
Mills, mrs C
Mills, miss Carrie O
Monday, C E
Monday, R A

5

Monday, miss Charlotte
Monday, miss Anna
Monday, miss Mary
Moody, miss Martha J
Morgan, mrs Eva
Morris, mrs Mary
O'Connor, mrs P
Orme, mrs Lucy
Payne Edward
Payne, mrs J B
Payne, mrs Carrie
Payne, mrs Elizabeth
Payne, mrs Margaret
Peck, Willis
Peck, mrs Anna E
Peck, Wm F
Peck, John B
Peck, mrs Martha A
Pegg, Dr W H
Pegg, mrs Martha
Pegg, miss Cynthia
Pendley, mrs Jane
Pilgrim, mrs N J
Pittman, mrs Martha C
Pitts, Columbus A
Pitts, mrs Emeline
Powell, mrs Dr C
Powell, J
Powell, miss G S
Purtell, mrs H A
Reynolds, J C
Reynolds, mrs C G
Rives, Frank
Roberts, Elisha
Roberts, mrs A
Robinson, miss Susan E
Robson, S B
Robson, miss Anna

Rollins, A P
Rollins, mrs C P
Rust, mrs Margaret
Sasseen, E R
Sasseen, E R, Jr
Sasseen, George
Seymour, Isaiah
Seymour, mrs Olive
Silvey, mrs A
Simmons, Dr J N
Simmons, mrs E C
Smith, B D
Smith, mrs Lizzie
Smith, mrs Cornelia E
Smith, Dr C H
Smith, Jno A
South, mrs J
Stegall, mrs Nancy
Stewart, miss L
Starnes, Joel
Starnes, mrs Mary
Starnes, mrs Anna
Starnes, miss Fannie
Starnes, miss Mattie
Strong, mrs Elizabeth B
Talley, A S
Taylor, mrs Susan
Taylor, mrs L
Varner, mrs Rebecca
Venable, miss Julia
Walker, Henry C
Walker, mrs Sallie S
Warren, mrs Amanda
Watley, mrs Anna
Watson, A R
Watson, mrs Fannie
Watts, mrs M L
West, mrs Jane E

West, miss Alberta
West, miss Laura
Westmoreland, mrs Dr H
Whitaker, mrs J
Whitaker, miss Mattie
Whitehead, Geo W M
Willingham, miss M E
Willingham, miss J
Wilson, Dr Henry
Wilson, mrs Mary
Wilson, mrs Marian
Wilson, miss Chatharine
Winship, Joseph

Winship, mrs Eudosia
Winship, Robert
Winship, mrs Mary F
Winship, George
Winship, mrs Eugenia
Winship, miss Ellen C
Witt, H H
Witt, mrs A A
Wood, Winston
Wood, mrs Mary
Yarbrough, Joel
York, B W
York, mrs C A

SABBATH SCHOOL.

Aggregate, Teachers and Pupils,   - -   250
Average Attendance,   - - - -   175

LEWIS LAWSHE, } Superintendents.
E. R. SASSEEN, }

B. W. York, Librarian.

GEORGE H. HAMMOND, } Ass't Librarians.
GEORGE SASSEEN, }

TRINITY, M. E.

South Side Mitchell Street, opposite City Hall.

(AGGREGATE MEMBERSHIP 257.)

Church Meetings 1st Sabbath in each Month, at 3 o'clock, P. M.

Communion 1st Sabbath in each Month.
Services every Sabbath at 10½ A. M., and at Night.

REV. WM. M. CRUMLEY, *Pastor.*

GEORGE ROBINSON, *Secretary Church Meeting.*

FORMER PASTORS.

Rev. John P. Duncan, 1854.
Rev. J. M. Austin, 1854.
Rev. Samuel Anthony, 1855.
Rev. Jesse Boring, 1855.
Rev. H. J. Adams, 1856.
Rev. Lewis J. Davies, 1857.
Rev. Robert N. Lester, 1858. and 1859.
Rev. Wm. M. Crumley, 1860.
Rev. John C. Simmons, 1861.
Rev. George G. N. McDonald, 1862.
Rev. H. H. Parks, 1863 and 1864.
Rev. Atticus G. Haygood, 1865 and 1866.
Rev. Wm. M. Crumley, 1867.

BOARD OF STEWARDS.

E. E. Rawson,
C. L. Redwine,
W. F. Harris,
F. M. Richardson.
J. M. C. Reed,
L. S. Salmons,
Robt Crawford.

TRUSTEES.

E. E. Rawson,
D. F. Hammond,
L. S. Salmons,
F. M. Richardson,
J. M. C. Reed,
W. F. Harris.

COMMUNICANTS.

Aiken, Francis M C
Aiken, mrs Susan
Allman, mrs Parmelia
Allman, miss Nannie
Anderson, Wm C
Anderson, mrs
Anderson, James H
Anderson, mrs Mary M
Anderson, miss Laura A
Anderson, miss Rosa M

Archer, mrs Caroline
Atkinson, S L
Austin, Joseph M
Bass, mrs Mary R
Bandy, mrs Emily
Baugh, Robert
Beck, Lewis
Beggorly, mrs Sarah P
Bell, miss Addie
Bell, miss Sarah
Bennett, Benj F
Bennett, mrs Mary E
Bennett, mrs Tallethia
Berry, mrs Catherine
Black, R D
Black, mrs R D
Booth, W K
Booth, mrs Anna
Boring, mrs Lorena
Bosworth, mrs Eliza
Bradbury, W S
Bradbury, mrs Elizabeth
Bradshaw, mrs Emily
Browning, mrs Hannah
Bruckner, Jas O
Bruckner, mrs Fannie
Bruckner, mrs Mary
Bruckner, miss Mattie
Buice, Elisha
Buice, mrs Addie
Boynton, C E
Caldwell, mrs Frances
Caldwell, miss R
Caldwell, miss Cammilla
Cheshire, C
Cheshire, mrs E D
Chester, W P
Chester, mrs Mary R

Chester, mrs Emma
Clancy, Michael J
Clancy, mrs Mary A
Clancy, miss Emma
Clancy, miss Mary M
Clancy, master Wm P
Colley, miss Sarah J
Cook, mrs Docia
Cook, miss Esther
Corbin, P V
Crawford, Robert
Crawford, mrs Adelia W
Davis, mrs Christiana
Day, Mattie R
Dermott, mrs Georgia C
Dodd, Green T
Dougherty, mrs Achsah
Doughty, mrs
Dunlap, miss Eleanor
Dunlap, miss Rebacca
Douglas, miss Annie
Earnest, F W
Earnest, mrs F W
Earnest, Elijah
Echols, Abner A
Edwards mrs
Ferguson, D P
Ford, Rev Jas J
Ford, mrs Emily
Ford, James C
Frizzell, John H
Gallagher, C H
Goudy, mrs E A
Hammond, Rev Dennis F
Hammond, mrs Adelia
Hammond, William
Hammond, miss Octavia
Hampton, John R

Haney, mrs Elizabeth
Hardage, Jas N
Hardage, mrs Louisa
Harris, Rev W F
Harris, mrs Martha
Haslett, John
Haslett, Elizabeth
Haygood, mrs Mary T
Haynes, W A
Haynes, mrs Lizzie
Hester, miss Mattie
Hilton, mrs Minerva
Holbrook, John M
Holbrook, mrs Hannah
Holbrook, Jesse C
Holbrook, mrs Elizabeth
Holmes, miss Fannie
Holmes, miss Margarett
Honecker, Christian
Honecker, mrs Martha
Honecker, miss Martha
Honecker, master William
Humphreys, Narcissa
Haygood, mrs N A
Haygood, miss Laura A
Haygood, miss Almira A
Haygood, Rev A G
Haygood, mrs M Y
Jeffries, LaFayette
Johnson, Mark W
Johnson, mrs L P
Johnson, mrs Martha
Johnson, Eliza
Jones, Oliver H
Jones, mrs Rebecca
Jones, Dr Geo W
Jones, mrs Zenobia

Knight, John
Knight, mrs Ann
Langford, mrs Magaret B
Lester, mrs
Livingston Jos H
Livingston, mrs
Long, mrs Harriet E
Lyon, mrs Judge
Lyon, mrs Ruth E
Lyon, miss Julia
Martin, Mary
McCormack, Hettie
McDade, mrs Rebecca
McFarland, mrs
McLean, mrs Jane
Mangum, mrs M L
Mangum, miss martha
Mangum, Wheeler
Morgan, A E
Muse, E H
Muse, mrs A S
Muse, Llewellen
McLendon, Mary L
Mobley, E D L
O'Donnally, Rev John
O'Donnally, mrs John
O'Donnally, master Robert
Ogletree, Samuel
Ogletree, mrs Mary F
Ogletree, miss Sallie
Ogletree, mrs Bersheba
Owens, John D
Owens, mrs E R
Owens, miss Sue W
Owens, miss Amelia C
Ozburn, J R D
Ozburn, mrs Elizabeth

Peacock, Lewis B
Pettus, mrs
Porter, J T
Porter, mrs Maria L
Powell, Dr T S
Powell, mrs Julia
Price, Dr Jas W
Patillo, mrs Sallie E
Quillian, George
Ramey, mrs Mary A
Rawson, E E
Rawson, mrs E W
Rawson, miss Mary P
Rawson, miss Laura
Rawson, miss Emma
Ray, mrs Isabella
Ray, miss Lizzie
Ray, master Henry
Reed, mrs Mary
Redwine, Dr C L
Register, mrs Tamesia
Register, mrs Ellen H
Reid, J M C
Reid, mrs Sarah
Reynolds, T S
Reynolds, mrs Mary
Richards, mrs L V
Richardson, Francis M
Richardson, mrs Sarah E
Richardson, master F H
Robinson, Geo M
Rogers, John C
Rhudy, miss Josephine
Rush, miss Margaret
Salmons, L S
Schenck, mrs Pauline
Scrutchin, mrs M A
Sherwood, mrs Samuel

Small, mrs W J
Smith, Ed A
Smith, mrs Elizabeth
Smith, miss Ophelia
Spillman, mrs
Stinson, mrs Julia
Stovall, mrs
Stoy, Thaddeus W
Stoy, mrs Emma
Thomas, Lovick P, sen
Thomas, mrs Martha A
Thomas, miss Sallie E
Thomas, Lovick P, jun
Thomas, mrs Jane
Thomas, Robt F
Thomas, mrs Eliza
Thomas, Jane E
Thompson, mrs Martha
Thrower, Thomas
Thrower, mrs Mattie
Thrower, Osgood A
Thrower, Benjamin
Thurman, miss Sarah
Towns, miss Jennie
Treadwell, miss Eliza J
Tuttle, Joel
Todd, Robt
Todd, Mary A E
Wade, mrs Josephine
Ware, mrs Nancy
Warren, Dr T A
Warren, mrs S E
Wellborn, Rev C B
Wells, mrs
Wells, miss Lizzie
Wells, mrs L C
Wells, miss Lucy
West, mrs

White, Virgil M
White, mrs Mary A
Willy, mrs Julia D
Wilson, mrs Jane
Wood, Coleman F
Wood, mrs Mary
Wood, miss Lou
Wood, mrs Candice
Woodruff, John C

Woodruff, mrs Mattie
Wing, mrs Emily
Zachry, Jas L
Zachry, mrs Mary J
Zachry, miss Luta C
Zachry, miss Carrie E
Zachry, Wm J
Zachry, mrs Martha A

SABBATH SCHOOL.

Aggregate, Teachers and Pupils,   -   -   300
Average Attendance,   -   -   -   -   225

F. M. RICHARDSON, Superintendent.

J. N. HARDAGE,
MRS. HETTIE M'CORMICK, } Librarians.

FIRST BAPTIST.

Corner Forsyth and Walton Streets.

Conference First Saturday in each Month.
Communion First Sabbath in each Month.
Services every Sabbath at 10½ o'clock.

H. C. HORNADY, *Pastor.*

*List of Names not accessible.

Total, Teacher and Pupils, - - - 500
Average Attendance, - - - . 350

A. K. SEAGO, Superintendent.

CHARLES J. KICKLIGHTER, Librarian.
A. P. STEWART, Assistant Librarian.

SECOND BAPTIST.

Northwest Corner of Washington and Mitchell Sts.

(AGGREGATE MEMBERSHIP 196.)

Conference—Saturday before the 2d Sabbath in each Month.
Communion—Sabbath following Monthly Conference.
Services every Sabbath at 10½ o'clock, A. M..

W. T. BRANTLEY, *Pastor.*

JOHN MILLEDGE, JR., Clerk

DEACONS.

B F Bomar,   Edward White,
I O McDaniel,   James H Callaway.

COMMUNICANTS.

Adair, G B   Armstrong, Dr W S
Alexander, mrs A E   Atkinson, mrs Anna E
Anderson, mrs E B   Bagby, W R
Andrews, Ezra   Bagby, mrs A H
Andrews, mrs Fannie   Barnard, mrs Mary

Bell, F R
Bell, mrs Mary
Benton, miss Susan
Blanchard, M C
Blanchard, mrs Martha S
Bomar, B F
Bomar, mrs J E L
Bomar, John
Bomar, mrs Anna
Brantley, miss Louisa
Brown, Jos E
Brown, mrs Elizabeth
Brown, C I
Brown, mrs Mary
Butt, Wm M
Butt, mrs Wm M
Butt, mrs Rebecca
Butt, Jesse
Butt, Timothy
Butt, miss Fannie
Butt, miss Elizabeth
Calaway, Jas H
Calaway, mrs Sarah
Chisolm, mrs Rebecca
Chisolm, miss Ellen
Chisolm, miss Cornelia
Chisolm, miss Martha
Clarke, Jas
Clarke, J W
Clarke, mrs Lydda
Clarke, miss Mary
Clarke, mrs Parmelia
Clarke, miss Alice
Clarke, miss Eugenia E
Connor, Geo C
Connor, mrs Louisa
Cuthbert, Robert
Cutting, J L

Cutting, mrs Eliza
Davis, mrs Ada A
Dorsey, mrs M E
Dubose, mrs M
Dunn, mrs Laura C
Echols, mrs Ruth W
Eyell, miss Caroline
Fleming, mrs Maria
Fleming, mrs O E
Franklin, J H
Frick, mrs Caroline
Gardner, mrs Rebecca
Gaskill, Rev V A
Gaskill, mrs M A
Gee, Wm
Gee, mrs S A
Glenn, H H
Glenn, Howell
Glenn, Thos J
Glenn, mrs Mildred
Glenn, miss Sallie
Goldsmith, mrs Sarah
Gregory, F M
Gregory, Ferdinand
Gregory, mrs S A
Gregory, miss Catharine
Grubb, Samuel
Grubb, mrs Ellen A G
Grubb, mrs Eliza. H W
Hamilton, miss M A E
Hammond, mrs L T
Harris, mrs Judge
Harris, miss Franecs
Harris, miss Josephine
Harris, miss Matilda
Henderson, miss Sallie E
Higginbotham, Mark
Hill, John R

Hill, mrs Dartha
Hillyer, Henry
Holmes, mrs Hester A
Holmes, mrs Martha
Hulsey, mrs Josephine
Humphreys, mrs Rebecca
Hunt, J W
Hunt, mrs Martha A
Hunter, mrs P R
James, John H
Johnson, miss Eliza
Jones, miss Lucy
Kendrick, S S
Kendrick, mrs E H
Kidd, mrs N
Knott, Rev Richard
Knott, mrs Sarah E
Knott, miss L P
Knott, miss Martha A
Krogg, mrs Jane
Lane, mrs Rebecca
Lee, Sanders W
Lee, mrs Anna
Lee, miss Mary
Love, mrs Tabitha
Luckie, mrs
Lynn, mrs Amanda M
Lynn, miss Mary
Lynn, miss Susan
Marshall, Rev A E
Martin, T A
Massey, Dr R J
Massey, mrs R J
Massey, mrs Sophia
Mathews, A B
McBride, A J
McDaniel, I O
McDaniel. Egbert

McDaniel, P E
McDaniel, Ira
McDaniel, mrs C J
McDaniel, mrs R J
McDaniel, mrs L C
McDaniel, miss Vesta J
Meredith, mrs Georgia
Meredith, miss Cordelia
Miller, mrs Mary
Nace, mrs Anna B
Neal, John
Neal, miss Emma
Nelson, mrs Nancy
Newman, mrs A E
Nix, mrs Ann
Nunnally, A F
Nunnally, mrs A F
O'Keefe, D C
O'Keefe, mrs Sarah
Patch, mrs Elizabeth
Pittman, M
Pittman, mrs Lou
Pope, mrs W
Potts, miss Lavinia
Pound, mrs
Reeves, mrs N J
Richards, J J
Richards, S P
Richards, H H
Richards, mrs S P
Richards, mrs Ellen
Richardson, mrs
Roach, Dr E J
Roach, mrs Dr E J
Rucker, mrs L V
Scruggs, Wm L
Scruggs, mrs Judith
Seals, mrs John H

Sisson, Henry
Smith, Samuel
Smith, T T
Smith, mrs T T
Smith, mrs Joseph
Smith, miss Elizabeth
Spear, mrs Elizabeth
Spear, miss Sallie
Spiller, miss Eddie
Stubner, mrs Anna
Taylor, mrs Susan
Tippen, J B
Toon, J J
Toon, mrs J J
Verdery, S A
Verdery, M R
Ware, Dr J E H
Watkins, mrs R D

Welborn, A R
Wells, mrs Elizabeth
Werner, mrs
West, Thos W
West, mrs Mary J
West, Henry A
Whitaker, J I
Whitaker, mrs Nannie E
Whitaker, miss Isabella J
White, Edward
White, mrs Mary A
White, miss M D
Wiker, mrs Catherine
Williams, mrs Mary L
Willis, Charles
Zimmerman, R P
Zimmerman, mrs Bethie M

SABBATH SCHOOL.

Aggregate Number of Teachers and Pupils, - 250
Average Attendance, - . - - - 200

J. J. TOON, Superintendent.

IRA McDANIEL, Librarian.

———•••———

FIRST PRESBYTERIAN.

South Side Marietta, between Forsyth 'and Spring Streets.

(AGGREGATE MEMBERSHIP 162.)

Communion, First Sabbath in March, June, September, and December.
Preaching every Sabbath at 10½ o'clock A. M.

REV. JOHN S. WILSON, D. D., *Pastor.*

ELDERS.

Joel Kelsey.
Berryman Shumate.
Wm. Markham.
Wm. McMillan.
S. B. Hoyt,
James Hoge,

L. B. Davis,
W. P. Inman,
V. Thompson,
Joseph L. King,
Wm. M. Lowry.

DEACONS.

J. R. Wallace,
L. M. Dimmick,
W. J. Houston,

J. S. Oliver,
W. A. Powell,
Charles Harmsen,

COMMUNICANTS.

Adams, Sarah S
Alexander, Martha
Allen, miss Clara C
Austell, mrs F A
Baine, Donald
Baine, mrs Rebecca W
Barry, Charles M
Barry, mrs Jane E
Barry, miss Sarah J
Bassford, mrs L L B
Bellingrath, Leonard
Bellingrath, mrs Catharine
Bellingrath, Albert
Bellingrath, mrs Mary
Blackburn, mrs E J J
Braumuller, H
Braumuller, mrs A
Brockman, Jas P
Brockman, mrs Ruth
Brockman, miss Lucy J
Clark, Robert C

Clifford, mrs Caroline
Cocke, mrs Margaret E
Cole, mrs Mary C
Collier, James M
Collier, mrs Frances M
Corry, mrs Harriet
Corry, miss Sarah J
Daniels, mrs Mary A L
Daniels, miss Jane
Edwards, Martha
Farrar, mrs Mary B
Farrar, mrs A
Ficken, Henry
Gamble, Sarah
Garmany, Mary
Gilbert, mrs Catharine
Glatz, Julius
Glatz, mrs Sarah Ann
Glenn, John
Glenn, mrs Eliza
Glenn, miss N E
Gordon, mrs Elizabeth A

Gordon, miss Alice
Green, mrs Mary
Harden, C
Harmsen, Charles
Harmsen, mrs Julia M
Hayden, Julius A
Hayden, mrs Harriet E
Hayden, miss Leslie
Haynes, Mary
Heely, Thomas G
Heely, mrs Olive M
Helms, Temperance A
Hetzel, Wilhelm
Hetzel, mrs Henrietta
High, mrs M
Hill, mrs Elizabeth C
Hill, Parmelia P
Hoge, James
Hoge, mrs Catharine
Hoge, miss M E
Hoge, miss Kate S
Hoge, miss Mary Jane
Horton, Theresa
Houston, W J
Houston, mrs Anna
Houston, mrs Amanda C
Houston, miss Flora
Hoyt, S B
Hoyt, mrs L M
Inman, W P
Inman, mrs H C
Inman, Shadrick W
Inman, mrs Catharine Ann
Inman, Hugh P
Jones, mrs Lavinia C
Kelsey, Joel
Kelsey, mrs Diana
Kelsey, Joel, Jr

King, Joseph L
King, Mrs Catharine
Kontz, Christian
Kontz, mrs Eliza
Kontz, miss E Amelia
Langley, Franklin
Langston, T L
Ligon, Thomas H
Ligon, mrs Martha
Lowry, Wm M
Lowry, mrs Julia
Lyon, George
Markham, Wm
Markham, mrs A D
McDiarmid, mrs M S
McFier, Mary A
McMillan, Wm
McMillan, mrs R D
McMillan, Jane
Morrison, M
Mulligan, Berry
Mulligan, mrs Susanna
Oliver, J S
Oliver, mrs Cynthia
Oliver, miss Georgia Ann
Parks, mrs Amanda M
Parks, miss Mary J
Payne, L M
Peck, mrs Josephine
Plaster, B F
Powell, mrs Louisa A C
Powell, W A
Rawlings, mrs Mary G
Rhinehart, Christian
Rhinehart, Mary A
Rice, mrs Louisa E
Robinson, James
Robinson, mrs Jane C

Robinson, mrs Martha M
Rouski, Hetty M
Rucker, J W
Rucker, mrs M J E
Saunders, F H
Sawtell, Ephraim
Saye, Richard
Scott, Mary
Shepherd, mrs M A
Shumate, Berryman
Shumate, mrs Nancy
Shumate, mrs Sarah W
Shumate, R C
Shumate, mrs Pryalla A
Sims, Philip B
Sims, mrs Jane
Smythson, Elizabeth
Strickland, Isaac
Strickland, mrs Mary F
Strickland, miss Laura
Thompson, V
Tomlinson, mrs A

Tuller, W H
Tuller, mrs F H
Underwood, mrs Loucinda
Vandergriff, mrs Elizabeth
Venable, S C
Waits, mrs Nancy E
Wallace, John R
Wallace, mrs Elizabeth a
Ware, Mary A E
White, John C
White, mrs Laura
Wiley, mrs
Williams, mrs Agnes
Williams, Lou
Wilson, Sarah
Wilson, mrs Mary A
Wilson, mrs Juliet
Willborn, mrs J S M
Wilson, miss Victoria D E
Wright, mrs Dorick
Wright, Martha C

SABBATH SCHOOL.

Total, Teachers and Pupils, -   -   -   -   120
Average Attendance, -   -   -   -   -   80
Volumes in Library, -   -   -   -   -   350

L. B. DAVIS, Superintendent.

JAS. HOGE, Ass't Superintendent.

T. C. LANGSTON, Librarian.

CENTRAL PRESBYTERIAN.

Wset Side Washington Street, opposite City Hall.

(AGGREGATE MEMBERSHIP 125.)

Sacramental Meetings First Sabbath in January, April, July, and October.

Preaching every Sabbath at 10½ o'clock, A. M., and in the Afternoon, or at Night.

REV. RUFUS K. PORTER, *Pastor.*

ELDERS.

Dr Joseph P. Logan,	Wm McNaught,
Julias M. Patton,	John C. Whitner.
Moses Cole,	

DEACONS.

W. P. Robinson,	P. P. Pease,
Geo. S. Thomas,	Charles Whitehead.
W. P. Harden,	

COMMUNICANTS.

Alexander, mrs Georgia J	Boyd, Martha A
Alexander, miss Harriet E	Boyd, Mary R
Anderson, mrs M A	Brown, mrs Mary L
Ansley, John U	Brown, miss Maria L
Ansley, mrs Mary	Calhoun, mrs Lucy
Bard, mrs Martha	Calhoun, miss Georgia
Barrick, James R	Calhoun, miss Florida
Barrick, mrs L B	Calhoun, mrs Mary J
Barth, C F	Campbell, mrs Virginia O
Boyd, miss Nancy E	Clack, mrs Elizabeth
Boyd, miss Martha C	Clarke, John M

Clarke, mrs J M
Clarke, Edward Y
Clarke, Thos M
Clayton, miss C
Cole, Moses
Cole, mrs Maria
Coleman, mrs Sallie H
Combs, miss Mary
Cooley, mrs Mary
Corley, miss Mary
Craig, James
Craig, mrs Julia A
Crew, mrs J L
Crook Joseph W
Crook, miss Mary W
Crook, miss Amanda M
Dabney, Wm A
Dabney, mrs Martha
DuBose, Dr W
DuBose, mrs Anna
Edwards, mrs Virginia M
Elliott, mrs Isabella
Ellis, John
Farrow, Henry P
Farrow, mrs Cornelia S
Forsyth, William
Forsyth, mrs Ann
Gardner, mrs Caroline E
Gilbert, Theodore
Gilbert, mrs Henrietta
Grant, Lemuel P
Grant, mrs L L
Grant, miss Anna
Grant, miss Lizzie S
Gullatt, mrs Josephine
Hanleiter, mrs A E
Harden, Dr W P
Harden, mrs Sarah J

Holly, mrs Sarah B
Hall, mrs Mary C
Jeffries. Dr. Francis M
Kilby, Wm J
Kilby, mrs Wm J
Kirkpatrick, mrs H A
Kirkpatrick, miss C E
Knight, George W
Lichtenstadt, mrs M M P
Lockhart, Joseph D
Logan, Dr Joseph P
Logan, mrs Ann E
Logan, miss Annie
Lines, Sylvanus D
Lines, mrs Jennie A
Lyon, mrs Mary E
McDowell, Thos
McDowell, mrs Elizabeth
McGuire, mrs Anna M
McNaught, William
Mullen, mrs Mary Alice
Newton, Charles S
O'Keefe, mrs S H
Orme, Dr Henry S
Parr, mrs S D
Patton, Julius M .
Patton, miss Mary D
Pease, Philander P
Pease, mrs P P
Phillips, H T
Ripley, mrs Laura D
Robinson, W P
Robinson, mrs Kate W
Rodes, mrs Sallie
Rogers, mrs Emily C
Rushton, William
Rushton, mrs Martha
Rushton, miss Mary A

6

Rushton, miss Eva
Sawtell, mrs Eliza V
Sewell, William F
Shaw, miss Calderwood
Sneed, miss Sarah F
Steele, mrs Mary
Thomas, George S
Thompson, Dr Joseph
Towns, George W
Toy, mrs James M
Van Epps, A C
Wallace, Alex M
Wallace, mrs Fannie G
Whitner, John C

Whitner, mrs Sarah M
Whitney, mrs Joshua
Whitney, miss Frank
Whitehead, Charles
Whitehead, mrs Julia C
Wiley, mrs Nancy H
Williams, mrs Carrie
Willis, J M
Willis, mrs Julia
Winn, Dr E E
Winn, mrs E E
Word, Dr Robert C
Word, mrs A E
Wyly, mrs Sarah H

SABBATH SCHOOL.

Total, Teachers and Pupils,   -   -   -   -   120
Average Attendance,   -   -   -   -   -   100

MOSES COLE, Superintendent.

J. C. WHITNER, Assistant Supt.

J. A. BARRY, Librarian.

ST. PHILIP'S, EPISCOPAL.

North-East Corner Washington and Hunter Streets.

(NUMBER OF COMMUNICANTS 127.)

Services every Sabbath at 10½ o'clock A. M.

REV. CHARLES W. THOMAS, *Rector.*

WARDENS.

Dr. J. M. JOHNSON, Senior Warden.
SAMUEL HAPE, Junior Warden.

VESTRYMEN.

JAMES M. BALL,	Dr. L. H. ORME,
JAMES ORMOND,	H. G. BELL,
DR. HOLMES SELLS,	ISAIAH PURSE,
CHARLES POWELL, Treas'r,	S. W. GRUBB, Secretary.

CONVENTION DELEGATES FOR 1866.

RICHARD PETERS, Esq.,   SAMUEL HAPE, Esq.

COMMUNICANTS.

Allen, mrs M	Cooper, miss G G
Angier, mrs E A	Croft, miss Ellen
Austin, mrs ——	Croft, miss Susan
Ball, J M	Currier, mrs C A
Bard, Dr Samuel	Douglass, Dr George
Barrow, mrs Claude	Douglass, mrs George
Bateson, Christopher H	Dunning, mrs C
Baugh, John	Erskine, Judge John
Beaumont, mrs M J	Erskine, mrs John
Bell, H G	Flynn, mrs Jane
Bell, mrs M A	Ford, Dr A C
Browning, C H	Ford, mrs Emily
Bryant, mrs E	Frazer, George P
Bryant, mrs J	Garcia, mrs B
Buckhardt, mrs G A	Gibbons, mrs George
Burton, mrs ——	Gray, mrs William
Cassin, mrs C P	Green, George
Clancy, miss ——	Green, mrs George
Clarke, mrs Joan	Grubb, Samuel W
Clarke, mrs M M	Hape, Samuel
Clayton, W F	Hape, mrs Orvilla
Crane, mrs Sallie C	

Henderson, John
Henderson, mrs John
Hewitt, mrs M J
Hill, mrs ——
Holroyd, miss Sarah
Holroyd, miss M A
Hunnicutt, mrs Joseph M
Hutchinson, mrs S B
Johnson, Dr J M
Johnson, Rev Richard
Johnson, mrs Richard
Johnson, miss L W
Johnson, miss S
Johnson mrs William
Jones, mrs Hiram T
Jones, miss A
Judson, miss L F
Judson, William
Judson, mrs E
Judson, miss Allie
Leonard, mrs ——
Leonard, miss E
Leyden, mrs R C
Martin, mrs S W
M'Arthur, T W
M'Arthur, mrs E A
Moore, mrs A G
Oatman, S B
Ogilsby miss Mary
Ormond, James
Ormond, mrs James
Ormond, Joseph
Ormond, miss Helen
Orme, W P
Orme, mrs W P
Orme, Dr L H
Orme, mrs F H
Parsons, Edward

Peters, Richard
Peters, mrs M J
Peters, mrs E
Peters, Richard, jr
Pinney, miss G C
Poole, miss Margaret
Powell, Charles
Powell, mrs M A
Powell, miss Ada
Powell, miss M A
Pratte, mrs E G
Riley, T G
Riley, mrs Anora
Robinson, mrs Matt
Romaré, Paul
Romaré, mrs Lucy A
Seaman, miss H C
Sells, Dr Holmes
Sells, mrs A H
Smith, mrs J J
Smith, mrs Mary C
Snook, P H
Snook, mrs P H
Solomon, William
Solomon, mrs S L
Solomon, miss S
Sosnowski, Julius
Spalding, miss L P
Taylor, miss C
Tierney, mrs M
Thomas, mrs E J
Thompson, miss L
Walker, mrs E B
Walker, mrs Thomas
Warwick, miss C
Watkins, miss M D
Watts, mrs M
Westmoreland, mrs M J

Williams, I D
Wilson, mrs ——
Wood, T S
Wood, mrs Mary

Wright, mrs L B
Wright, miss J A
Wright, miss L Rosa
Young, W Euclid

SABBATH SCHOOL.

Total number Teachers and Pupils, - - 72
Volumes in Library, - - - - - 400

SAMUEL HAPE, Supt.

H. G. BELL, Librarian.

CHRISTIAN CHURCH.

*New Church Building in course of erection, on Hunter
Street.*

*Services, for the present, in building nearly opposite
1st Baptist Church, on Walton Street.*

JNO. T. HALL, *Elder.*

S. J. SHACKELFORD, }
THO. W. CHANDLER, } *Deacons.*
J. I. MILLER, }

CATHOLIC CHURCH—IMMACULATE CONCEPTION.

South-East corner of Floyd and Hunter Streets.

* (TOTAL ADULT MEMBERSHIP ABOUT 500.)

Services every Sabbath, at 10½ o'clock, A. M.

CONVENT SCHOOL of the Sisters of Mercy, east side of
Lloyd Street, between Hunter and Mitchell.

*An accurate list of names not accessible.

MASONIC.

NOTE.—The following Masonic bodies meet at present in Odd Fellows' Hall, but will occupy "Masonic Temple," corner Marietta and Broad Streets, as soon as completed, which will probably be in June next.

ATLANTA LODGE, NO. 59, F. A. M.

Organized under Dispensation, April 13, and Chartered October 26, A. D., 1847, A. L. 5847.

REGULAR COMMUNICATIONS, 2d and 4th Thursday nights in each month.

OFFICERS.

THOS. W. CHANDLER, W. M.
W. H. TULLER, Sen. W.
L. R. LANIER, Jr. W.
ED. A. WERNER, Treas.
J. M. BORING, Sec'y.
H. C. BARROW, Sen. D.
G. A. HUWALD, Jr. D.
W. D. LUCKIE, } Stewards.
C. E. STEPHENS, }
J. G. McLIN, Tiler.

MASTER MASONS.

Adamson, W L	Baker, Rev R S
Anderson, W C	Baker, A
Andrews, Ezra	Bankston, H
Bacon, R A	Barnwell, V T
Barrett, W J	Bell, J L

Bennett, B F	Fechter, D
Biggers, S T	Fay, Calvin
Biggers, J M	Fleck, Daniel
Bookout, J M	Flynn, Jno H
Bramlet, J F	Ford, A C
Brenton, D A	Fuller, W A
Bridges, A S	Fuller, J H
Brooks, W E	Gartrell, L J
Bryant, J M	Giles, J T
Buice, D	Glenn, H H
Burr, G W	Goodhue, Nathaniel
Bush, B	Grady, A B
Butt, Wm M	Graff, J H
Calhoun, I P	Gramling, J R
Campbell, C T	Grant, W W
Camp, G W	Gredig, Abraham
Castleberry, M T	Griffin, J D
Center, G W	Gross, C G
Chapman, Rufus	Hackett, Wilson
Chapman, Henry	Hammond, A W
Chase, G H	Hammond, Geo H
Connally, T W	Hancock, W S
Cook, I	Harris, W W
Cook, G W D	Harris, T M
Cornell, J M	Harrell, J H
Coulter, F F	Hays, I N
Crane, J E	Hazlett, S D
Craven, V M	Herring, W F
Crussell, T G W	Hestley J S
Davis, C C	Hetzel, William F
Davis, J C	Hightower, T J
Doby, J B	Hill, Wm M
Doby, G J	Holbrook, J M
Dougherty, D H	House, F C
Durand, S A	Houston, W J
Edwards, J R	Howell, H P
Earnest, E E	Hoyt, S B
Embry, J F	Hook, Rev D

Hughes, Columbus
Hunnicutt, C W
Hunnicutt, E T
Ivy, M J
Jackson, J B
James J H
Jenkins, J J
Jentzen, J H
Johnson, R J
Johnson, J M
Johnston, F M
Jones, H W
Krous, Harry
Landsberg, A
Lanier, W P
Lawshé, Rev Lewis
Lawshé, Er
Leyden, A
Lowe, W B
Manning, A M
Manning, W H
Marshall, H
Martin, T A
Martin, M H
McPherson, James
McWilliams, G W
McEntyre, W R
McCool, J A
Mead, L S
Mead, W T
Mell, E S
Mills, J G M
Mims, J T
Mitchell, W D
Moore, B F
Morris, J F
Morris, T A
Morris, W L

Munday, E W
Murphy, E C
Murphy, Anthony
Nelson, James M
Oatman, S B
O'Connor, Thomas
O'Keefe, D C
Orme, Henry S
Oslin, Rev R E
Owen, Powell
Ozburn, J R D
Parsons, Edward
Pate, J A
Payne, C M
Peel, John
Perdue, F P
Phillips, L B
Pittman, Daniel
Plummer, E T
Pound, J G
Powell, Chapman
Price, J W
Purtell, J H
Ransom, J H
Rice, A G
Roach, E J
Robinson, R J
Rogers, Rev B P
Roony, Nicholas
Rosser, J P
Rucker, J W
Sasseen, E R
Sawtell, I Y
Seavy, J H
Sewell, J W
Sewell, A C
Shearer, W
Shipley, J S

Silvey, John
Sitton, P M
Smith, A M
Smith, B D
Spinks, L D
Stephens, W H
Strickland, Henry
Strong, C H
Suttles, A G
Taylor, J A
Thrasher, J J
Thrower, T L
Thurman, B
Touchstone, B B
Toy, James M
Trimble, M H
Walker, D A
Walker, T E
Ware, J E H

Waters, W T
Welch, George
Wells, J Y
Westbrook, J L
Whitaker, A S
White, R A
Wiley, J M
Williford, B N
Willis, J M
Wilson, W A
Wilson, J S
Wise, John S
Witt, H H
Wood, Winston
Young, John
Young, Rev D
Young, W Euclid
Young, Robert

FULTON LODGE, NO. 216, F. A. M.

Organized October, 1857.

REGULAR COMMUNICATIONS 1st and 3d Thursday nights in each month.

OFFICERS.

W. W. BOYD, W. M.
H. W. BROXTON, Sr. W.
M. V. D. CORPUT, Jr. W.
C. D. JACKSON, Treas.
C. F. BARTH, Sec'y.
L. COHEN, Sr. D.
T. E. WHITAKER, Jr. D.
J. W. KEELY, } Stewards.
G. H. GRAMLING, }
A. McLELLAN, Tiler.

MASTER MASONS.

Bass, U D
Bellingrath, L
Bomar, B F
Bowman, J T
Brauham, D H
Brewer, W
Broscius, J W
Bush, R P
Chapman, E B
Dallas, D G
Dean, L
Erskine, John
Farrow, H. P.
Frank, M
Frank, S
Garner, L C
Glenn, L J
Gramling, J A
Hagan, F
Hammock, C C
Harmsen, Charles
Hayden, F
High, W L
Holland, W C
Howard, R A
Hudson, J H
Jennings, W
Joiner, H
Kennedy, T J
King, A L
Kuhrt, H G

Lansdell, W A
Lichtenstadt, M L
Love, S B
Maier, John
Massey, R J
Mayer, David
McDaniel, I O
McDaniel, P E
Mitchell, A W
Peck, J C
Phinizy, J F
Pratte, B A
Rich, William
Smith, C H
Spenceley, J
Stanton, W H
Steinheimer, J
Thomas, G S
Turner, D R
Venable, D C
Walker, E B
Watkins, W
West, W D
Whitaker, J I
Williams, J E
Williams, E G
Williams, J N
Wilson, W
Wilson, M M
Wing, H L

MOUNT ZION ROYAL ARCH CHAPTER, NO. 16.

Chartered May 3d, A. D., 1847, A. I., 2377.

REGULAR CONVOCATIONS, 2d and 4th Monday nights in each month

OFFICERS.

THOS. W. CHANDLER, M. E. H. P.
H. C. BARROW, E. K.
H. MARSHALL, E. S.
HENRY S. ORME, Capt. H.
W. W. BOYD, Prin. Soj.
L. R. LANIER, R. A. C.
E. J. ROACH, M. 3d V.
V. T. BARNWELL, M. 2d V.
CALVIN FAY, M. 1st V.
C. D. JACKSON, Treas.
GEO. H. HAMMOND, Sec'y.
A. McLELLAN, Sen'l.

ROYAL ARCH MASONS.

Anderson, W C
Albert, J F
Austell, A
Bacon, R A
Baker, R S
Biggers, S T
Bookout, T A
Boring, J M
Bostain, H W
Brooks, W E
Broxton, H W
Connally, T W
Crussell, T G W
Cunningham, J D

Davis, C C
Fleishel, David
Frank, M
Fuller, W A
Glenn, L J
Gross, C G
Hammock, C C
Hays, J W
Hendrix, J C
Holt, A K
Houston, W J
Hughes, Columbus
Hunnicutt, C W
Hunnicutt, E T

Lansdell, W A
Lattimer, H B
Lawshé, Lewis
Leyden, A
Maier, Jno
Mayer, David
McLin, J G
Mead, W T
Mills, J G W
Moore, B F
Moore, W C
Morris, T A
Owen, P
Ozburn, Jas R D
Page, W J
Peck, J C
Pegg, W H
Pounds, J G

Ransom, Joseph H
Rich, William
Rosser, J P
Rushton, W
Sitton, P M
Strong, C H
Thomas, A G
Tuller, W H
Turner, W H
Werner, E A
Whitaker, J I
Whitaker, T E
Williams, J E
Williams, J N
Williford, B N
Willis, J M
Winn, E E
Witt, H H

JASON BURR COUNCIL, NO. 13.

ROYAL MASTERS AND SELECT MASONS OF 27.

Organized in April 1855.

REGULAR CONVOCATIONS, 3d Monday night in each month.

OFFICERS.

W. W. BOYD, T. Ill.
THOS. W. CHANDLER, H. T.
H. C. BARROW, H. A.
N. D'ALVIGNY, Treas.

J. M. BORING, Rec.
HENRY S. ORME, C. G.
A. McLELLAN, Steward.
J. G. McLIN, Sen'l.

MEMBERS.

Aderhold, W V
Albert, J F
Barnwell, V T

Ladd, A C
Lankford, J A
Lawshé, Rev Lewis

Blackie, C S   Love, J M
Brooks, V E   Marshall, H
Clarke, I. H W   Mead, W T
Crussell, G W   Mills, J G W
Davis, C   Moore, W C
Embree, L   Richardson, F M
Fay, Calv   Sitton, P M
Hammon Geo H   Thomas, A G
Hill, Wn I   Tuller, W H
Hood, R D   Whitaker, J I
Jones, G   Willis, J M
Key, Re W   Zachry, Bertrand

CŒUR : LION COMMANDERY, NO. 4.—K. T.

Ch ered Sept. 17, *A. D.,* 1859, *A. O.,* 741.

REGUL CONCLAVE, 1st Monday night in each month.

OFFICERS.

THOS. W. CHANDLER, P∴ C∴ Em. Com.
ALVIN FAY, Gen.
W. W. Boyd, P∴C∴—G∴Gen∴Capt. Gen.
H. MARSHALL, Prelate.
I. M. WILLIS, S. W.
W. H. TULLER, J. W.
LEWIS LAWSHE, Treas.
W. H. TURNER, Rec.
HENRY S. ORME, Warder.
P. M. SITTON, Std. Br.
H. HODGES, Swd. Br.
A. M. MANNING, 1st Gd.
C. C. DAVIS, 2d Gd.
COLUMBUS HUGHES, 3d Gd.
J. G. MCLIN, Sen'l.

KNIGHTS TEMPLAR.

Aderhold, W V	Leyden, A
Anderson, G T	Manning, G S
Albert, J F	McLellan, A
Barnwell, V T	McPherson, James
Barrow, II C	Mead, W T
Beaumont, T M—P∴C∴	Mills, J G W
Bostain, II W	Moore, B F
Brassell, J	Morris, T A
Brooks, W E	Newman, Wm G
Cleveland, W L	Peacock, D W K
Corput, Max V D	Pratte, Bernard
D'Alvigny, N	Sage, B Y
Dent, Joseph E	Smith, II F
Dent, W B W	Steadman, E
Fuller, W A	Richardson, F M
Hancock, W II	Whitaker, T E
Jackson, C D	Wilkinson, U B
Jones, G L	Wise, J S

WHITE EAGLE CHAPTER, NO. 1.

Rose Croix, A. and A. R.   *Chartered July* 3, 1866.

W. W. Boyd, M∴ W∴	II. C. Barrow, M∴ C∴
Tho. W. Chandler, S∴W∴	Calvin Fay, S∴ Exp.
A. J. Blair, J∴ W∴	II. S. Orme, J∴ Exp.
W. H. Tuller, Ora.	M. Frank, Gd. of Tem.
N. D'Alvigny, Alsno.	II. G. Kuhrt, Tiler.
W. T. Mead, Sec'y.	

MOUNT ZION COUNCIL OF GOOD SAMARITANS

Meets first Tuesday Night in each Month.

W. W. Boyd, Master of Ceremonies.

Geo. H. Hammond, Sec'y.

I. O. O. F.

CENTRAL LODGE, NO. 28.

Organized October 7, 1848.

MEETS EVERY TUESDAY NIGHT, IN ODD FELLOWS' HALL.

OFFICERS.

M. BUICE, N. G.　　　W. D. WEST, V. G.
J. C. ROGERS, Treas.　　B. F. BENNETT, Sec'y.

MEMBERS.

Anderson, Robert	Dunbar, J H
Ashley, W G	Eddleman, F M
Bacon, R A	Elyea, C H
Bailey, W H	Fechter, D
Baine, Donald	Fife, R A
Baker, J W	Fleishel, David
Bender, William	Fowler, J W
Boyd, W W	Franklin, H
Bright, G L	Garnett, Thos.
Broxton, H W	Gramling, W G
Caldwell, M P	Gramling, J A
Carnell, James M	Gross, C G
Center, Geo W	Guess, H P
Chapman, W B	Hanleiter, W R
Clarke, L H	Haynes, T F
Cranford, H L	Hembree, H D R
Crawford, F A	Henderson, J C
Croft, D W	Holcombe, H C
Daiber, John	Husketh, L S

Jackson, C D
Jarrall, Willis
Jones, J T
Keltner, Wm
Keltner, Dan'l E
Keltner, T W
Kerr, J L
Kilby, W J
Kirkland, W L
Klotz, J P
Lee, M D
Lynch, J
Mays, J P
McDaniel, W P
Middleton, J A
Mitchell, W D
Mitchell, W E
Mott, James B
Munday, E W

Oliver, W T
Pair, J H
Phillips, L B
Pittman, R A
Plummer, E T
Rich, William
Rogers, J C
Rogers, J J
Smith, James T
Spinks, L D
Spinks, H T
Thompson, J R
Tyler, Charles
Wallace, J R
Weaver, J M
Whitaker, T E
Young, Dr David
Youngblood, M M

BARNES LODGE NO. 55.

Organized March 5, 1863.

MEETS EVERY FRIDAY NIGHT, IN ODD FELLOWS' HALL.

OFFICERS.

J. M. HUNNICUTT, N. G.   C. E. STEPHENS, V. G.
E. P. McCown, Treas.   S. W. GRUBB, Sec'y.

MEMBERS.

Autry, J H
Autry, F M
Barnes, A L
Barnwell, V T
Barrick, James R
Bennett J K
Bowen, J C

Bradley, Wm
Brannan, John C
Bridges, R H
Brown, Lee
Bush, Geo W
Bush, R P
Barrow, H C

Chandler, Thos W
Chase, Geo H
Cox, F A
Cox, James B
Crane, J E
DeLay, H R
Dickson, W E
Dockum, O, p g
Edwards, J L
Farrar, R M, p g
Fletcher, W H
Fleming, T P, p g
Freck, A
Gammage, T M
Glenn, Luther J, p g
Grant, W W
Griffin, J L
Grist, B A
Grist, M T
Grubb, S W, p g
Grubbs, W W
Henderson, John
Hill, A J
Hill, John A
Hughens, Jno H
Hunnicutt, J M
Ikerd, H M

McCown, E P, p g
McCown, R W
Mead, L S
Middleton, W G
Millwood, W R
Mitchell, I S
Murphy, E C
Myers, C F
Ogletree, Geo T
Orme, Henry S
Patillo, S H
Porter, J T
Queen, David M
Riley, Thos G
Shaw, S H
Smith, Jesse
Stapler, R F, p g
Stephens, C E
Thompson, B W
Thompson, J T
Watson, A R
Whitmire, W C
Willis, J M
Wing, James M
Wilson, Hugh A
Wilson, Henry
Young, John

EMPIRE ENCAMPMENT, NO. 12.

Chartered December 13, 1860.

MEETS ON THE 2D AND 4TH WEDNESDAY NIGHTS OF EACH MONTH,
AT ODD FELLOWS' HALL.

OFFICERS.

T. P. FLEMING, C. P.   J. W. BAKER, Jr. W.
B. F. BENNETT, H. P.   S. W. GRUBB, Scribe.
JOHN A. HILL, Sen. W.   M. BUICE, Treas.

7

MEMBERS.

Bailey, W H, P C P & P H P   Jones, John T
Baker, John W   Kilby, W J, P H P
Barnes, W H, P G P   Lower, A
Barnwell, V T   Mays, John P
Bennett, B F   McCown, E P, P C P & P H P
Boyd, W W, M W G P   Mitchell, W D
Brown, Lee   Munday, E W
Buice, M   Pair, J H
Chandler, T W   Plummer, E T
Crawford, A R   Riley, Thos G
Croft, D W   Stapler, R F
Dockum, O, P C P & P H P   Terry, Geo W
Farrar, R M   Thompson, J R
Fleming, T P, P C P & P H P   Wallace, John R
Gramling, W G, P H P   Whitaker, T E
Grubb, S W, P C P & P H P   Willis, J M
Hembree, H D R   Young, John
Hill, John A   Youngblood, M

UNITED STATES GOVERNMENT.

THE EXECUTIVE.

Andrew Johnson, of Tennessee, President, salary $25,000
LaFayette S. Foster, of Conn., acting Vice President, salary........................ 8,000

THE CABINET.

Wm. H. Seward, of N. Y., Sec. of State, salary $ 8,000
Hugh McCulloch, of Indiana, Sec. of Treas. " 8,000
Edwin M. Stanton, of Penn., Sec. of War, " 8,000
Gideon Wells, of Conn., Sec. of Navy, " 8,000
Orville H. Browning, of Ill., Sec. of the Interior, salary................................... 8,000
Henry Stanbury, of Ohio, Att'y Gen'l, salary... 8,000
Alex. W. Randall, of Wis., P. M. Gen'l, salary... 8,000

THE JUDICIARY.

SUPREME COURT OF THE UNITED STATES.

Salmon P. Chase, of Ohio, Chief Justice, salary, $ 6,500

Associate Justices—Salary $6,000.

Nathan Clifford, of Maine.   David Davis, of Illinois.
Samuel Nelson, of N. Y.   Noah H. Swayne, of Ohio.
Robt. C. Grier, of Penn.   Samuel F. Miller, of Iowa.
Jas. M. Wayne, of Ga.   Sthephen J. Field, of Cal.

Court meets 1st Monday in December, at Washington.

UNITED STATES DISTRICT COURT.

The United States District Court for Georgia, consists of two Districts, the Northern and the Southern, and is held as follows :
Northern District—At Atlanta, second Monday in March and September.

Southern District—At Savannah, second Tuesday in February, May, August, and November.

OFFICERS OF COURT.

John Erskine, Judge; salary $4,000.
H. H. Fitch, U. S. Attorney.
W. G. Dickson, U. S. Marshal.
C. H. Elyea, U. S. Deputy Marshal.
H. C. Holcomb, Clerk, Southern District.
W. B. Smith, Clerk, pro tem., Northern District.

UNITED STATES COMMISSIONERS.

Northern District.—James L. Dunning; W. B. Smith
Southern District.—H. C. Holcomb; A. W. Stone.

GEORGIA STATE GOVERNMENT.

EXECUTIVE DEPARTMENT.

Charles J. Jenkins, Governor, salary............ $4,000
R. L. Hunter, Sec. Ex. Department, salary....... 1,800
H. J. G. Williams, Sec. Ex. Department, salary.. 1,800
Z. D. Harrison, Messenger Ex. Dept., salary..... 950

STATE HOUSE OFFICERS.

N. C. Barnett, Sec. of State, and Surv. Gen'l, salary $2,000
Jno. T. Burns, Comptroller General, salary...... 2,000
John Jones, Treasurer, salary.................. 2,000
J. G. Montgomery, Librarian, salary............ 1,200
Jesse Horton, Capt. State House Guard, salary... ——

JUDICIARY.—Judges Supreme Court.

Joseph Henry Lumpkin, of Athens, Chief J., salary $3,500
Iverson L. Harris, of Milledgeville, salary........ 3,500
Dawson A. Walker, of Dalton, salary.......... 3,500

Logan E. Bleckley, Reporter, salary $1,000.
C. W. DuBose, Clerk.

Sessions held semi-annually, at Milledgeville: First Monday in June and December.

PENITENTIARY.

W. C. Anderson, Principal Keeper, salary........ $2,000
C. G. Talbird, Assistant Keeper, salary........ 1,200
A. M. Nisbet, Book Keeper, salary............ 1,200

LUNATIC ASYLUM.

Dr. T. F. Green, Supt. and Resd't Physician, salary $2,500
Dr. T. O. Powell, Assistant Superintendent.

COWETA CIRCUIT.

Hirm Warner, Judge, salary................... $2,500
W. H. Hulsey, Solicitor, salary............... 300

COUNTIES, AND TIMES OF HOLDING COURTS.

Troup—3d Monday in May and November.
Meriwether—3d Monday in February and August.
Fayette—2d Monday in March and September.
Clayton—1st Monday in May and November.
Fulton—1st Monday in April and October.
DeKalb—4th Monday in April and October.

OFFICERS OF FULTON COUNTY.

JUSTICES OF THE INFERIOR COURT.

E. M. Taliaferro,　William Watkins,　I. O. McDaniel.
C. C. Green,　　　(One Vacancy.)

Court.—Third Monday in June and December.

Ordinary—Daniel Pittman.
Judge County Court—B. D. Smith.
County Solicitor—George S. Thomas.
Sheriff—B. N. Williford.
Clerk Superior Court—W. R. Venable.
Clerk Inferior Covrt—J. W. Manning.
County Treasurer—D. P. Ferguson.
Receiver Tax Returns—Samuel Grubb.
Tax Collector—John M. Harwell.
County Surveyor—Thomas A. Kennedy.
Coroner—William Kile.
Special Bailiff, County Court—Jo. S. Smith.

JUSTICES OF THE PEACE.

Atlanta District—Wm. M. Butt, A. A. Gaulding.
Black Hall—Adam S. Pool, F. M. White.
Stone's—Joseph Willis, A. A. Wilson.
Casey's—John A. Casey, J. T. Akridge.
Buck Head—S. H. Donaldson, Hiram Casey.
Oak Grove—Wm. Power, Starling Goodwin.

POSTAL INFORMATION.

Post Office.—Corner Albama and Broad Streets.
T. G. Simms, P. M.; L. F. M. Mills, Assistant P. M.

Office Hours.—From 8.00 A. M., to 12.30 P. M., and from 2.00 to 6.00 P. M., every day except Sunday.

Open on Sundays, from 8.00 to 10.00 A. M., and from 5.00 to 5.30 P. M.

LETTER POSTAGE.

The law requires the postage on all letters to be pre-paid by stamps or stamped envelopes, payment in money being prohibited. All drop letters must also be pre-paid.

The rate of letter postage is three cents per half ounce throughout the United States, and three cents for each additional half ounce or fraction thereof.

The rate of postage on drop letters is two cents per half ounce or fraction thereof, at all offices where free delivery by carrier is established. Where such free delivery is not established, the rate is one cent.

NEWSPAPER POSTAGE.

The following is the postage on newspapers, when sent from the office of publication to regular subscribers:

Postage on daily papers to subscribers, when pre-paid quarterly, or yearly, in advance, either at the mailing office or office of delivery, per quarter, 35 cents.

Six times per week, per quarter.... ....30 cents.
For Tri-Weekly, " " ....15 "
For Semi-Weekly, " " ....10 "
For Weekly, " " .... 5 "

Weekly Newspapers (one copy only) sent by the publisher to actual subscribers, within the county where printed and published, free.

POSTAGE ON TRANSIENT MATTERS.

BOOKS AND CIRCULARS.

Books, not over 4 ounces in weight, one address, 4 cents; over 4 ounces, and not over 8 ounces, 8 cents; over 8 ounces and not over 12 ounces, 12 cents; over 12 ounces and not over 16 ounces, 16 cents.

Circulars, not exceeding three in number, to one address, 2 cents; over three and not over six, 4 cents; over six and not over nine, 6 cents; over nine, and not exceeding twelve, 8 cents.

OFFICES RE-OPENED IN GEORGIA UP TO MARCH 1867.

APPLING—Scriven, Miss Annie Clements.
BAKER—Newton, D L Parker.
BALDWIN—Milledgeville, W E Quillian.
BANKS—Erastus, Miss Mary M Burgess; Homer, Mrs E P Dodd; Middle River, W T Martin.
BERRIEN—Nashville, Sarah R Shepeard.
BIBB—Macon, J H R, Washington.
BROOKS—Quitman, D B Norman.
BRYAN—Way's Station, T A Owens.
BULLOCH—Statesborough.
BURKE—Alexander, Miss J P Brickett; Girard, C L Mobbiie; Holcombe, E J C Hull; Lawtonville, Geo B Hack; Millen, J H Daniel; Midville, S Goodwin; Waynesboro, C E Blount.
BUTTS—Indian Springs, G G Hardaway.
CALHOUN—Morgan, W G Pierce.
CAMDEN—Jeffersonton; St Mary's.
CAMPBELL—Campbellton, Mrs S L Butt; Fairburn, S Harvey; Palmetto, Miss M G Burch; White Hill, Paul E Black.
CARROLL—Bowden, T S Garrison; Carrolton, W B Conyers; Hickory Level, James L Baskin; Villa Rica, S W Noland.
CASS—Adairsville, J L Gash; Allatoona, J S Hopper; Cartersville, T M Compton; Cassville, Miss F M Brown; Etowah, Elijah Sprigg; Kingston, F M Whitborn; Pine Log, W Allen; Stilesboro', J F Sproul.
CATOOSA—Greysville, G C Wheeler; Ringgold, B C Yates.
CARLTON—Trader's Hill, B F Jones.
CHATHAM—Savannah, A L Harris, (Acting.)

CHATTAHOOCHEE—Cusseta, Mrs S R Cobb.
CHATTOOGA—Mellville, L J Mosteller; Summerville, Geo M C Branner.
CHEROKEE—Canton, L Holcomb; Woodstock, Laura A Harden.
CLARKE—Athens, S Williford; Watkinsville, Miss L E Grady.
CLAY—Fort Gaines, Emsley Lott.
CLAYTON—Jonesboro', Mrs M F Hanes; Lovejoy's Station, Mrs M C Stephens.
CLINCH—Homersville, G Lastingar; Lawton, W H Clifton.
COBB—Acworth, T A Roony; Bollonville, B F Moulding; Marietta, D M Young; Powder Springs, A J Kiser; Roswell, T D Adams.
COFFEE—McIntire.
COLQUITT—Moultrie.
COLUMBIA—Berzelia, H D Leitner; Lombardy, Mrs E Wood; Saw Dust, G L Reville; Thompson, R W Neal.
COWETA—Grantville, W B Smith; Newnan, Mrs D Wheelan; Turin, Mrs F O Gay.
CRAWFORD—Knoxville, Miss E W Torrence.
DADE—Morganville, R A Morgan; Rising Fawn, M F Cowen; Trenton, O C Johnson.
DAWSON—Dawsonville, Mrs M V Perkins.
DECATUR—Bainbridge; Cairo.
DeKALB—Cross Keys, Miss M C Polk; Decatur, W C Rosseau; Lithonia, G M Phillips; Stone Mountain, G P Bradley.

DOOLY—Byronville, J S Byron; Gum Creek, Wm Culpepper; Vienna, Robt N Coppedge.

DOUGHERTY—Albany, Miss M J Richardson.

EARLY—Blakely, J P Powers.

EFFINGHAM-Eden, M Humphreys; Guyton, G H Eaton; Springfield, A F Rahn.

ELBERT—Elberton, A L Vail; Ruckersville, T B Cleveland.

EMANUEL—Cannoochee, Miss M D Binson; Swainsboro', T H Kibbel.

FANNIN—Hot House, Elisha Anderson; Morganton, Andrew J Stone.

FAYETTE—Fayetteville, Miss P Smith.

FLOYD—Cave Springs, S Hammil; Floyd Springs, M rs E C McCullough; Rome, A R Smith; Yarborough, Mrs M F Wyatt.

FORSYTH—Cumming, S R Knox; Big Creek, Miss Lucretia J Douglass; Vickery's Creek, J W Orr.

FRANKLIN—Bold Spring, Miss A A Alexander; Carnesville, Pleasant Holley; Franklin Spring, Rich d W Royston.

FULTON—Atlanta, T G Simms; East Point, N H Bacon; Irbyville.

GILMER—El'ijay, Mrs C J Jarrett.

GLASSCOCK—Gibson.

GLYNN—Brunswick, B C Franklin; Bethel, S T Gordon.

GORDON—Calhoun, W H Thompson; Fair Mount, Haywood McKuhan; Resaca, J Hill.

GREENE—Greensboro', J W Godkin; Penfield, Miss Dinah Phipps; Union Point, R A Newson; Woodville, J Willingham.

GWINNETT—Cain's F Waldrup; Lawrenceville, A F Davis; Yellow River, L Nash.

HABERSHAM—Clarkesville, J R Stanford; Loud ville, Hamilton Allison.

HALL—Gainesville, J W Murphy.; Gillsville, C Q Chandler.

HANCOCK—Sparta, J H Burnett.

HARALSON—Buchanan.

HART—Air-Line, Miss Sarah Askia; Hartwell, H N Mulkey.

HARRIS—Cataula, Miss M W Pitchford; Ellerslie, Mrs M Harrison; Hamilton, Mrs M C Adair; Mountain Hill, Miss J C Duke; Mulberry Grove, Mrs A L Smith; Waverly Hill, J G Edwards; Whitesville, W Weekes; Wisdom's Store, W H Bass.

HEARD—Franklin, W Wilson; St Cloud, T J Bird.

HOUSTON—Byron, T B Gough; Fort Valley, J A McKav; Pardue's C Churchnell; Perry, E M Hulsey; Powersville, W E Warren.

HENRY—Bear Creek, T McMahon; McDonough, S E Daily; Flat Rock.

IRWIN—Irwinville, D J Feun.

JACKSON—Harmony Grove, W Vauhn; Jefferson, J Warren.

JASPER—Monticello, Miss J Hawk.

JEFFERSON—Bartow, J W Carswell; Bethany, J B Randall; Louisville, E J Pound.

JOHNSON—Wrightville, M E McNayat.

JONES—Clinton, Miss R A Worsham.

LAURENS—Dublin, John J Keen.

LEE—Flat Pond, James H Johnson; Renwick, G T Ellison: Starkville, Nancy Heald.

LIBERTY—Hinesville, Mrs C E Allen; McIntosh, S A Frazer; Riceboro', F R Lyons; Taylor's Creek, Mrs S A Wilson; Walthourville, N Brown.

LINCOLN—Lincolnton, ——; Clay Hill; Goshen.

LOWNDES—Naylor, Miss L E Stephens; Ousley, Benj H Witherington; Valdosta, J Walker.

LUMPKIN—Auraria, J Williamson; Crossville, R Boons; Dahlonega, J T Paxson; Pleasant Retreat, H D Poteet.

McINTOSH - Darien, A A DeLorme.

MACON—Marshalville, E E Bryan; Montezuma, J F Morris; Oglethorpe, J O Loyd; Winchester, T Holcomb.

MADISON—Fort Lamar, Catherine Andrew.

MARION—Buena Vista, Miss Sarah Kemp; Danielsville, E S Cobb.

MERIWETHER—Greenville, Miss J H McLares; Jones' Mills, A S Drewry; Luthersville, Mrs Fanny Teagle; Rocky Mount, W H Lofton; Woodbury, J T Lawrence; Warnersville, Milton A Dupree.

MILLER—Colquitt, F M Platt.

MILTON—Alpharetta, O P Skelton.

MITCHELL—Camilla, C M Burtz.

MONROE—Colaparchee, S F Story; Culloden, Wm H Dewees; Forsyth, Mrs M L Snead; Russellville, W C Ballard; Unionville, Catherine Darden.

MONTGOMERY—Mount Vernon.

MORGAN - Buckhead, Miss M A Dobbins; Madison, L Markbam; Rutledge, A R Tribble.

MURRAY—Spring Place, W Anderson.

MUSCOGEE—Columbus, T M Hogan.

NEWTON—Covington, T S Womack; Conyers, W E McCalla; Newton Factory, W H Pennington; Oxford, J O H P Heuderson.

OGLETHORPE—Baird-Town, O A McLaughlin; Crawford, N M Stanford Lexington, E C Shackelford; Millstone

Mrs. E F Glenn; Maxey, J E Bell; Point Peter, G W Alexander; Stephens, W Brook; Winterville, J Winter.

PAULDING—Dallas, J B Adair.

PICKENS—Jasper, L W Hall; Talking Rock, Thos J Bryan.

PIERCE—Blackshear, W Brunt.

PIKE—Barnesville, A H Barnes; Liberty Hill, J P Brown; Milner, E Bradshaw.

POLK—Cedar Town, H W Watts.

PULASKI—S F Salter.

PUTNAM—Eatonton, Miss S J Prudden.

QUITMAN—Georgetown, Mrs. M J Neal; Morris Station, Miss R Wall.

RABUN—Clayton.

RANDOLPH—Cuthbert, S N Hurd; Nochway J W Bone.

RICHMOND—Augusta, F Blodgett; Allens, Pat F Murphy; McBeen Depot, J M Shaw; Richmond Factory, D B Hack.

SCHLEY—Ellaville, M H Scovill.

SCRIVEN—Cameron, Geo Marland; Halcyondale, Jesse Franklin; Mo' ley Pond, Simeon Hilks; Scarbrough, W C Wright.

SPALDING—Griffin, D H Johnson.

STEWART—Green Hill R F Gawley; Lumpkin, J K Yarbrough.

SUMTER—Americus, W C Goodwin; Andersonville, Thos J Goodman; Plains of Dura, H H Nunn.

TALBOT—Bellevue, G A Reedy; Bluff Spring, T J Whitley; Box Spring, D H Funderburk; Geneva, G W Jordan; Pleasant Hill, Mrs Ann C Evans; Talbotton, Mrs J B Collier.

TALIAFERRO——Crawfordsville, Catherine C Trippe; Sharon, D O'Keefe.

TATNALL—Bull Creek, D Barnard; Long Branch, M M Moody; Reidsville, A W Delay.

TAYLOR—Butler, C Mulkey; Howard, M P Brown; Reynolds, H Hodges.

TELFAIR—Jacksonville.

TERRELL—Dawson, M H Baldwin; Dover, Miss S A Lynch; Powers, Miss E C Felder

THOMAS—Thomasville, Miss M E Hall.

TOWNS—Hiawassee, W T Cram.

TROUPE—Antioch, H H Cary, Hogansville, W Hammel; LaGrange, F Ball; Mountville, J N Carleton; O'Neal's Mills, Wm J Smith; Vernon, G M White; West Point, G H Jones.

TWIGGS—Marion. Mrs A Jordan; Twiggsville, R C Carroll.

UNION—Blairsville, W J Conley.

UPSON—Thomaston, A T Shackelford, jr; The Rock, J F Black.

WALKER—Cedar Grove, W B Gray; Cassandra, J C Lee; High Point, Jno Parrish; LaFayette, R N Dickerson; Rock Spring, James R Jones.

WALTON—Logansville, E M Brand; Monroe, J W Baker; Social Circle, A M Colton.

WARE—Tebeanville, M M Grovenstine.

WARREN—Double Wells, Ed. L O Bolen; Mayfield, J T Whaley; Warrenton, J A J Mc onough.

WASHINGTON—Davisborough, W A Morgan; Oconce, Wm W Cox; Saundersville Mrs L M Pournelle.

WAYNE—Doctor Town, D S Dillan; Waynesville, Miss A Highsmith.

WEBSTER—Preston, Mrs N A R Davenport.

WHITE—Cleveland, (e h,) Wm Warwick; Nacoochee, J R Dean, Sen.

WHITFIELD—Dalton, T M McHan; Red Clay, R W Weatherby; Tilton, Step Roberts; Tunnel Hill, J D Stephens; Varnell's Station, L N Spear.

WILCOX—Adams, G M B McDuffie; Abbeville, H L Davis; House Creek, S Stanley.

WILKES—Danburg, Miss H T Danforth; Washington, Mrs C B Robinson.

WILKINSON—Erwinton, P Ward; Toombsboro', C M Lindsay.

WORTH—Isabella.

RAIL ROADS.

J. H. PORTER, General Ticket Agent.

WESTERN & ATLANTIC RAIL ROAD.
Campbell Wallace, Superintendent.
Jno. B. Peck, M. Tr.   Jno. M. Bridges, Ag't.

Distances from Atlanta.

To	Marietta	20 miles.	To	Resaca	84 miles.
"	Acworth	35 "	"	Tilton	90 "
"	Allatoona	40 "	"	Dalton	100 "
"	Etowah	45 "	"	Tunnel Hill	107 "
"	Cartersville	47 "	"	Ringgold	115 "
"	Cass	52 "	"	Johnson	121 "
"	Kingston	59 "	"	Chickamauga	126 "
"	Adairsville	69 "	"	Chattanooga	138 "
"	Calhoun	79 "			

ATLANTA & WEST POINT RAIL ROAD.
JOHN P. KING, President.
L. P. Grant, Supt.   R. M. Farrar, Agt.

Distances from Atlanta.

To	East Point	7 miles.	To	Grantville	51 miles.
"	Fairburh	19 "	"	Hogansville	58 "
"	Palmetto	25 "	"	LaGrange	71 "
"	Powells	33 "	"	Long Cane	80 "
"	Newnan	39 "	"	West Point	86 "

GEORGIA RAIL ROAD.

JNO. P. KING, Pres't.

E. W. COLE, Supt.   G. T. ANDERSON, Agt.

Distances from Atlanta.

To Decatur......	6 miles.	To Union Point..	95 miles.
" Stone Mountain	16 "	" Crawfordville .	107 "
" Lithonia	24 "	" Barnett	114 "
" Conyers	31 "	" Camack	125 "
" Covington	41 "	" Thomson	134 "
" Social Circle...	52 "	" Dearing	142 "
" Rutledge......	59 "	" Saw Dust.....	146 "
" Madison	68 "	" Berzelia	152 "
" Buckhead.....	76 "	" Belair	162 "
" Greensboro....	88 "	" Augusta......	171 "

ATHENS BRANCH—From Union Point

To Woodville	5 miles.	To Lexington....	24 miles.
" Maxey's	13 "	" Athens	40 "
" Antioch.......	17 "		

WASHINGTON BRANCH—From Burnett

To Raytown..... ..	5 miles.	To Washington. ..	21 miles.
" Ficklin	10 "		

WARRENTON BRANCH—From Camack

To Warrenton.... 5 miles. To Mayfield.. ... 21 miles.

MACON & WESTERN RAIL ROAD.

A. J. WHITE, Pres't.

E. B. WALKER, Supt.   R. A. ANDERSON, Agt.

Distances from Atlanta.

To East Point ... 7 miles.	To Milner ....56 miles.
" Rough &Ready13 "	" Barnesville .....62 "
" Forrest........15 "	" Goggins ......67 "
" Morrow's .....19 "	" Collins ....72 "
" Jonesboro'....23 "	" Forsyth ......78 "
" Lovejoy's .....29 "	" Smarr's ....83 "
" Bear Creek.....34 "	" Crawford's....89 "
" Fayette ....38 "	" Howard's .....96 "
" Griffin........44 "	" Macon ....103 "
" Thornton's .....50 "	

SCHEDULE.—(*March* 1.)

Passenger Trains leave Atlanta as follows:

W. &. A. R. R.	8.50 A. M. 7.00 P. M.
Ga. R. R	8.55 " 7.15 "
A. & W. P. R. R....	" 12.15 "
M. & W. R. R	7.15 " 8.15 "

Arrive:

W. A. A. R. R.	1.35 A. M. 1.15 P. M.
Ga. R. R	10.05 " 6.00 "
A & W. P. R. R............	8.37 " — "
M. & W. R. R.......	2.00 P. M. 4.35 "

MISCELLANEOUS.

BANKS.

ATLANTA NATIONAL BANK.

A. AUSTELL, President.   W. H. TULLER, Cashier.

Directors.—A. Austell, M. G. Dobbins, Wm. R. Phillips, Jesse McKendon, J. H. James.

GEORGIA NATIONAL BANK.

JOHN RICE, President.   E. L. JONES, Cashier.

Directors—W. W. Clayton, E. E. Rawson, S. A. Durand, John Collier.

LOAN AND BUILDING ASSOCIATIONS.

GATE CITY.

Organized April 10, 1866. Regular meeting 10th of each month.

J. R. Wallace, Pres't.   W. J. Houston, Treasr.
N. R. Fowler, Sec'y.   N. J. Hammond, Att'y.

Directors.—F. M. Richardson, Thos. Spencer, L. C. Wells, Wm. Rushton.

FULTON.

Organized, June 8, 1866. Regular meeting 8th of each month.

Perino Brown, Prest.   N. R. Fowler, Treasurer.
C. F. Wood, Sec'y.   Dan'l Pittman, Attorney.

Directors.—C. F. Wood, E. R. Sasseen, John Glen, F. P. Rice.

STONEWALL.

Organized August 4, 1866. Regular meeting 4th of each month.

S. A. Verdery, Prest.   B. F. Moore, Treasurer.
J. S. Peterson, Sec'y.   L. J. Glenn, Att'y.

Directors.—John A. Doane, R. P. Zimmerman, J. W. Clayton, J. M. Ball.

MECHANICS.

Organized October 6, 1866. Regular meeting 12th of each month.

L. C. Wells, President.   W. J. Houston, Treas'r.
S. W. Grubb, Sec'y.   N. J. Hammond, Att'y.

Directors.—J. R. Wallace, Thos. Spencer, F. M. Richardson, J. E. Gullott.

RATES OF DRAYAGE.

Molasses per hogshead......... ....$1.00
Sugar, per hogshead............ 75
Flour, meal, bacon, etc., and all kinds of bulk freight,
 that can be safely transferred, per load of 1800 lbs. 60
For a one horse dray load of 900 lbs............... 30
For all parts of loads, and small articles, charges
 may be made in proportion; but no change ex-
 cept by special agreement, required to be less than 25

WEIGHTS AND MEASURES.

Bushel.	Lbs.	Bushel.	Lbs.
Wheat	60	Blue Grass Seed	14
Shelled Corn	56	Buckwheat	52
Corn in the ear	70	Dried Peaches	38
Peas	60	Dried Apples	24
Rye	56	Onions	57
Oats	32	Salt	50
Barley	47	Stone Coal	80
Irish Potatoes	60	Malt	38
Sweet Potatoes	55	Bran	20
White Beans	60	Turnips	55
Castor Beans	46	Plastering Hair	8
Clover Seed	60	Unslacked Lime	80
Timothy Seed	45	Corn Meal	48
Flax Seed	56	Fine Salt	55
Hemp Seed	44	Ground Peas	25

A box 24 by 16 inches, 22 deep, contains 1 barrel.
A box 16 by 16½ inches, 8 deep, contains 1 bushel.
A box 8 by 8½ inches, 8 deep, contains 1 peck.
A box 4 by 4 inches, 4⅓ deep, contains half gallon.
A box 4 by 4 inches, 2½ deep, contains 1 quart.

PURCHASERS' PILOT.

NOTE.—In compiling the following pages for the guidance of purchasers, we have endeavored to represent every branch of business, consulting, at the same time, the interests of buyers. While the List of Articles, &c., will be found brief, and but few Firms named under each head, it is believed the catalogue will prove sufficiently full to enable any person, though unacquainted in the city, readily to determine where and of whom to make their purchases.

For location of Parties see "Citizens List."

Agents, Collecting.
  T S Garner.
  J F Shecut.
  [See also Attorneys.]
Agents, Insurance.
  M C Blanchard.
  W P Patillo.
  C B Wellborn.
  John C Whitner.
  W H Hancock.
  Jennings & Crane.
  Wm. Jennings.
  L B Davis.
Agents, Manufacturers'.
  J W Clayton & Co.
  M R Bell & Co.
  King, Hardee & Co.
  P P Pease & Co.
Agents, Real Estate.
  Bell & Bell.
  T S Garner.
  V A Gaskill.
  G W Adair.
  Edward Parsons.
  J. O. Harris.

Agricultural Implements.
  T M & R C Clarke.
  King, Hardee & Co.
  Tommey & Stewart.
  Johnson & Echols.
  P P Pease & Co.
  Clayton & Adair.
Ammunition.
  Heinz & Berkele.
  J C Rogers.
  T M & R C Clarke.
  Phillips & Flanders.
Aprons & Jewels, Masonic.
  Chandler & Barrow.
Anti-Friction Metal.
  J E Gullatt.
  Hunnicutt & Bellingrath.
Architects.
  Fay & Corput.
  Columbus Hughes.
Artists, Photographic.
  Dill & Maier.
  O R Lane.
  F. Kuhn.
  S H Davis.

8

Attorneys at Law.
J M Calhoun & Son
Gartrell & Jackson
Hill & Candler
Wm H Hulsey
William Ezzard
M A Bell
John Milledge, Jr
Hammond, Mynatt &
    Wellborn
S Weil
Collier & Hoyt
V A Gaskill
Alston & Winn
Tidwell & Fears
George S Thomas
A W Hammond & Son
L E Bleckley
L J Glenn & Son
Brown & Pope
W L Goldsmith
N S Craven
John L Hopkins
George Hillyer
H J Sprayberry
Robert Baugh
Farrow & Simpson
Jared Irwin Whitaker.
J W Duncan
Daniel Pittman
Marshall J Clarke
J M Clarke
Atlanta Daily Intelligencer
Jared I Whitaker, pro.
Auctioneers.
William M Hill
Shackelford & Ketcham
C Powell

Axles, Iron.
T M & R C Clarke
Tommey & Stewart
Bacon, Bagging and Rope
G L Anderson & Co
M R Bell & Co
Clayton & Adair
Orme & Farrar
Roberts, Reid & Co
King, Hardee & Co
McDaniel, Strong & Co
Meador Brothers
P P Pease & Co
Phillips & Flanders
A K Seago
R H McCrosky
J W Clayton & Co
Wylie, Johnson & Co
Bakers.
G W Jack
W C Loughmiller
Banks and Bankers
Atlanta National Bank
Georgia National Bank
John H James
Bedsteads
A Ergenzinger
George P Frazer
Morgan & Co
Phillips & Flanders
Bellows, Bells, Belting
T M & R C Clarke
Tommey & Stewart
Black and White Lead
Taylor & Davis
McCamy & Co
Massey, Swanson & Co
J T Jenkins & Co

Blank Books.
Jared I Whitaker
J J Toon
[See Bookesllers]

Blacksmiths.
Ford & Booth
J E Gullatt
Hunnicutt & Bellingrath
William Forsyth

Blacksmiths' Tools.
T M & R C Clarke
Tommey & Stewart

Boarding Houses.
A W Brown
Mrs Eliza Johnson
Mrs S H Coleman
Bell Mansion
Covington House
Mechanic House
Mrs G B Douglass
T M Jones
John T Hall
George Powers
Mrs A J Simms
Mrs N N Kidd
Mrs H C Hathaway
Mrs Elizabeth Hanye
W W Wallace

Boiler Makers.
J E Gullatt
Joseph Winship & Co
Porter & Butler
Gate City Foundry, &c

Bonnets and Trimmings
Mrs W G Knox

Book Binderies.
J J Toon
Jared I Whitaker

Book Sellers.
M Lynch & Co
J J & S P Richards
Sheldon & Connor
B B Crew & Co

Boot and Shoe Merchants
Banks, Eddleman & Co
Force & Co

Bottler
T W West

Brass Finisher
Hunnicutt & Bellingrath

Brass Founder
J E Gullatt

Brick Makers
J F Phinizy
Thomas G Heely
A B Ragan
Lewis Lawshe

Britania Ware
T R Ripley

Bridles, Collers, etc
Tommey & Stewart
Mitchell & O'Connor
Andrews, Rogers & Co

Brokers
J M Willis & Co
John H James
M G Dobbins & Co
E R Laws
W P Chisolm

Builders' Hardware
T M & R C Clarke
Tommey & Stewart
Heinz & Berkele

Builders' Material
King, Hardee & Co
A K Seago

Builders.
  S B Sherwood.
  T G Heely
  G T Ogletree
  John Boutell
Cabinet Makers' Material
  Geo. P Frazer
  A Ergenzinger
  Morgan & Co
Canes
  J M Holbrook
Candy Manufacturer
  G W Jack
Card Pictures
  O R Lane
  F Kuhn
  Dill & Maier
  [See, also, Book Sellers]
Carpenters' Tools
  [See Hardware, etc.]
Carpet Dealers
  S S Kendrick & Co
  Talley Brown & Co
Carriage Hardware
  [See Builders' Hardware]
Carriage Makers
  Ford & Booth
Champagne
  Cox & Hill
  George Sharpe, Jr
  Burns & Dryer
Chandeliers
  Hunnicutt & Bellingrath
Childrens' Shoes
  Banks, Eddldman & Co.
  Paige Fleishel & Co
  Force & Co
  Scott & Freeman

China Ware, etc.
  T R Ripley
Clocks and Watches
  B Herman & W Bollman
  Er Lawshe
  E E Earnest
Clothiers
  Friedman & Loveman
  Paige, Fleishel & Co
  Wm Rich & Co
  Reeve & Co
  Herring & Leyden
Coal
  A C Ladd
Combs and Brushes
  Talley, Brown & Co
  Silvey & Dougherty
Coffee
  [See Com. Merchants]
Confectioners
  G W Jack
  F Cora & Co.
  E Van Goidsnoven
  G Paoliello
  T G Riley
  John T Hagan
  Simmons & Henderson
Commercial College
  G Walton Knight
Commissioners of Deeds
  H P Farrow
  C B Wellborn
Commission Merchants
  A K Seago
  G L Anderson & Co
  R H McCrosky
  M R Bell & Co
  Clayton & Adair

Fains & Parrott
Johnson & Echols
King, Hardee & Co
McDaniel, Strong & Co
Meador Brothers
P P Pease & Co
Oliver & Waddail
Phillips & Flanders
Roberts, Reid & Co
C B Wellborn
Witt & Norman
Wylie, Johnson & Co
Zimmerman & Verdery
Langston, Crane & Hammock
L H Hope & Co
Abbott & Brothers
P & G T Dodd
Adair & Lee
Wiley & Carroll
Cofer & McCalla
A M Wallace
I O McDaniel
R J Lowry & Co
J C Rogers
Skinner & Co
Ford & Hightower
Arnold, Dunlap & Cane
West & Guthrie
J L King & Son
L S Salmons & Co
Johnson, Snow & Co
Steadman & Simmons
A J Robert & Co
Pratte, Edwards & Co
James L Zachry
Glenn, Wright & Carr
Tidwell & Holliday

Smith & Richmond
J L Zachry
Henderson, Chisolm & Co
Garrett & Brother
Chapman & Rucker
L C & T L Wells
Orme & Farrar
John Harris & Sons
Butler & Peters
Van Epps & Tippin

Contractors
S B Sherwood
Willis Peck
G T Ogletree
T G Heely
J A Hayden
John Boutell

Coppersmiths
J E Gullatt
Hunnicutt & Bellingrath.
F M Richardson
Langford, Seay & M'Crath

Cords, Tassels, etc.
S S Kendrick & Co
J E Godfrey
Talley, Brown & Co
Silvey & Dougherty
Scott & Freeman

Cotton Yarns
Tommey & Stewart
P P Pease & Co
Zimmerman & Verdery
A K Seago
Phillips & Flanders
King, Hardee & Co
Clayton & Adair

Southern Mutual Ins. Co
W P Patillo, Agt.

Cotton Presses
  Tommey & Stewart
Crockery .
  T R Ripley
  Silvey & Dougherty
  Scott & Freeman
  McBride, Dorsett & Co
  Henry Seltzer
  J C Rogers
  Phillips & Flanders
Cracker Manufactory
  G W Jack
Curtains, Cornice, etc.
  S S Kendrick & Co
Dentists
  J T Cambell
  H Marshall
  Ford & Hape
Dentists' Materials
  Samuel Hape
Diplomas, Masonic
  Chandler & Barrow
Domestics
  P P Pease & Co
  Zimmerman & Verdery
  Silvey & Dougherty
  Phillips & Flanders
Dress Makers
  Mrs Payne & McAllister
  Mrs Shepherd & Ingles
  Mrs C W Sherwood
Druggists
  Massey, Swanson & Co
  J T Jenkins & Co
  McCamy & Co
  Taylor & Davis
  A Howell & Co
  Redwine & Fox

Dry Goods, etc.
  Talley, Brown & Co
  Silvey & Dougherty
  Scott & Freeman
  Paige, Fleishel & Co
  J H White & Co
  Peck, Thompson & Co
  William Rich & Co
  E E Winn
  Phillips & Flanders
  W H Brotherton
  John Thomas
  John M Gannon
  John Ryan
  Ransford & McNulty
  Flynn & Dooly
  Chamberlin, Cole & Boynton
  P H Snook
  Moore & Marsh
  E W Munday
  L Cohen
  Friedman & Loveman
  Wight, Meador & Co
  Herring & Leyden
Eating Saloons
  George Johnson
  Granberry & Pease
  Joe Berman
Enameled Cloth & Leather
  Tommey & Stewart
  Andrews, Rogers & Co
  Micthell & O'Connor
Engineers, Civil
  Fay & Corput
  Columbus Hughes
  James F Cooper
  W B Bass

Envelopes
M Lynch & Co
Sheldon & Connor
J J & S P Richards
Exchange
John H James
J M Willis & Co
M G Dobbins & Co
W P Chisolm
F N Chisolm
Atlanta National Bank
Georagia National Bank
Extension Tables
Morgan & Co
Geo P Frazer
A Ergenzinger
Fairbanks' Scales
T M & R C Clarke
Fancy Goods
G W Jack,
F Corra & Co
Beermann & Kuhrt
Feathers—bed
A Ergenzinger
Feathers—Fancy
Mrs W G Knox
Fillings — Cotton,   Wool,
and Linen
King, Hardee & Co
Factory Yarns
A K Seago
P P Pease & Co
Phillips & Flanders
Zimmerman & Verdery
Fancy Dry Goods
Silvey & Dougherty
Wm Rich & Co
Scott & Freeman

Talley, Brown & Co
Paige, Fleishel & Co
Friedman & Loveman
J H White & Co
Flynn & Dooly
Fertilizers
M R Bell & Co
Clayton & Adair
Johnson & Echols
P P Pease & Co
Tommey & Stewart
King, Hardee & Co
A K Seago
Flour Dealers
Glenn, Wright &.Carr
A K Seago
G L Anderson & Co
R H McCrosky
P & G T Dodd
M R Bell & Co
Oliver & Waddail
Flouring Mills
Chas E Grenville
W G Peters & Co
Flowers—Artificial
Mrs W G Knox
Ford's Phos and Fertilizer
M R Bell & Co—p 160
Furniture Dealers
Geo P Frazer
Morgan & Co
A Ergenzinger
Gas Fitters
J E Guilatt—p 268
Hunnicutt & Bellingrath
Georgia State Lottery
W W Boyd, Principal
Manager.

Gent's Furnishing Goods
J H White & Co
Silvey & Dougherty
Paige, Fleishel & Co
Freedman & Loveman
Peck, Thompson & Co
E E Winn
Wm Rich & Co
Reeve & Co

Glass-Ware
T R Ripley

Globe Valves
Hunnicutt & Bellingrath
J E Gullatt

Glue
[See Druggists]

Grain Dealers
A K Seago
M R Bell & Co
G L Anderson & Co
L C & T L Wells
Bell & Ormond
P P Pease & Co
Clayton & Adair
Oliver & Waddail
J W Clayton & Co
Alex M Wallace

Grindstones
[See Hardware]

Grocers—Family
J C Rogers
C B & D R Lyle
Witt & Norman
Garner & Johnson
R H McCrosky
Larendon Bros
Wade & Kean
Phillips & Flanders

Haslett & Jones
B Garcia

Guano
Clayton & Adair
Johnson & Echols
P P Pease & Co

Gun and Lock Smiths
Heinz & Berkele

Hair Braiding
Mrs A Braumuller

Hardware, Cutlery, etc
T M & R C Clarke
Lewis Cook
Heinz & Berkele
Tommey & Stewart
McNaught, Ormond & Co
J M & J C Alexander

Hat and Cap Store
J M Holbrook

Hotels
National Hotel
Planters' Hotel
American Hotel
Bellevue Hotel

Hollow Ware
F M Richardson
Franklin & Mihalovitch
Roberts, Reid & Co

Hominy
Witt & Norman
Johnson & Echols
J C Rogers
R H McCrosky

Hosiery and Gloves
Wm Rich & Co
Paige, Fleishel & Co
Talley, Brown & Co
J H White & Co

Silvey & Dougherty
Scott & Freeman
Hubs, Rims, and Spokes
T M & R C Clarke
Tommey & Stewart
Ice Cream
G W Jack
F Corra & Co
T G Riley
Ice Dealers
A F Burnett & Co
India Rubber Shoes
Banks, Eddleman & Co
Force & Co
Indigo
[See Druggists and Family Grocers]
Insurance Agents
M C Blanchard
W P Patillo
J C Whitner
C B Wellborn
W H Hancock
Iron Founders
Joseph Winship & Co
Porter & Butler
J E Gullatt
Atlanta Mining & Rolling Mill Co
Gate City Foundry
Iron, Steel, etc
T M & R C Clarke
Tommey & Stewart
Lewis Cook
Iron Pipe
Hunnicutt & Bellingrath
J E Gullatt

Japanned Ware
F M Richardson
Jewelry and Silver Ware
Er Lawshé
E E Earnest
B Herman & W Bollman
H N Allen
Leitner & Fricker.
Job Printing Offices
J I Whitaker
J J Toon
T S Reynolds
Sam'l Bard
Kerosene Oil
J C Rogers
[See also Druggists]
Laces and Embroideries
[See Dry Goods, etc]
Ladies' Hats
Mrs W G Knox
Ladies' Furs
J M Holbrook
Lamps, Burners, etc
T R Ripley
[See also Druggists]   .
Lawyers
Marcus A Bell
J M Calhoun & Son
Wm Ezzard
Farrow & Simpson
Gartrell & Jackson
V A Gaskill
George Hillyer
Wm H Hulsey
S Weil
Tidwell & Fears
Geo S Thomas

Collier & Hoyt
W L Goldsmith
Hammond, Mynatt &
  Wellborn
A W Hammond & Son
John Milledge, Jr
L J Glenn & Son
N S Craven
Brown & Pope
Jno L Hopkins
H J Sprayberry
Hill & Candler
L E Bleckley
Michael Ivey

Lead- Sheet
  [See Lead Pipe]

Lead Pipe
  Hunnicutt & Bellingrath
  J E Gullatt

Leather Belting
  T M & R C Clarke
  Tommey & Stewart

Leather Dealers
  Tommey & Stewart
  Cofer & McCalla
  Banks, Eddleman & Co

Lightning Rods
  A C Ladd

Lime
  Tommey & Stewart
  A K Scago

Liquors
  Burns & Dwyer
  Cox & Hill
  Geo Sharpe Jr
  J W Clayton & Co
  John H Lovejoy

Livery Stables
  Tennessee Sale & Livery
  Tattersalls
  Eclipse
  O H Jones's

Looking Glass Plate
  Morgan & Co
  Geo P Frazer
  A Ergenzinger

Lumber Dealers
  T M Bryson
  Means & Roberts
  S A Durand
  F P Rice
  King, Hardee & Co
  A K Scago

Machine Shops
  J E Gullatt
  Joseph Winship & Co
  Porter & Butler
  Gate City

Marble Dealers
  S B Oatman
  D N Judson

Masonic Books, etc
  Chandler & Barrow

Mattresses, etc
  A Ergenzinger
  Geo P Frazer
  Morgan & Co

Mattings, etc
  S S Kendrick & Co

Meerschaum Pipes
  Beermann & Kuhrt

Metalic Burial Cases
  Charles Bohnefeld
  J W Gaut

Metal Roofers
  F M Richardson
Millinery Goods
  Mrs W G Knox
  O'Connor & Hardage
  Mrs R Gouldsmith
  Miss Sarah Holroyd
Milling Material
  King, Hardee & Co
Molasses
  A K Seago
  J C Rogers
  Johnson & Echols
  Witt & Norman
Monuments
  S B Oatman
Mouldings, Gilt, etc
  A Ergenzinger
  Morgan & Co
  Geo P Frazer
Musical Merchandize
  H Braumuller
  Sheldon & Connor
  J J & S P Richards
Musicians
  Charles Harmsen
  W L Hensler
  W F Clarke
Newspapers and Periodicals
  Scott's Monthly Magazine
  Atlanta Daily Intelligencer
  Christian Index & South-Western Baptist
  The Daily New Era

The Ladies' Home
The Daily Opinion
The Atlanta Med Journal
Oil, Linseed, Tanner's, Lard, etc
  Taylor & Davis
  Massey, Swanson & Co
  J T Jenkins & Co
  McCamy & Co
Ornamental Work—Metal
  Hunnicutt & Bellingrath
  J E Gullatt
Oysters, Dealers in
  A F Burnett & Co
  Cox & Hill
  G W Jack
Painters, House and Sign
  W S Bradbury
  O Dockum
  Cox, Huwald & Co
Painters—Portrait
  Jno Maier [Dill & M]
Pawnbrokers
  E R Laws
  J M Willis & Co
Penmanship
  G Walton Knight
Percussion Caps
  Heinz & Berkele
  P & G T Dodd
  J C Rogers
Photograph Albums
  Sheldon & Connor
  J J & S P Richards
  [See also Photographers.]
Photographers
  F Kuhn

Photographers
O R Lane
Dill & Maier
S H Davis

Physicians
G L Jones
J M Boring
J G Westmoreland
W F Westmoreland
H Westmoreland
J M Johnson
D C O'Keefe
N D'Alvigny
S S Beach
John Goodman
S T Biggers
W C Asher
R C Word
Edwin S Ray
H S Orme
Jas F Alexander
H L Wilson
T S Powell
J Gilbert
J R Harris
R Q Stacy
Geo G Crawford
O Stovall
W T Goldsmith
W S Armstrong
L H Orme
F H Orme
J W Price

Piano-fortes
Carl F Barth

Pistols, Guns, etc
Heinz & Berkele
T M & R C Clarke

Planing Mills
Landsberg & Harris
Joseph Winship & Co
Peck & Markham
Gate City

Plaster, Paris
Samuel Hape

Plated Ware
E E Earnest
Er Lawshe
H N Allen
T R Ripley
B Herman & W Bollman

Pocket Cutlery
Tommey & Stewart
Heinz & Berkele
T M & R C Clarke
J J & S P Richards

Printers, Book and Job
J J Toon
Jared I Whitaker
Samuel Bard

Produce Dealers
M R Bell & Co
Clayton & Adair
P P Pease & Co
A K Seago
G L Anderson & Co
Fains & Parrott
J W Clayton & Co
J C Rogers
R H McCrosky
Witt & Norman
Phillips & Flanders
Wade & Kean

Pumps, Force, etc
Smith & Richmond
Hunnicutt & Bellingrath

Raisins
  G W Jack
  J C Rogers
  Johnson & Echols
Regalia—Masonic, etc
  Chandler & Barrow
Restaurants
  Geo Johnson
  Granberry & Pease
  Joe Berman
Ribbons, etc
  Mrs W G Knox
  J E Godfrey
  Talley, Brown & Co
  Silvey & Dougherty
Roofing Materials
  F M Richardson
Rope and Bagging
  P P Pease & Co
  Phillips & Flanders
  A K Seago
  M R Bell & Co
  Orme & Farrar
Rubber Tube
  Hunnicutt & Bellingrath
Rugs and Matts
  S S Kendrick & Co
Saddles and Harness
  Mitchell & O'Connor
  Andrews, Rogers & Co
Saw-Mills
  T M Bryson
  S A Durand
  F P Rice
Scales and Balances
  Clayton & Adair
  T M & R C Clarke
  Tommey & Stewart

Schools
  Peters street High School
  West-End Academy
  Atlanta High School
School Books, etc
  J J & S P Richards
  M Lynch & Co
  Sheldon & Connor
Seedsmen
  E Van Goidsnoven
  J C Rogers
  B D Lester
Segars
  Beermann & Kuhrt
  Cox & Hill
  Geo Sharp, Jr
  Smith & Richmond
  Meador Brothers
  J W Clayton & Co
  Clayton & Adair
Sewing Machines
  E E Earnest
  W Lichtenstadt
Sheet Iron
  Hunnicutt & Bellingrath
  F M Richardson
Sheet Music
  Sheldon & Connor
  J J & S P Richards
  H Braumuller
Shirt-Fronts and Collars
  Wm Rich & Co
  Freedman & Loveman
  J H White & Co
Shoe Pegs and Thread
  Force & Co
  Banks, Eddleman & Co

Shoemakers' Tools
  Tommey & Stewart
  Heinz & Berkele
  T M & R C Clarke
Shot
  Heinz & Berkele
  J C Rogers
Shovels
  [See Hardware]
Show-Cases
  Morgan & Co
  Geo P Frazer
  A Ergenzinger
Silver-Plated Ware
  Er Lawshe
  ?T R Ripley
  E E Earnest
  B Herman & W Bollman
Shirts
  Talley, Brown & Co
  Silvey & Dougherty
  J H White & Co
  Paige, Fleishel & Co
  Peck, Thompson & Co
  Phillips & Flanders
  Wm Rich & Co
Snuff and Snuff Boxes
  Beermann & Kuhrt
Soap
  J C Rogers
  Johnson & Echols
  R H McCrosky
Soda Water
  T G Riley
  T W West
Southern Express Co
  E Hulburt, Supt.
  V Dunning, Agt.

Sofas
  A Ergenzinger
  Morgan & Co
  George P Frazer
Spectacles
  Er Lawshe
  E E Earnest
  B Herman & W Bollman
  H N Allen
Spelter Solder
  Hunnicutt & Bellingrath
  J E Gullatt
  F M Richardson
Stables, Livery & Sale
  W J Wootten
  Whitaker & Sasseen
  O H Jones
Stationery, etc.
  Sheldon & Connor
  M Lynch & Co
  J J & S P Richards
Staple Dry Goods
  Silvey & Dougherty
  Scott & Freeman
  Talley, Brown & Co
  J H White & Co
  E E Winn
  Wm Rich & Co
  Peck, Thompson & Co
Stills
  Hunnicutt & Bellingrath
Stoves, etc.
  F M Richardson
  Johnson & Echols
Steel
  Tommey & Stewart
  T M & R C Clarke
  Lewis Cook

Sugar and Syrup
A K Seago
M R Bell & Co
Wylie, Johnson & Co
R H McCrosky
Clayton & Adair
G L Anderson & Co
P P Pease & Co
Witt & Norman
Langston, Crane & Hammock
Johnson & Echols
J C Rogers
Phillips & Flanders
Wade & Kean

Table Cutlery
T R Ripley
Silvey & Dougherty
J C Rogers
McBride, Dorsett & Co
Phillips & Flanders

Tables, Safes, etc.
A Ergenzinger
Morgan & Co
George P Frazer

Tailors, Merchant
J H White & Co
Herring & Leyden
J H Purtell
Gross & Schramm

Teachers, Book-keeping
G Walton Knight

Teachers, Dancing
J S Nichols

Teachers, Music
W L Hensler
Charles Harmsen
W F Clarke

Tinsmiths' Material
F M Richardson

Tobacco
Beermann & Kuhrt
Meador Brothers
Smith & Richmond
J W Clayton & Co
Clayton & Adair
Witt & Norman

Toilet Preparations
[See Druggists]

Tomb Stones
S B Oatman

Toys and Fancy Articles
G W Jack

Trunks
J M Holbrook

Umbrellas
J M Holbrook
Silvey & Dougherty

Undertakers
Charles Bohnefeld
J W Gaut

Upholsterers
A Ergenzinger
Morgan & Co
George P Frazer

Varnishes
Taylor & Davis
J T Jenkins & Co
Massey, Swanson & Co
McCamy & Co

Wagon Makers
Ford & Booth

Wall Paper
J J & S P Rishards
Sheldon & Connor
M Lynch & Co

Washing Machines
Tommey & Stewart
T M & R C Clarke

Watch Makers' Tools and Materials
Er Lawshe

Watchmakers and Jewelers
E E Earnest
B Herman & W Bollman
H N Allen
Er Lawshe
T Gilbert
A Thieme
J M Bookout

Water Cocks
J E Gullatt
Hunnicutt & Bellingrath

Wax Figures, etc
G W Jack

White Goods
Talley, Brown & Co
Silvey & Dougherty
Scott & Freeman
J H White & Co
Wm Rich & Co
Peck, Thompsom & Co
Paige, Fleishel & Co

Wholesale Grocers
M R Bell & Co
Fains & Parrott
A K Seago
G L Anderson & Co
Clayton & Adair
P P Pease & Co
Zimmerman & Verdery
Langston Crane & Hammock
Phillips & Flanders

Wylie, Johnson & Co
McDaniel, Strong & Co
Witt & Norman
Roberts, Reid & Co
Meador Brothers
Glenn, Wright & Carr
A M Wallace
A J Robert & Co
Chapman & Rucker
John Harris & Sons
Wyley & Carroll
L L Landrum
Pratte, Edwards & Co
King, Hardee & Co
Abbott & Brothers
P & G T Dodd
Henderson, Chisolm & Co
Arnold, Dunlap & Cain
Steadman & Simmons
L C & T L Wells

Wholesale Tobacconists
Smith & Richmond
Meador Brothers

Willow Ware
G W Jack

Yankee Notions
Silvey & Dougherty
Scott & Freeman
Talley, Brown & Co

Yarns, Cotton
Tommey & Stewart
A K Seago
Phillips & Flanders
P P Pease & Co

Zinc
F M Richardson
Hunnicutt & Bellingrath.
T M & R C Clarke

ATLANTA CITY DIRECTORY.

A

ABBOTT & BROS., gro mer, w s Whitehall, b Hunter and Mitchell.

Abbott, L. L., (A & Bros,) bds at Mrs. S. H. Coleman's.

Abbott, W. L., (A & Bros,) cor Luckie and Harris.

Abbott, B. F., (A & Bros,) West End, nr Green's Ferry Avenue.

Abrams, Mrs. A., s s Jones, b Martin's and Connelly.

Acton, T. M., gro mer, n s Walton, b Bartow and Foundry alley.

ADAIR, GEO. W., Real Estate Agnt., s ec R R and Whitehall, res w s Peters, near new corporate line.

Adair, Jas., gro mer, bds at Mrs. E. White's.

ADAIR & LEE, gro mer, s s Mitchell, b Whitehall and Forsyth.

Adair, J. A. (Adair & Lee.)

Adair, G. B., bds at Mrs. R. E. Chisolms.

Adams, A. Q., eng State Road, n s Rhodes, nr W & A R R shop.

Adams, Benson, e s East-Peachtree, nr old corp line.

Adamson, J. G., gro mer, bds at W. L. Adamson's.

Adamson, J. C., carp State shop, lives on Delay.

Adamson, Wm. L., gro mer, n s Luckie, b Spring and Bartow.

ADCOCK, JOHN J., eng W & A R R, e s Fowler, b Green & Rhodes.

AGRICOLA, RICHARD, fam gro, w s Peters, nr G. W. Adair's.

Aikin, F. M. C., bk m, e s Nelson, near Race.

Aikin, Michael, clk, bds at James Lycnh's.

9

Aikin, R. W., bk m, w s Peters, s of Walker.

AINSWORTH, S. M., tchr, n s Peters, b Whitehall and Forsyth.

AINSWORTH, MRS. S. M., tchr music, n s Peters, b Whitehall and Forsyth.

ALBRIGHT, A. shoemaker, e s Thompson, nr Hunter.

Aldredge, J. Stephen, s w c Garnett and Thompson.

ALEXANDER & ORME, physicians, office 2d floor, w s Broad, b R R and Marietta.

Alexander, Dr. J. F., (A. & Orme,) res cor Peachtree and Oslin.

ALEXANDER, DR. A., (A R M & Min Co,) e s Peachtree, b Cain and Harris.

Alexander, John, blk smith, State shop, e s McDonough, b Fair and Jones.

Allen, E. T. & F. M., fam gro, w s Whitehall, nr Hunter.

Allen, W. B., fireman S Road, s s Thurman, e of Fowler.

Allen, James M., s w c Thurman, and W & A R R.

ALLEN, H. N., (see p 132)—jeweler, n w cor Whitehall and R R

Allen, R., carp, s of Delay, w of Mangum.

Allen, E. A., carp, n w c Fair and Crew.

Allred, Mrs. M. A., s w c Magazine and Fowler.

Ament, Robert, mldr, w s Calhoun, b Decatur and Georgia R R.

AMERICAN HOTEL, White & Whitlock, pros, s e c Alabama and Pryor.

ANDERSON, R. A., Ft Agt M & W R R Depot.

ANDERSON, G. L. & CO., (see p 130)—gro and com mer s s Mitchell, b Whitehall and Broad.

ANDERSON, Gen. G. T., Ft Agt, Ga R R Depot, res n w cor Collins and Ga R R.

Anderson, J. H., (G L A & Co,) w s Pryor, nr Garnett.

Anderson, Capt. G. W., bds at J. W. Lloyd's.

Anderson, Wm. C., w s Terry, b Ga R R and Hunter.

Anderson, Mrs. J. E., bds with R. B. Campbell.

Anderson, G. L., (G L A & Co,) bds with J. H. A.

ANDREWS, ROGERS & Co., saddlery &c, s s Marietta, w of Broad.

Andrews, Ezra, (A. Rogers & Co.,) c Pryor and Fulton.
ANGIER, DR. N. L., n e c Washington and Mitchell.
Archer, C. C., fam gro, cor Decatur and Pratt.
Armstead, Joel, s s Decatur, b Randolph and Gartrell.
Armstead, George W., blk s, bds at Wm. Armstead's.
Armstead, D. A., carp, bds at Wm. Armstead's.
Armstead, W., carp. n s Houston, b Calhoun and Butler.
Armstead, Jas. M.,blk s, bds at Wm. Armstead's.
Armstead, W. J., w s Bloyd, b Baker and Oslin.
Armstrong, Joseph, wks gas works, s s Delay, w of Rock.
ARMSTRONG, DR. W.S, office e s Whitehall, nr Hun-
  ter—bds at Planters' Hotel.
Arnold, D. S., clk s e cor Calhoun and Harris.
Arnold, Reuben, atty, s w cor Collins and Oslin.
Asher, Mrs. M. L., with Capt. Wm. A. Fuller.
Ashford, R. A., mail agt, bds at Planters' Hotel.
ASHLEY, W. G., formn W & A R R car shop, bds at
  Mrs. S. A. Lester's.
ATKIN, JAS., Col Int Rev, post office bldg, cor Broad
  and Alabama, res e s Forsyth, s of Garnett.
Atkins, Mrs. S. E., w s Peters, w of M & W R R
Atkinson, Mrs. Mary H., cor Race and Haynes.
Atkinson, Samuel, carp, n s Stockton, e of Mangum.
ATLANTA NATIONAL BANK, A. Austell, Prest, W.
  H. Tuller, cash, s s Alabama, nr Whitehall.
ATLANTA GAS LIGHT COMPANY—Works, w s
  W & A R R, b Foundry and Thurman, J. W. Duncan,
  President.
ATLANTA HIGH SCHOOL, cor Collins and Ellis, W.
  M. Janes, W. R. Jones, and R. A. Richardson, tchrs.
ATLANTA MEDICAL COLLEGE, John G. West-
  moreland Dean of Faculty, n w c Butler and Jenkins.
ATLANTA MEDICAL & SURGICAL JOURNAL,
  J. G. Westmoreland, W. F. Westmoreland, and J. M.
  Johnson, Editors,—Office e s Whitehall, nr Hunter.
ATLANTA DAILY INTELLIGENCER, w s White-
  hall, b R R and Alabama, Jared Irwin Whitaker, pro.
ATLANTA & WEST Pt. R. R. Ft. Depot., n s Ga. R.
  R., opp Pratt st, M. J. Small, agt.

PERINO BROWN. V. WILDMAN·

BROWN & WILDMAN,

BANKERS,

Southwest cor. Broad and Marietta Streets,

ATLANTA, - - - - - - - - - - GEORGIA.

:0:

PARTICULAR ATTENTION GIVEN TO COLLECTIONS.

REFER TO

The National Park Bank New York.

Banks and Bankers Generally of Georgia.

BEERMANN & KUHRT,

WHOLESALE AND RETAIL DEALERS IN

HAVANA AND DOMESTIC SEGARS,

Smoking and Chewing Tobacco,

Meershaum Pipes and Segar-Holders, (Warranted Genuine,)

BRIAR, INDIA RUBBER, CLAY & CHINA PIPES

Of All Descriptions,

AMBER, WEICHSEL, CHERRY, AND FANCY STEMS,

SNUFF, AND SNUFF BOXES,

Fancy Goods,

&c., &c., &c.,

Whitehall Street, Two Doors from the Rail Road,

ATLANTA, - - - - - - - - GEORGIA·

ATLANTA & WEST PT. R. R. General Office, s s Alabama, b Pryor and Hunter, L. P. Grant, supt.

Austell, A, Pres A N Bank, s s Marietta, b Forsyth and Spring.

Austin, J. M., carp, e s Peachtree, b Baker and Oslin.

AUTEN, R. M., painter, n s Nelson, w of Mangum.

Autry, J. H., carp, W & A R R shop.

Autry, James, carp, bds at Mrs. L. A. King's.

Ayer, Rev. F., n w cor Calhoun and Houston.

Ayres, Wm. H., peddler, w s Forsyth, opp Grenville's Mill.

B

Badger, Ralph B., dentist, e s Whitehall, b Alabama and Hunter.

Bagby, Wm. K., e s Cooper, b Fair and Jones.

BAILY, W. H., frmn. Int. Job office, res w s Peters nr M & W R R.

BAINE, DONALD, tailor, s s Boothe's Alley.

Baker, Charles, stone m, n s Whitehall, at old corp line.

Baker, B. H., fireman W & A R R, bds with Mrs. E. W. Grubbs.

Baldwin, Mrs. E., w s Forsyth, b Alabama and Hunter.

Baldwin, G. A., fam gro, w s Frazer, s of Rawson.

Baldwin, W. L., w s Frazer, s of Rawson.

Ball, James M., n w c McDonough and Rawson.

Ball, John, carp, w s Terry, b Fair and Jones.

Ballard, W., e s Peachtree, b Ellis and Cain.

Ballard, Mrs. Mary, cor Decatur and Moore.

Banarsdell, C., bds at Planters' Hotel.

Banks, Mrs. M., e s Ivy, b Gilmer and Wheat.

Banks, J. T. bds at Mechanic House.

Banks, James W., n s Rock, b Fowler and Mangum.

BAPTIST CHURCH, 1st, Rev. H. C. Hornady, pastor, n w cor Forsyth and Walton.

BAPTIST CHURCH, 2d, Rev. W. T. Brantley, pastor, n w cor Washington and Mitchell.

Barker, J. W., e s Frazer, b Jones and Rawson.

Barker, Brader, clk with F. M. Richardson.

Barnes, James J., (Middlebrook & B.)
Barnes, J. D., n w c Martin and Rawson.
Barnes, Joseph F., police, s w cor Fowler and Green.
Barnes, Mrs. Mary, s w cor Nelson and M & W R R.
Barnes, A. L., bds with Mrs. Mary B.
Barrett, James S., blk s, s s Rock, b Fowler and Mangum.
Barrett, Wm. I., n s Simpson, opp Hull.
Barrett, John H., bk k, s s Pryor, b Wheat and Houston.
Barrett, F. S., clk, bds at Mechanic House, e s Lloyd, b
    Alabama and Hunter.
Barrett, Mrs. E. C., s s Rock, b Fowler and Mangum.
BARRICK, JAS. R., (McCamy & Co.)
BARROW, H. C., (Chandler & B,) w s Broad, two
    doors n of bridge.
BARTH, C. F., dlr in pianos, e s Whitehall, b Alabama
    and Hunter.
Bartlett, Isaac E, s s Decatur, b Moore and Bell.
Barton, Robert, carp, n s Rawson, b McDonough and
    Crew.
Barry, C. M., wchmn, cor Fair and Terry.
Bass, Walter, bds with G. T. Anderson.
Bass, U. D., cond, A & W P R R, bds with G. T. Ander-
    son.
Bassford, W. S., asst editor " Ladies' Home," bds at M.
    A. Bell's.
Baughan, Ben., ptr, w s Calhoun, b Ga R R and Decatur.
BEACH, SOLOMON S., M. D., office and res n w cor
    Decatur and Moore.
Beasley, James, e s Walker, opp Stonewall.
Beavers, W. C., n w cor Mangum and Thurman.
Beck, Lewis H, clk at Stewart and Tommey's.
BEERMAN & KUHRT, (see p 134—dlrs in cigars,
    tobacco, &c.,) w s Whitehall, b R R & Alabama.
BEERMAN, CHAS., (B. & Kuhrt,) Whitehall, c Fair
    and Grenville's alley.
Berman, Joseph, bar k, n s Mitchell, b Pryor and Lloyd.
Belcher, Thos. Jeff., lab, w s Peters, s of Walker.
BELLEVUE HOUSE, Drs. J. W. Price and son, pro's,
    s s Alabama, b Lloyd and Washington.

Bellenger, John, bg mstr, W & A R R, bds with Mrs. S. A. Lester.

Bellingrath, Leonard, (Hunnicutt & B,) res on Marietta road, outside city.

BELL-JOHNSON OPERA HALL, n e cor Alabama and Broad.

Bell Mansion, s e cor Collins and Wheat.

BELL & ORMOND, gro mer, Whitehall street.

Bell, H. G. (B & Ormond,) bds with Mrs. H. C. Hathaway.

BELL, M. A., (see p 132)—atty, s e c Collins and Wheat.

Bell, Mrs. Minerva, bds with M. T. Castleberry.

Bell, J. L., s s Hunter, b King and Terry.

BELL, M. R. & Co., (see p 136)—gro and com mer, w s Broad, 1st door north of bridge.

Bell, A. P., (B., M. R. & Co.,) w s Cone, b Walton and Luckie.

Bell, M. R., (B., M. R. & Co.,) bds with A. P. B.

Bellah, J. W., n s Walton, b Bartow and Foundry.

Bellows, Eli, carp, n w c Lloyd and Jones.

BENNETT, B. F., frmn Franklin Printing House.

Bennett, John W., eng Ga R R, w s Butler, b Gilmer and Jenkins.

Bennett, P. M., boot mkr, McDonough, nr old corp line.

Bergstron, A., bds at Mechanic House.

Berkele, Henry, (Heinz & B.,) bds with Chas. Heinz.

Berkele, John, (Heinz & B.,) bds with Chas. Heinz.

Berry, Cary W., eng Ga R R, s w c Pratt and Gilmer.

Berry, F. M., eng W & A R R, e s Calhoun, b Decatur and Gilmer.

Berry, John, clk, bds with A. W. Brown.

Berry, Mrs. Catharine, e s Butler, b Ga R R and Hunter.

BERRY, W. PATT, Druggist, with Taylor and Davis.

Berry, W., eng, w s Calhoun, b Decatur and Gilmer.

Bessent, P. G., gro mer, w s Calhoun, opp Med College.

Biggers, Stephen T., bo phys, n w c Luckie and Cone.

Billingslea, L. C., clk, bds at Mrs. Sarah Mead's.

Billings, H. C. frmn "Ladies' Home" printing office.

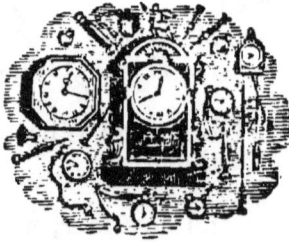

Bills, Lewis, blk s, n w c Frazer and Richardson.

Bird, J B, butcher, e s Frazer, b Richardson and Fulton.

Black, Jacob, bds at Planters' Hotel.

Black, George W, bds with Elias B.

Black, Elias, carp, w s Fowler, n of Foundry.

Blackburn, J M, carp, s s Decatur, b Butler and Calhoun.

Blackburn, J W, carp, w s Frazer, opp jail.

Black, G D, e s Pryor, b Peters and Garnett.

Blackman, J A J, n s Peters, b Thompson and M & W R R.

Blackman, L R II, with J A J B.

Blackstock, J J, stone m, w s Peters, s of Walker.

Blackstock, R, lab, w s McDaniel, e of Whitehall.

Blackstock, W W, stone m, w s McDaniel, e of Whitehall.

Bleckley, Logan E, atty, cor East Peachtree and Currier.

BLANCHARD, M C, (see p 138) Ins Agt, n s Stockton, e of Mangum.

Blanchard, Chas, n s Rock, near Mangum.

Blunt, Mathew, e s Collins, b Gilmer and Jenkins.

Bohnefeld, Chas, undertaker, n s Luckie, b Forsyth and Cone.

BOLLMAN, Wm, (B, Herman & Wm B,) w s Whitehall, s of and near R R.

Bollman, B, bds at Planters' Hotel.

BOLTON, M L, n w c Calhoun and Ga R R.

BOMAR, Dr B F, trader, n w c Green and Haynes.

Bomar, F J, pol, s s Nelson, w of M & W R R.

BONE, J C, cond W & A R R, n w c Luckie and Simpson.

BOND, PETER, mach Ga R R sh, bds with E C Downs.

Booth, Robt, clk, with J H White & Co.

Boothe, W K, wagon mkr, n s Ga R R, between Collins and Calhoun.

BOOKOUT, J M, jeweler, w s Peachtree, nr Marietta, res s s Nelson, w of M & W R R.

BORING, J M, M D, Office and res w s Forsyth, nr Hunter.

Bosworth, Mrs Eliza, e s Walker, nr Nelson.

Bosworth, J M, bds with Mrs E B.

Boutell, N A, carp, bds with Levi Stansell.

BOUTELL, JNO, bldr, s w c Collins and Ellis.

Bowen, Hiram, carp, n e c Peters and Garnett.

BOWEN, J C, carp, w s Forsyth, nr Grenville's mill.

BOWEN, GEO W, pol, w s Forsyth, b Garnett and Grenville's alley.

BOWEN, REV CHAS A, s s Stephens, w of Race.

Bowles, M W, ptr, e s Whitehall, b Mitchell and Peters.

Boyd, A L, n s Stonewall, w of Race.

BOYD, Col W W, Manager Ga State Lottery, res e s East-Peachtre, at old corp line.

Boyd, T J, cond W & A R R, w s Collins, b Decatur and Ga R R.

Boyd, Jno, clk M & W R R Depot, bds with R B Campbell.

Boyd, W E, gro mer, e s McDonough, b Fair and Jones.

Boyd, A W, (W W Wall & Co,) w s Peters, s of M & W R R.

Boynton, C E, (Chamberlin, Cole & B,) bds at American Hotel,

BRACKEN, PETER, mach W & A sh, n s Rhodes, nr Mangum.

BRACKEN, T J, eng W & A R R, n s Hunter, b Terry and King.

BRADBURY, W S, ptr, e s Crew, s of Rawson.

Bradbury, T S, carp, w s Walker, s of Boothe's al.

Bradfield, Dr Joe, Drug, n e c McDonough and Rawson.

BRADLEY, J M, s s Nelson, e of Walker.

Bradley, M H, carp, n w c Spring and W & A R R.

Branham, J, eng W & A R R, bds with Henry Buice.

Brannin, Columbus, bds with Mrs Eliza Bosworth.

Brannin, J T, mattress mkr, bds with Mrs N E Robbins.

BRANTLY, REV W T, Pastor 2d Baptist Church, res n w c Washington and Jones.

Braswell, Mrs L J, s s Hunter, b Butler and Terry.

BRAUMULLER, H, music store, w s Whitehall, b Alabama and Hunter, res w s Forsyth, n of Hunter.

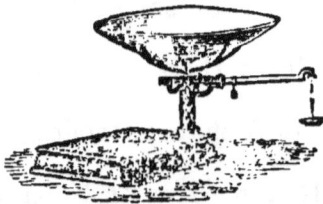

BRAUMULLER MRS A., Mil and Fancy Goods, at music store of H B.

BRAUN, F, cooper, s s Stockton w of M & W R R.

BRAY, W M, tchr, w s Whitehall, near junction of Forsyth.

Brewer, J L, ptr, S sh, s s Foundry, w of W & A R R.

BRIDGES, JOHN M., Ft Agt, W & A R R Depot, res e s Fowler, near Green.

Bridges, J, clk Ins office, bds at J C Whitner's.

BRIDWELL, CICERO, fam gro, cor Stockton and M & W R R.

Bridwell, Zion, printer, near c Fowler and Green.

Bridwell, Jno A, stone m, s s Green, b Fowler and Mangum.

Bridwell, Mrs Harriet, s s Stockton, w of M & W R R.

Brinkley, S B, gro mer, n w c Decatur and Randolph.

BROTHERTON, W H, Dry Goods, s w c Whitehall and Mitchell, res w s Forsyth, b Garnett and Grenville's al.

BROWN, C I, s w c Peters and Crew.

BROWN, A W, bdg h, w s Lloyd, b Hunter and Mitchell.

Brown, G C, tin smith, Pryor, b Hunter and Mitchell.

Brown, Jno, carp, W & A R R shop, at jn Fair and Hunter.

BROWN, J W (Talley, B & Co.)

BROWN & WILDMAN, (see p 134) Bankers, s w c Marietta and Broad.

BROWN, PERINO, (B & Wildman,) res w s East-Peachtree, opp Oslin.

BROWN & POPE, attys, s e c Broad and M & W R R

BROWN, Joseph E, (B & Pope,) s w c Washington and Jones.

BROXTON, H W, carp, w s McDonough, b Jones and Rawson.

Bruce, R, carp, n s Houston, b Calhoun and Butler.

BRUCKNER, J O, bk k, with F M Richardson, res n s Pryor, b Peters and Garnett.

10

Bruckner, Mrs Mary, s w c Spring and Luckie.

Brunk, A, National Hotel.

Bryan, H, bds at L. G. Holland's.

BRYAN, WILLIAM, Ins Agt, bds with A W Brown.

BRYANT, J M, s s Boothe's alley.

Bryant, Wm M, carp, s e c Peters and Thompson.

BRYSON, J W F, clk, American Hotel.

BRYSON, T M, dealer in lumber, with John Silvey.

Buchanan, A J, blk s, s e c Fair and Frazer.

Buckalew, Jas, carp, S sh, s of Delay, w of Mangum.

BUCKHARDT, G A, fam gro, n w c Washington and Hunter.

Buckner, Thos, emp W & A R R, bds with Russell Crawford.

Buffington, Mrs S C., w s Pryor, b Peters and Garnett.

BUICE, J D, tin smith, e s Peachtree, opp Walton, res s e c Wheat and Pryor.

BUICE, J M & BROTHER, fam gro, e s Peachtree, opp Walton.

BUICE, M, fam gro, res e s Thompson, b Hunter and Mitchell.

Buice, Elisha, mer, w s Crew, b Fair and Jones.

Buice, Henry, s s Butler, b Ga R R and Hunter.

Burke, T, gro mer, w s Calhoun, b Decatur and Ga R R.

BURNETT, Robt, cond M & W R R, n s Decatur, b Moore and Pratt.

BURNETT, A F & CO., (see p 138)—Ice, Oysters, &c., old postoffice bldg, e s Whitehall, s of R R.

BURNS & DWYER, (see p 138)—Wines and Liquors, n s Ga R R, e of and near Whitehall.

BURR, GEO W, frmn Richardson's tin shop, e s Whitehall, b Hunter and Mitchell.

BUSH, BROOKS, painter W & A R R sh, res e s McDonough, near old corp line.

BUSH, R P, emp W & A R R, bds with Brooks, B.

Bussey, Geo, bds at Covington House.

Bussey, G H, National Hotel.

BUTLER, JAS E, gro mer, n w c Marietta and Cone.

Butler, J P, butcher, bds at American Hotel.
Butler, T J, clk, s s Decatur, b Collins and Calhoun.
BUTT, WM M, J P, office cor Alabama and Forsyth, res
    e s McDonough, s of Rawson.
Buzby, Mrs Melinda, w s W & A R R, b Rock and Delay.
Buzby, Willis, emp S road, with Mrs M B.
Busby, W T, fam gro, w s West-Peachtree, b Hunnicutt
    and Mills.
BYINGTON, Judge ——, bds with Mrs E Johnson.

C

CAIN, JEFF, eng S road, n s Rhodes, near W & A R R.
CALDWELL, JAS, res n e c Mitchell and Thompson.
CALHOUN, Dr E N, s e c Peters and Washington.
CALHOUN, J M, atty, s w c Alabama and Washington.
CALHOUN, W L, atty, n s Hunter, b Lloyd and Wash-
    ington.
Calhoun, C A, fireman S road, bds at Bellevue House.
Callahan, Daniel, eng S road, bds with Mrs A D Rhodes.
Callahan, Dennis, w s Lloyd, b Hunter and Mitchell.
Callahan, Owen, eng, bds with Mrs A D Rhodes.
Callaway, Jas H, bds with R A Howard.
Callaway, Mrs Martha, s s Hunter, b Calhoun and Butler.
Camp, Geo W, carp, s s Baker, b Butler and Bloyd.
CAMPBELL, J B, w s East Peachtree, opp Currier.
CAMPBELL, Dr. J T, (see p 140)—Dentist, office e s
    Whitehall, b Alabama and Hunter.
CAMPBELL, RICHARD B, chf clk, M & W R R
    Depot, res w s M & W R R, near Depot.
Campbell, C T, Expressman, bds with J C Robinson.
Campbell, Mrs. Thomas, with John M Bridges.
Campbell, Monroe, clk W & A R R Depot, bds with
    R B C.
Campbell, Clinton, bds with R B C.
Cannon, Patrick, e s Lloyd, b Mitchell and Hunter.
CANNON, C A, carp, s s Decatur e of Peck and Mark-
    ham's Plaining Mill.
Carbine, P V, mach, bds at Bellevue House.
Carbine, Jno, blr mkr, bds at Bellevue House.

Carden, C B, Watchman, M & W R R Depot.

Carder, Mrs Ellen, with J C King.

CARLTOAN, S M, breaksman S road, n s Race, w of Haynes.

Carlton, J M B, e s Bartow, b Marietta and W & A R R.

Carmichael, Jonathan, carp, with Z A Clarke.

CARPENTER, E C, pattern mkr, bds with Mrs L A King.

CARR, E A, (Glenn, Wright & Co.,) bds at Bell Mansion.

Carroll, W S, gro mer, e s Ivy, near junction with Peachtree.

Cason, Thos, bk m, w s Race, s of Haynes.

Cason, Jno, w s Terry, b Fair and Jones.

CASSIN, C P, mer, s s Nelson, w of M & W R R.

CASTLEBERRY, M T, fam gro, e s Peters, w of M & W R R.

CATHOLIC CHURCH, Immaculate Conception, s e c Hunter and Lloyd, Rev Thos O'Reilly, Pastor.

CENTER, GEO W, clk with Bell & Ormond, res e s Collins, b Wheat and Houston.

Center, E A, pol, with Geo W C.

Center, P W, clk, with G W C.

CHAMBERLIN, COLE & BOYNTON, Dry Goods, Rawson's bldg, s e c Whitehall and Hunter.

Chamberlin, E P, (C, Cole & Boynton.)

CHANDLER & BARROW, (see 142)—Regalia &c, w s Broad, b Marietta and Railroad.

CHANDLER, THOS W, (C & Barrow,) n w c Luckie and Hunnicutt.

Chandler, David, Asst Surv Ga A L R R, bds at Bell Mansion.

CHAPMAN & RUCKER, gro and com mer, w s Whitehall, b Hunter and Mitchell.

Cheatham, Marcus, bds with Mrs E Haney.

CHESTER, JOHN S, mach S shop, n w c Haynes and Rhodes.

CHESHIRE, E D, clk at Talley, Brown & Co's, n e
c Windsor and Fulton.

CHISOLM, MRS R E, bdg h, e s Pryor, near Garnett.

Chisolm, F N, (Henderson, C & Co,) n e c Walton and
Cone.

Chisolm, Willis P, broker, e s Whitehall, b Alabama and
Hunter.

CHISLOM, J C, gun smith, bds with J A Hancock.

Christian, W C D, emp W & A R R, cor Collins and
Butler.

CHRISTIAN CHURCH, n s Hunter, b Pryor and
Lloyd.

CHRISTIAN INDEX & SOUTH-WESTERN BAP-
TIST, Franklin Printing House, Dr D Shaver, editor.

Christiphine, Frank, n w c Luckie and Spring.

CITY FLOURING MILLS, n e c Bartow and W &
A R R, W G Peters & Co, pros.

CITY HALL SQUARE, bounded on e by Calhoun, w
by Washington, n by Hunter, and s by Mitchell streets.

CITY HOSPITAL, in Fair Grounds, cor Fair and Hill,
Dr E J Roach, City Physician.

CITY CEMETERY, e of Elmore, b Fair street and Ga
R R, G A Pilgrim, Sexton.

CHANCY, M J, near n w c McDonough and Fair.

Clarke, Jas, w s Washington, b Fulton and Richardson.

CLARKE, J M, Atty, e s McDonough, b Rawson and
Clark.

CLARK, MRS LYDIA, e s Whitehall, b Mitchell and
Peters.

CLARK, W F, printer and musician, with Mrs Lydia C.

Clark, V B, bar k, bds at American Hotel.

Clark, J D, cond A & W P R R, bds at American Hotel.

Clarke, A A, clk A & W P R R Depot, s s Marietta, b
Bartow and Foundry alley.

Clarke, J D, ptr, n e c Wheat and Pryor.

Clarke, Mrs Elizabeth, n s Crape's alley, w of Race.

CLARKE, T M & R R C, (see p 144)—Hardware, cor
Peachtree and Line.

CLARKE, THOS M, (T M & R C C,) res n w c Mitchell and Forsyth.

CLARKE, R C, (T M & R C C,) bds with T M C.

CLARKE, WM H, com mer, bds with Mrs Eliza Johnson.

CLARKE, Z A, plasterer, e s Marietta, opp Gas Works.

CLAYTON, J W, Agt So Manuf, s w c Houston and Gilmer.

CLAYTON & ADAIR, (see p 146) gro and com mer, s s Alabama, b Pryor and Lloyd.

CLAYTON, WM W, (C & Adair,) n w c Marietta and Spring.

Clotz, J P, s s Alabama, near Broad.

Clower, Thos L, s s Irwin, near Bloyd.

Clower, W W, bk m, s s Harris, b Collins and Calhoun.

COCHRAN, J A, trader, w s Whitehall, near junction of Forsyth.

COFER & McCALLA, Leather and com mer, n s Decatur, b Peachtree and Pryor.

Cofer, E G, carp, s w c Fowler and Magazine.

Coggin, W T, bk m, n s Rock, b Fowler and Mangum.

Coggin, Harris W, telgh watchman, n s Rock, w of Mangum.

COHRON, JOSEPH, printer, Intelligencer office, e s Race, s of Haynes.

Cohen, John, carp, e s Walker, s of Stephens.

Cohen, James, s s Washington, b Jones and Rawson.

COHEN, L, Dry Goods, e s Whitehall, b Alabama and Hunter.

Cole, W E, bds with J M C Monday.

Cole, Moses, bds with Dr N L Angier.

COLEMAN, MRS S H, bdg h, o s Whitehall, b Hunter and Mitchell.

COLLIER & HOYT, attys, w s Whitehall, b Alabama and Hunter.

Collier, John, (C & Hoyt,) w of and fronting M & W R R, s of Stockton.

Collier, T M, saloon k, bds at Planters' Hotel.

Collins, R S, bk m, bds at Mechanic House.

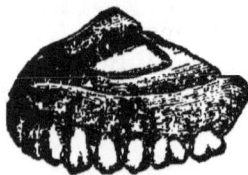

COMPTON, W W, mer, bds at American Hotel.

CONCORDIA HALL, e s Whitehall, b Hunter and Mitchell.

Conger, T, carp, n s Magazine, e of Fowler.

Connally, Jno, s s Hunter, b Butler and Terry.

Connally, Arthur, s s Hunter, b Butler and Terry.

Conner, E C, (Sheldon & C,) bds with Mrs G B Douglass.

CONSODINE, T, boot mkr, n s Decatur, b Pryor and Ivy.

Conway, A C, carp, with W J Gee.

Cook, Miss Esther, n s Fair, near Martin alley.

COOK, GEO W D, (J Winship & Co,) n s Walton, b Spring and Bartow.

Cook, J L, pol, e s Walker, s of Boothe's alley.

COOK, L, hardware, s w c Whitehall and Alabama.

Cooley, Mark, bar k, n e c Mitchell and Broad.

COOPER, JAS F, City Surv, e s Pryor, b Wheat and Line,

Corbit, M, bk m, e s Forsyth, b Alabama and Hunter.

Corey, F W, (Pond & C,) National Hotel.

CORPUT, Max V D, (Fay & C,) n s Decatur, b Collins and Calhoun.

Corput, Gustavus, clk with M V D C.

CORRA, F & Co, conf, e s Whitehall, b Alabama and R R.

Corra, F, (C, F & Co,) McDonough, s of Rawson.

Corrigan, Michael, w s Lloyd, b Hunter and Mitchell.

Corey, Mrs Harriet, s w c Cone and Luckie.

Cothran, E A, printer, bds at Mechanic House.

Coulter, Lewis, n s Gilmer, b Collins and Calhoun.

COURT HOUSE, (Fulton County,) in City Hall Square.

COVINGTON HOUSE, Mrs E White, pro, s s Decatur, b Lloyd and Collins.

Cowan, W H C, gun smith, e s McDonough, at junction of Butler.

COWART, R J, atty, bds at Covington House.

Cowart, George, bds at Covington House.

Cowart, Charles, bds at Covington House.

Cox, F A, eng W & A R R, s s Hayden, near Harris.

Cox Jas E, s s Nelson, e of Walker.

COX & HILL, (see p 148) Wines and Liquors, e s Peachtree, n of Line.

COX, CAPT W B, (C & Hill,)—e s Ivy, b Harris and Baker.

Cox, J B, ptr, n s Hunter, near City Cemetery.

Coyen, Jas, fam gro, s s Marietta, b Bartow and Foundry alley.

Cozart, Mrs W H, n s Peters, b Forsyth and Thompson.

Crane, Benj E, (Langston, C & Hammock,) bds with Wm W Clayton.

Crane, G D, (Jennings & C,) bds with J T Hall.

Craven, V W, ptr, n s Gilmer, b Ivy and Collins.

Craven, N S, atty, bds with V W C.

CRAVEN, Rev ISAAC N, s w c Gilmer and Collins.

CRAWFORD, ROBT, Com Pub Works, s e c Terry and Ga R R.

Crawford, Elisha, carp, n w c Lloyd and Jones.

Crawford, Russell, pol, s s Marietta, near Gate City Foundry.

Crawford, W H, plasterer, n e c Foundry and Fowler.

CRENSHAW, J L, pol, e s Butler, b Ga R R and Hunter.

• Crew, B B & Co, bk slrs, e s Whitehall, b R R and Marietta.

Crew, B B, (C, B B & Co.,) bds with D N Judson.

Cromley, Mrs Catherine, Milliner, s s Marietta, near Gate City Foundry.

Crow, Thos J, carp, n s Stonewall, w of Race.

Crockett, David M, carp, u w c Calhoun and Ga R R.

Crockett, D A, mach, bds with David M C.

CROFT, DAVID W, cond M & W R R, res s s Stockton, w of M & W R R.

Crook, Miss Amanda, tchr, with J W C.

Crook, J W, n e c McDonough and Fair.

Crosby, Isaac, pattern mkr, s s Ga R R, b Butler and Terry.

Cruise, Wm, well digger, n w c Luckie and Mills.
CRUMLEY, Rev W M, Pastor Trinity M E Church, bds with J H Anderson.
CRUSSELL, T G W, bk m, n e c Peachtree and Ellis.
Culverson, J II, carp, s s Decatur, near A & W Pt Depot.
Curtis, Mrs M E, dress mkr, n s Peters, near Whitehall.

D

DAILY NEW ERA, Dr Samuel Bard, pro, cor Marietta and Peachtree.
Dallas, G J, mer, bds at American Hotel.
Daly, Martin, bar k, n s Owens, near M & W R R.
D'ALVIGNY, N, M D, n s Jenkins, b Collins and Calhoun.
D'Alvigny, C F S, med student, with Dr N D.
Daniel, C, clk P O, bds at G B Roberts.
Daniel, Jas, mach, bds with Mrs Jane Walsh.
Daniel, Joshua, s w c Collins and Harris.
Daniel, Jno B, clk, bds with J D.
Darby, Archibald, emp Ga R R, bds with E C Downs.
Darnold, Jas, carp, s s Marietta, b Bartow and Foundry alley.
Davidge, C II, in Revenue office, bds at American Hotel.
Davis, J C, s e c Peachtree and Cain.
DAVIS, C C, Fam Gro, cor Trebursey and Race.
Davis, S II, cor Crew and Fulton.
Davis, John, mach, S shop, bds with Mrs A D Rhodes.
Davis, John J, tailor, w s Broad, near Mitchell.
DAVIS, LARKIN II, s e c Davis and Race.
Davis, John F, blk s, e s Frazer, b Jones and Rawson.
Davis, Kinson, pdlr, bds with Hardy Treadwell.
Davis, Mrs M J, bds with H Westmoreland.
Davis, T J, bds with II Westmoreland.
Davis, Joseph, bk k, bds with W W Clayton.
Davis, L B, Purchasing Agt, s w c Forsyth and Church.
Davison, Wm, clk, bds with D N Judson.
Day, Mrs Frank, s w c Whitehall and Garnett.

11

Day, D H, bk k, n w c Gilmer and Pratt.

Day, E F, with D H D.

Dean, Dr Elbert M, n s Thurman, w of Mangum.

Dean, Lemuel, gro mer, s s Marietta, opp Mangum.

Deckard, Wm, mach, S shop, bds with John S Chester.

Delany, T N, Mechanic House, e s Lloyd, b Alabama and Hunter.

Delay, Mrs Mary C, n s Marietta, near Gate City Foundry.

Delay, H R, ptr, s w c Grubb and Simpson.

Denham, Robt, carp, Race street, near old corp line.

Denniger, John, printer, w s Spring, b Walton and Luckie.

Deno, Geo C, mail agt, bds at Bellevue House.

Dewberry, David, carp, n e c Hunter and Butler.

Dewberry, Giles, gas fitter, s e c Decatur and Moore.

Dickey, Dr W J, bdg h, n s Mitchell, b Whitehall and Pryor.

DILL & MAIER, (see p 168) Photo Gallery, w s Whitehall, b Alabama and Hunter.

Dill, C W, (D & Maier,) with N E Gardner.

Dimmick, Loderick M, shoe mer, w s East Peachtree, b Baker and Oslin.

DOANE, JOHN A, bds with Dr J M Boring.

Dobbs, J H, clk, bds at American Hotel.

DOCKUM, O, Painter, s s Fair, near King.

Dodd, P & G T, Grocers, n e c Whitehall and Mitchell.

Dood, Green T, (D, P & G T,) s s Mitchell, b Whitehall and Pryor.

Dodd, Philip, (D, P & G T,) bds with G T D.

Doncaster, ——, bk m, bds with E E Winn.

DOOLY, M H, Supervisor, W & A R R, n e c Mangum and Green.

Doonan, Mrs Ellen, n w c Whitehall and Garnett.

Doonan, John J, clk, W & A R R, with Mrs E D.

Dougherty, W A, atty, bds at Bell Mansion.

DOUGHERTY, DAVID, (Silvey & D.)

Doughty, Mrs M E, n s Decatur, b Calhoun and Butler.

Douglass, Mrs G B, bdg h, s w c Mitchell and Washignton.

Douglass, T, blk s, n w c Luckie and Foundry alley.

DOUGLAS, Mrs E, dress mkr, w s Whitehall, b Hunter and Mitchell.

Dove, Levi, blaster, s s Delay, w of Haynes.

Downing, Wm, clk, w s Mitchell, b Lloyd and Washington.

DOWNS, WM, cond W & A R R, bds at Mrs C L Kile's.

Downs, J H, emp Ga R R, bds with E C Downs.

Downs, E C, carp, n s Ga R R, b Calhoun and Butler.

Downs, John U, fireman, W & A R R, bds with E C D.

Downs, Lemuel, bar k, American Hotel.

Drake, Jacob, plas, n s Harris, e of Butler.

Drake, Vines, n s Rock, w of Mangnm.

Drake, J F, emp W & A R R, s s Marietta, b Bartow and Foundry alley.

BuBOSE, Dr W S, n s Hunter, b Lloyd and Washington.

Ducker, Wm N, cab mkr, n s Garnett, b Whitehall and Forsyth.

Dudley, Mrs J D, s w c Harris and Collins.

DUNCAN, J W, Atty, s w c Marietta and Broad, res n w c Peachtree and Harris.

Dunlap, P H, bds with Mrs Catherine Bell.

Dunlap, W W, bgge master, W & A R R, bds with Mrs C Bell.

Dunnigan, C J, w s Walker, near Peters.

DUNNING, JAS L, U S Com, N Dist Ga, s w c Lloyd and Mitchell.

DUNNING, VOLNEY, Agt So Ex Co, s s Alabama, b Pryor and Lloyd.

Dunning, R S, pat mkr, n w c Lloyd and Peters.

Dunphy, Richard, stone m, w s Collins, b Houston and Ellis.

Durand, S A, dealer in lumber, w s Whitehall, b Peters and Garnett.

Durand, Mrs M F, Mil and Fancy Goods, w s Whitehall, b Peters and Garnett.

Dyer, Washington, carp, bds with Hiram Bowen.

E

EARNEST, E E, (see p 152) Jewelry, &c., w s Whitehall, b Hunter and Mitchell.

Earnest, C E, plasterer, w s Mangum, b Nelson and Race.

Earnest, F W, gro mer, n e c Mangum and Race.

Echols, Robt M, mail guard, W & A R R, bds with Mrs S A Lester.

Echols, Thos, bds at Mrs R E Chisolm's.

Echols, James, bk m, w s Peters, n junction of Walker.

EDDLEMAN & BANKS, Boots and Shoes, e s Peachtree, opp Walton.

Eddleman, F M, (E & Banks,) res on Pryor, near Rawson.

Eddleman, John, clk at Eddleman and Banks'.

Eddleman, Frank, carp, S shop, n s Mechanic.

Eddleman, George II, bds with John E.

Edwards, Benj, Mail Agent, bds at Bellevue House.

Edwards, J R, cond M & W R R, bds with Mrs S A Lester.

Edwards, John, carp, bds with Mrs L A King.

Edwards, Jesse, s s Luckie, b Bartow and Foundry alley.

Edwards, B C, printer, bds at Mechanic House.

Edwards, B F, Mail Agent, A & W P R R, bds at Mechanic House.

Eeds, C W, printer, at Atlanta Daily Intelligencer.

Eischengreen, J, mer, bds at Planters' Hotel.

Eiseman & Bro, clothing, e s Whitehall, near Hunter.

Eiseman, M J, clothing, bds at Planters' Hotel.

Eisenhut, John, shoe mkr, e s Fowler, b Green and Rhodes.

Ellison, James, carp, bds with Hardy Treadwell.

Elsworth, John, eng, S road, with Jacob Weaver.

ELYEA, C H, U S Dept Marshall, n s Wheat, b Collins and Calhoun.

EMPIRE STEAM PLANING MILL, n s Decatur, e of Bell, Peck & Markham, pros.

English, J W, National Hotel.

Euwright, Mrs C M, w s Crew, b Jones and Fair.

EPISCOPAL CHURCH, St Philip's, n e c Washington and Hunter, Rev Chas W Thomas, Rector.

Ergenzinger, Alex, upholsterer, bds at Mrs S H Coleman's.

Evans, George, bk m, w s Crew, s of Rawson.

Evans, John, ptr, n w c Frazer and Richardson.

EVERETT, WM S, clk, Talley, Brown & Co's, res n e c Windsor and Richardson.

EZZARD, WM, (see p 152) Atty, w s Broad, b R R and Marietta, res n w c Peachtree and Luckie.

EZZARD, WM L, w s Forsyth, b Luckie and Church.

F

FAINS & PARROTT, (see p 154) Gro and Com Mer, e s Peachtree, opp Walton.

Fain, W D, and Fain, John N, (F & Parrott.)

Faith, John, e s Frazer, s of Rawson.

FAIR GROUND, s s Fair st, b Connally alley and Hill.

FAMBROUGH, W P, Master Carp, n e c Walker and Boothe's alley.

Farnsworth, W T, carp, bds with Levi Stansell.

Farrar, Jesse C, cor Collins and Harris.

FARRAR, R M, (Orme & F,) cor Collins and Harris.

FARROW, H P, (see p 154) Atty, n e c Alabama and Whitehall, entrance n s Alabama, res cor Washington and Crumley.

Farley, Philip, s s Mechanic.

FAY & CORPUT, (see p 154) Arch, n e c Decatur and Ivy.

FAY, CALVIN, (F & Corput,) e s Whitehall, b Mitchell and Peters.

FERGUSON, D P, Fam Gro, n e c Whitehall and Mitchell, res e s M & W R R, s of Grenville's alley.

Few, Mrs Selina A, e s Walker, s of Boothe's alley.

Finch, H B, atty, bds with M L Harris.

FINDLEY, J J, Atty, n w c Cain and Randolph.

Findley, W V, carp, bds with J J F.

Fishback, W G, tailor, b Peachtree and Ivy, at junction of same.

Fish, Vines, trader, s s Nelson, near M & W R R.

Fisher, George, cab mkr, S shop, n s Magazine, w of Fowler.

Fitts, Robt C, mail clk "Int Office," bds at Dr J M Boring's.

Fitzgibbon, Thos, s s Fair, b McDonough and Frazer.

Fitzgibbon, Pat, keeper City Hall.

Flack, W B, bds at American Hotel.

Flash, A, e s Whitehall, b Garnett and Grenville's alley.

Fleck, Daniel, br k, w of W & A R R Round House.

Fletcher, Charles L, bds with Mrs A L Boyd.

Fleishel, David, (Paige, F & Co,) res w s Whitehall, s of Garnett.

Fleishel, Joseph, and Benj, with David F.

Fleming, A, s s McLin, near M & W R R.

Fleming, A F, salesman, with Smith & Richmond.

Fleming, L G, bds at Mechanic House.

Fleming, Thos P, with M R Bell & Co.

Floyd, John F, shoe mkr, w s Peters, n of junction of Walker.

FLYNN & DOOLY, Dry Goods, e s Whitehall, b Hunter and Mitchell.

Flynn, John H, master mach, W & A R R shop, n e c Collins and Gilmer.

Flynn, Jas, eng W & A R R, bds with M H Dooly.

Flynn, Thos, bds with M H Dooly.

FORCE & CO, (see p 156) Shoe Store, e s Whitehall, b Alabama and Hunter.

Force, G H, (F & Co,) bds at American Hotel.

Force, A W, (F & Co,) bds at D N Judson's.

FORD & HIGHTOWER, Gro Mer, n s Mitchell, b Whitehall and Broad.

GEO. HILLYER,

ATTORNEY AT LAW,

ATLANTA, GEORGIA.

Office, Atlanta National Bank building—up stairs.

JAMES M. CALHOUN.   WM. L. CALHOUN.

J. M. CALHOUN & SON,

ATTORNEYS AT LAW,

South-West corner Alabama and Washington Streets,

ATLANTA, GA.

Will attend to all professional business in their office. Also, practice in the U. S. District Court at Atlanta, and in the State Courts.

SEE P. 148.

Ford, Dr John J, (F & Hightower,) e s Peters, w of M & W R R.

FORD & BOOTH, (see p 158) Carriage Mkrs, s s Mitchell, near Whitehall.

Ford, Jas J, (F & Booth,) w s Washington, b Fair and Jones.

FORD & HAPE, (see p 156) Dentists, s s Alabama, b Whitehall and Pryor.

FORD, Dr ARTHUR, (F & Hape, bds at Planters' Hotel.

Forsyth, A B, s s Line, b Pryor and Ivy.

Forsyth, Wm, blk s, n w c Cain and Orme.

FOSTER, Gen IRA R, n s Marietta, near Gate City Foundry.

FOWLER, N R, Clk County Court, e s Peachtree, b Harris and Baker.

Fox, George, mach, S road, bds with Mrs A D Rhodes.

Fox, Amos, (Redwine & F,) w s Pryor, b Peters and Garnett.

FRANKLIN & MAHALOVITCH, House Fur Goods, w s Whitehall, b Alabama and R R.

Franklin, Herman, w s Forsyth, b Peters and Garnett.

Franklin, M, with Herman F.

FRANKLIN PRINTING HOUSE, J J Toon, pro, n s Alabama, b Whitehall and Pryor.

FRAZER, GEO P, (see p 158) Furniture, s s Marietta, near Whitehall.

FRIEDMAN & LOVEMAN, (see p 158) e s Whitehall, b Alabama and Hunter.

FRIZZELL, W H Frmn Empire Steam Plaining Mill, n s Decatur, e of Bell.

Fulsom, ——, (Joiner & F,) bds with Mrs A J Simms.

FULLER, Capt WM A, Cond W & A R R, n s Mechanic.

Fuller, A R, clk P O, bds with G B Roberts.

FULLER, J H, cond M & W R R, n e c Whitehall and Fair.

G

Gaines, M, shoe mkr, w s Race, s of Stonewall.

Gaines, R C, s s Fair, b Frazer and McDonough.

Gaines, Allen W, n s Magazine, e of Fowler.

GAMMAGE, THOS, Eng Ga R R, bds with T A Morris.

Gannon, Jno M, Dry Goods, n e c Whitehall and Hunter; residence, cor Pryor and Fair.

Gannon, Peter, n s Decatur, b Calhoun and Butler.

GARCIA, B, Fam Gro, w s Whitehall, b Mitchell and Peters.

Gardner, N E, s e c Hunter and Forsyth.

Gardner, M M, carp, n s Nelson, w of Haynes.

Garmany, J S, blr mkr, n s Decatur, b Moore and Pratt.

GARNER, T S, (see cover,) Real Estate Agent, room No 16, Empire Block, e s Whitehall, b Hunter and Mitchell.

GARNER & JOHNSON, Fam Gro, e s Whitehall, s of Mitchell.

Garner, J G, carp, w of Walker, near Peters.

GARRETT & BRO, Grocers, e s Whitehall, b Hunter and Mitchell.

Garrett, Young, (G & Bro,) w s Washington, b Fulton and Richardson.

Garrett, W J, (G & Bro,) e s Washington, s of Rawson.

Garrett, Dr Wm M, Dentist, s s Mitchell, w of M & W R R

GARTRELL, L J, (see p 162) Atty, w s Whitehall, b R R and Alabama, res n s Decatur, opp Rolling Mill.

Garvey, Mrs Mary, n s Gilmer, b Collins and Calhoun.

GASKILL, Rev V A, (see p 162) Atty and Real Estate Agt, e s Whitehall, near R R, res e s Forsyth, b Peters and Garnett.

Gather, Frank, shoe mkr, s w c Ivy and Harris.

GATE CITY FOUNDRY, Car and Machine Works, s s Marietta, opp Delay, (Henry.)

Gatins, Jno, clk, M & W Depot, cor Calhoun and Jenkins.

Gatins, Joseph, n s Gilmer, b Collins and Calhoun.

GAULDING, A A, J P, office n e c Alabama and Forsyth.

Gaven, John, bds with P H O'Neill.

Garvey, P, National Hotel.

Gavett, Samuel, mach, bds with Jno Kershaw.

Gay, E H, dry goods mer, e s Peachtree, opp Luckie.

Gay, Gustavus, dry goods mer, s s Church, b Forsyth and Cone.

Gay, J O A, w s Martin, b Jones and Rawson.

GENTRY, SAMUEL, yd master, M & W R R, on alley b M & W, and old Mon R R's, opp w end of Hunter.

Gee, W J, bldr, n s Green, w of Haynes.

GEORGE, JNO H, Plasterer, n s Harris, b Butler and Bloyd.

GEORGIA STATE LOTTERY, (see p 162,) for benefit of "Masonic Orphans' Home," W W Boyd, Principal Manager, office in Granite Block, w s Broad, b Marietta and R R.

GEORGIA RAILROAD FREIGHT DEPOT, cor Lloyd st and Ga R R, Gen G T Anderson, Agt.

GEORGIA NATIONAL BANK, s s Alabama, b Whitehall and Pryor, John Rice, Pres't, E L Jones, Cash.

Gibbon, Hugh, bds with John Connally.

Gibbon, George, s s Mitchell, b Crew and Washington.

Giddings, W B, bds with A P McPherson.

GILBERT, J, Phys, office and res cor Decatur and College.

Gilbert, Mathew, clk, bds with John Silvey.

Gilbert, T, watch mkr, w s Whitehall, b R R and Alabama.

Gilday, Thos, clk, bds with John Connally.

GILES, J L, with Phillips & Flanders.

Giles, J T, painter, n s Houston, b Collins and Calhoun.

Gilleland, W G, carp, cor Decatur and Moore.

Gillespie, R H C, clk, bds with John T Hall.

Glass, Robt, clk, bds with A Gray.

GLENN, L J, & SON, Attys, n e c Whitehall and Hunter.

Glenn, Luther J, (G & Son,) res cor Cooper and Rawson.

12

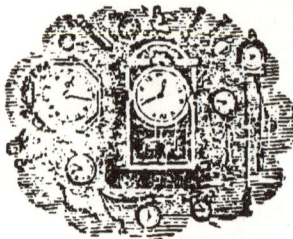

Glenn, John, Rec and For Agt Ga R R Depot.

Glenn, M T, carp, bds with Mrs N N Kidd.

Glenn, Mrs M E, s s Fair, near Fair Ground.

GODFREY, Rev J E, s w c Collins and Baker.

Godfrey, C W, bk k, with Rev J E G.

Godfrey, R J, clk at Revenue Office, bds with Rev J E G.

Golden, H, Tr Agt S Road, w s McDaniel, c of White-hall.

GOLDSMITH, W L, Atty, w s Whitehall, b Alabama and Hunter.

GOLDSMITH, W T, M D, w s Whitehall, b Alabama and Hunter.

GOODE, Maj HAMILTON, Tchr, s w c Marietta and Spring.

Goodman & Seymore, fam gro, e s Peachtree, n of Walton.

GOODMAN, Dr JOHN, n s Walton, b Bartow and Foundry alley.

Goodman, S P, clk, s s Luckie, b Bartow and Foundry alley.

Gordon, D L, bar k, s s Mitchell, b Whitehall and Pryor.

Gordon, Mrs E A, n s Ellis, b Peachtree and Ivy.

Goudy, Mrs E A, n w c Mitchell and Mangum.

Gouge, J, tin s, bds with W J Dickey.

Gouldsmith, R, cab mkr, w s Pryor, b Peters and Mitchell.

Gouldsmith, Mrs R, mil and fancy goods, e s Whitehall, b Alabama and Hunter.

Graff, Jacob, National Hotel.

Graham, Wm A, printer, Int Office.

Gramling, Geo, carp, bds with Mrs S A Lester.

Gramling, John, clk Silvey & Dougherty's, bds with J Silvey.

Gramling, Wm, clk Silvey & Dougherty's, bds with J Silvey.

GRAMLING, W G, Supt Car Factory, W & A R R, bds at American Hotel.

GRANT, Col L P, Supt A & W P R R, office s s Alabama, b Pryor and Lloyd, res s of City Cemetery, near old corp line.

Grant, A T, clk, bds with A L Grant.

Grant, W W, clk A & W P R R, bds with A L G.

Grant, A L, cor Decatur and Collins.

GRAY, W D, Marble Cutter, n s Fair, w of Cemetery.

Gray, W H C, bds with Mrs M W G.

Gray, Luke, car insp, bds with J M C Monday.

Gray, Mrs Lucinda, with M T Castleberry.

Gray, Mrs Martha W, n s Fair, opp Martin alley.

Green, W E, n s Cain, b Ivy and Collins.

Green, Geo, car insp, s e c Foundry and Mangum.

Green, Jesse C, cor Walker and Boothe's alley.

Greeson, Mrs T A, s s Ga R R b Butler and Terry.

GRENVILLE, CHAS E, Mer Miller, w s Whitehall, Fair.

Gresham, T G, Mail Agt W & A R R, s s Mechanic.

Gray, Jno D (A R Mill & Min Co,) w of R Mill.

Gray, Wm R, with J D Gray.

Gray, Chas W, with J D Gray.

Grier, J L, carp, s w c West Peachtree and Mills.

Griffin, Leroy, e s McDonough, near old corp line.

GRIFFIN, DR E E, bds with Jno T Hall.

GRIFFIN, J L, grocer, w s Whitehall, b Hunter and Mitchell.

Griffin, J D, carp, cor Butler and Harris.

Griggs, E W, bk m, n s Trebursey, w of Race.

Grist, B A, printer, New Era office, n s Mechanic.

Grizzard, T F, with Dr W H Pegg.

GROSS & SCHRAMM, Mer Tailors, w s Whitehall, b Alabama and Hunter.

Gross, C G, (G & Schramm,) bds at Planter's Hotel.

GRUBB, SAMUEL, Tax Rec, e s Frazer, s of Richardson.

GRUBB, SAMUEL W, Foreman "Daily Intelligencer," bds with Samuel G.

Grubbs, Thos J, w s Race, s of Haynes.

Grubbs, Mrs Elizabeth, s s Marietta, b Spring and Bartow.

Grubbs, Wilson L, carp, w s Race, s of Haynes.

Grubbs, Wm W, carp, w s Race, s of Haynes.

Grubbs, B F, carp, s s Marietta, b Bartow and Foundry alley.

Guess, H P, w s Peachtree, n of Walton.

GULLATT, JAMES E, Brass Founder, s e c Decatur and Butler.

Gullatt, Henry, mldr, w s Calhoun, b Gilmer and Jenkins.

H

HAGAN, JOHN T, Variety Store, w s Whitehall, b Mitchell and Peters.

Hayden, P, mer, n s Pryor, near Garnett.

HALL, H H, & BRO, Tin Smiths, w s Peters, near M & W R R.

HALL, J T, Painter, n s Peters, b Forsyth and Thompson.

HALL, JOHN T, bdg h, s s Hunter, b Whitehall and Pryor.

Hall, P M, shoe mkr, s s Hunter, b Calhoun and Butler.

HALL, J W, Fam Gro, n s Peters, b Forsyth and Thompson.

HAMBLETON, JAS P, M D, w s Peachtree, b Harris and Baker.

Hamilton, Murray, fireman W & A R R, s s Marietta, b Bartow and Foundry alley.

Hammock, C C, (Langston, Crane & H,) n w c McDonough and Jones.

HAMMOND & SON, Attys, s s Alabama, b Pryor and Lloyd.

Hammond, A W, (H & Son,) bds at Planters' Hotel.

Hammond, N J, (H & Son,) w s Peachtree, b Cain and Harris.

Hammond, Mrs R J, fam gro, s e c Peters and Garnett.

Hammond, W P, mer, e s Pryor, b Wheat and Houston.

HAMMOND, GEO H, bds with N J H.

HAMMOND, MYNATT & WELLBORN, Attys, w s Whitehall, b Alabama and Hunter.

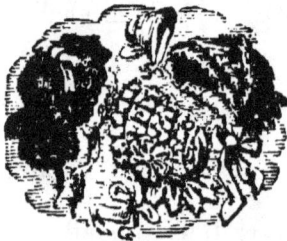

HAMMOND, D F, (H, Mynatt & Wellborn,) res West End.

HANCOCK, JAS A, Eng M & W R R, s s Peters, b Forsyth and Thompson.

HANCOCK, WM S, n s Peters, b Forsyth and Thompson.

HANCOCK, WM H, Ins Agt, n w c Whitehall and Alabama.

Haney, Thos, blk s, bds with Mrs A D Rhodes.

Haney, Henry, blk s, bds with Mrs A D Rhodes.

HANLEITER, WM R, bk binder, Franklin House, s w c Irwin and Randolph.

HAPE, Dr ALBERT, (Ford & H,) bds at Planters' Hotel.

HAPE, Dr SAMUEL, (see p 164) Dental Depot, s s Alabama, b Whitehall and Pryor, res s s Oslin, b Collins and Calhoun.

Haralson, A J, mer, n s Marietta, b Spring and Bartow.

Haralson, J H, butcher, bds with A J H.

Harbuck, John, gunsmith, s s McDaniel, b Whitehall and Windsor.

Harden, Mrs Clementine, n w c Forsyth and Peters.

Harden, M, butcher, w s Forsyth, b Luckie and Church.

Harman, Chas, bk k, e s Pryor, b Wheat and Houston.

HARRIS, HENRY D, Clk National Hotel.

HARRIS, JOHN, & SONS, Gro and Com Mer, w s Whitehall, b Hunter and Mitchell.

Harris, John P and Isaac P, (H, John & Sons.)

HARRIS, THEOPHILUS, Clk, 1st Market, e s Martin, s of Rawson.

Harris, W C, carp, w s Pryor, b Hunter and Mitchell.

Harris, Wm, mach, s s Ga R R, b Terry and King.

Harris, Mrs M L, e s Collins, b Cain and Harris.

HARRIS, W W, Cond M & W R R, w s Calhoun, b Decatur and Gilmer.

HARRIS, J O, Real Estate Agt, w s Collins, b Houston and Ellis.

HARRIS, McAFFEE & CO, Rock Querry, at w end of Foundry.

Harris, J R, phys, n s Decatur, b Collins and Calhoun.

HARRISON, Rev W P, Pastor Wesley Chapel, M E Church, res in parsonage, n of same.

Harrison, John, mach, w end of Foundry.

HARVEY & WARLICK, Tin Smiths, w s Peachtree, n of Walton.

Harvill, Wm H, wagon mkr, n w c Decatur and Pratt.

Harwell, Levi H, gro mer, n s Mechanic.

HARWELL, J M, Tax Col, n s Mechanic.

Haslett & Jones, gro mer, w s Whitehall, be Hunter and Mitchell.

Haslett, John, (H J & G H,) s s Fair, b McDonough and Frazer.

Hassell, Wm, carp, s s Peters, b Forsyth and Thompson.

Hathaway, Mrs H C, bdg h, cor Washington and Peters.

Haverty, Thos, gardener, n s Owens, near M & W R. R.

Haverty, Michael, bar k, n s Owens, near M & W R. R.

HAYDEN, JULIAS A, Contractor, n w c Marietta and Cone.

Haygood, Mrs, G B, n w c McDonough and Fair.

Haney, Mrs Elizabeth, bdg h, n e c Butler and Ga R R.

Haney, Wm E, clk A & W P R R Depot, bds with Mrs E H.

HAYNES, WM A, Watch Mkr at Er Lashe's jewelry store.

Haynes, Mrs Annette, s s Mitchell, c of Mangum.

Hays, A C, cab mkr, n s Walton, b Bartow and Foundry.

Hays, I N, ptr, n s Houston, b Collins and Calhoun.

Head, John C, e s Mangum, n of Rock.

HEALY, THOS G, Contractor, s w c Mangum and Race.

Hearn, Thomas, carp, bds with Hiram Bowen.

Hearn, Mrs P, n s Trebursey, w of Race.

Heartsill, A L, carp, w s Spring, b Marietta and W & A R R.

Heggie, A C, salesman with Smith & Richmond, bds at American Hotel.

HEINZ & BERKELE, (see p 164) Hardware, &c., w s Whitehall, b R R and Alabama.

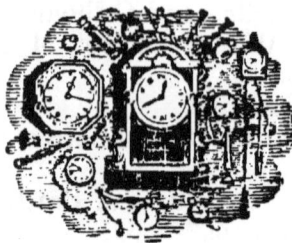

HEINZ, CHAS, (H & Berkcle,) res on **Pryor**, b Hunter and Mitchell.

HENDERSON, CHISOLM & CO, e s Whitehall, b Hunter and Mitchell.

Henderson, J T, (H, Chisolm & Co,) bds with Mrs S H Coleman.

Henderson, Jas, bk m, e s Crew, b Fulton and Crumley.

Henderson, D, carp, n s Mitchell, w of Haynes.

HENDRIX, J C, Trader, cor Luckie and Alexander.

Hendon, Jas W, clk, s s Mitchell, w of M & W R R.

HENSLER, W L, Prof Music, bds with Dr J N Simmons.

HENSON, FIELDING, Gas Fitter, n e c Mitchell and Lloyd.

Herpy, Daniel, carp, bds with W J Dickey.

HERRMANN B, & WM BOLLMAN, (see ps 140 and 178) Jewelers, cor Whitehall and Marietta, and w s Whitehall, s of and near R R.

HERNDON, JOSEPH, Carp, w s Walker, s of Stephens.

HERNDON, W G, bds with Joseph H.

HERRING & LEYDEN, Dry Goods, e s Whitehall, n of Hunter.

HERRING, WM (H & Leyden,) w s Peachtree, b Ellis and Cain.

Herrington, H H, mach, bds with Jacob Sponsler.

Heyes, H G, mach, n s Hunter, w of Forsyth.

Hicks, V, fam gro, s s Mitchell, w of Haynes.

Hicks, P, National Hotel.

Hillburn, F A, e s Walker, s of Boothe's alley.

Hill, John, mer, n s Line, b Pryor and Ivy.

Hill, J R, carp, n s Decatur, b Calhoun and Butler.

Hill, Wm, emp S road, bds with Mrs E McGibbonney.

Hill, John A, carp, W & A R R shop.

Hill, Isaac, carp, bds with W J Dickey.

HILL, WM M, Auctioneer, cor Peachtree and Marietta, res n s Decatur, b Ivy and Collins.

Hill, A J, clk, bds with Wm M Hill.

HILL, THOS W J, Atty, bds with Wm M H.

Hill, Wm R, (Cox & H,) s e c Collins and Baker.

HILLYER, GEORGE, (see p 172) Atty, s s Alabama, b Whitehall and Pryor, bds with R B Campbell.

HILLYER, HENRY, Atty, with George H.

Hilton, Aug, carp, n s Fair, b Terry and Martin.

Hinton, M J, photo, s s Decatur, b Calhoun and Butler.

Hirshberg, Maas & Co, w s Whitehall, b Alabama and Hunter.

Hitchins, G S, carriage mkr, s s Walton, b Forsyth and Cone.

Hitchins, F C, carriage mkr, with G S H.

Hitt, Abner, bds with H W Broxton.

Hoffman, Joseph R, bk m, bds with W J Dickey.

Hogan, Mrs Rebecca, with Mrs Celete A Jones.

HOGE, JAMES, Supt Gate City Foundry, res cor West-Peachtree and Hunnicutt.

HOGE, E F, Atty, n s Decatur, b Pryor and Ivy.

HOLBROOK, J M, (see p 166) Hat Store, w s Whitehall, b Alabama and Hunter, res s w c Peters and Washington.

Holbrook, Jesse C, n s Rawson, b Cooper and Pryor.

Holcomb, Robert, watchman, S shop, s w c Fowler and Magazine.

HOLCOMB, H C, clk U S Dist Court, s e c McDonough and Hunter.

Holland, E W, n s Marietta, b Spring and Bartow.

Holland, Ed, at Atlanta National Bank, bds with E W H.

Holland, Joseph, blk s, w s Mitchell, b Lloyd and Washington.

Holland, Moses, bk m, s s Hunter, b Terry and King.

Holland, L G, bk m, s s Decatur, b Moore and Bell.

Holland, Wm C, bds with Lewis Coulter.

Holley, Chas W, manuf ladies' shoes, e s Crew, s of Rawson.

Holliday, G H, (Tidwell & H.)

Hollingsworth, Mrs E M, e s Ivy, b Decatur and Gilmer.

Hollinshed, gro mer, bds with Marcus Johnson.

Holmes, H J, n s Rock, w of Mangum.

Holmes, R T, bds with R C Gaines.

Holmes, John D, printer, " Ladies Home " office.

Holmes, Miss Fannie, tchr, bds with Mrs Mary Bruckner.

HOLROYD, Miss SARAH, Mil and Fancy Goods, s s Alabama, b Whitehall and Pryor.

Holtzclaw, H J, policeman.

Honecker, Chaistian, n w c Mangum and Rhodes.

HOPKINS, J L, Atty, n s Decatur, e of Peachtree, res s s Wheat, b Ivy and Collins.

Hope, L H, com mer, n s Cain, e of Bloyd.

HORNADY, Rev H C, Pastor, 1st Baptist Church, res w s Forsyth, b Walton and Luckie.

Horton, W C, painter, e s Frazer, b Jones and Rawson.

Horton, Marion, bk m, s of Delay, w of Mangum.

House, Francis C, n s Peters, b Whitehall and Forsyth.

HOUSTON STREET FEMALE HIGH SCOOL, by Misses Carn and Clayton, n s Houston, b Ivy and Collins.

Howard, A G, salesman, with Smith & Richmond, bds at Planters' Hotel.

HOWARD, R A, n s Decatur, b Collins and Calhoun.

Howard, W H, Jr, bds at Planters' Hotel.

HOWELL, A, Druggist, bds at American Hotel.

HOYT, H O, Dealer in Lumber, n s Line, b Pryor and Ivy.

HOYT, S B, City Atty, (Collier & H,) w s Whitehall, b Alabama and Hunter.

HUBBARD, WM L, Dept Sheriff, w s Calhoun, b Decatur and Gilmer.

HUDSON, W J, bk k, Phœnix Planing Mill, res s w c Decatur and Calhoun.

HUGE, PETER, Trader, s s Mechanic.

HUGHENS, JOHN H, Cond A & W P R R, n s Decatur, b Moore and Bell.

·Hughes, Ed, mer, bds at American Hotel.

HULBERT, E, Supt So Ex Co, office s s Alabama, b Pryor and Lloyd.

BOOKS AND STATIONERY.

Constantly for Sale, at Wholesale and Retail,

A LARGE AND WELL SELECTED STOCK OF

STANDARD WORKS

IN EVERY DEPARTMENT OF LITERATURE.

ALSO,

SCHOOL BOOKS, BLANK BOOKS

PAPER, AND STATIONERY,

OF ALL KINDS.

M. LYNCH & CO.,

West side Whitehall, near R. R. Crossing.

Atlanta, · · · · · · · · Georgia.

T. L. LANGSTON.   BEN. E. CRANE.   C. C. HAMMOCK.

LANGSTON, CRANE & HAMMOCK,

COMMISSION MERCHANTS

AND

Wholesale Dealers in Groceries and Produce,

ALABAMA STREET, EAST OF WHITEHALL,

ATLANTA, · · · · GEORGIA.

Hulsey, A J, Asst Surv Ga Air Line R R, bds at Bell Mansion.

HULSEY, WM H, (see p 168) Atty, w s Broad, b Marietta and R R.

Humphrey, Dr Wm C, w s Frazer, b Rawson and Fulton.

HUNNICUTT & BELLINGRATH, (see p 170) Gas Fitters, s w c Alabama and Lloyd.

HUNNICUTT, C W, (H & Bellingrath,) n w c West Peachtree and Hunnicutt.

HUNNICUTT, E T, Gro Mer, s w c Forsyth and McLin.

HUNNICUTT, J M, Clk, Scott and Freeman's, w s Forsyth, at junction with Whitehall.

Hunt, F S, agt Vul Iron Works, bds at American Hotel.

Hunt, William, tchr, cor Mitchell and Washington, bds with Mrs G B Douglass.

Hunt, W R, arch, bds at American Hotel.

Hunt, James, carp, n s Stonewall, w of Race.

Husketh, James, carp, bds with W H Freeman.

Husketh, Luke, eng, M & W R R, bds with J J Adcock.

Hutchins, B J, n w c Collins and Gilmer.

Hutchins, Reuben, s s Decatur, b Calhoun and Butler.

Hutson, Wm M, n s Rock, e of Fowler.

I

Ikerd, H M, carp S shop, bds with Mrs E McGibboney.

Ingles, W C, contractor, s s Houston, b Ivy and Pryor.

Ingraham, W W, carp, s s Fair, b Frazer and Terry.

INMAN, S W, Trader, w s Forsyth, b Mitchell and Peters.

Irvine, Mrs Carrie, e s Forsyth, b Peters and Garnett.

IVINS, SAMUEL P, Assistant Editor "Atlanta Intelligencer."

Ivy, Henry P, blk s, n e c Pryor and Wheat.

Ivy, S, mldr, n s Wheat, b Pryor and Ivy.

Ivy, Michael, atty, bds with J G Trammel.

JOHN H. LOVEJOY,

WHOLESALE

DEALER IN

FOREIGN AND DOMESTIC LIQUORS,

SEGARS, &c., &c.,

Granite-Front, Peachtree St., Opposite Walton,

ATLANTA, GA.

J

JACK, G W, (see p 174) Confectioner, e s Whitehall, b Alabama and Hunter, res w s Whitehall, near junction of Forsyth.

Jack, F M, conf, bds with G W J.

Jack, W F, conf, bds with Mrs A J Simms.

JACKSON, C D, n s Line, b Pryor and Ivy.

JACKSON, WILLIAM, bk m, n s of Race, w of Haynes.

Jackson, Henry, atty, s s Alabama, b Whitehall and Pryor, bds at American Hotel.

Jackson, Thos C, Pryor, s of Rawson.

Jacobs, Dr ——, w s Whitehall, near old corp line.

JAMES, JOHN II, (see p 176) Banker, n e c Whitehall and Alabama, res cor Peachtree and Church.

Janes, John, blk s, bds with James Mann.

Janes, W M, A M, Atlanta High School.

Jarred, Andrew, carp, bds with W C Anderson.

JEFFRIESS, J S, bldr, e s Collins, n of Currier.

JENKINS, J T & CO, (see p 176) Druggists, s w c Alabama and Pryor.

Jenks, Ambrose, shoe mkr, s s Gilmer, b Ivy and Collins.

JENNINGS & CRANE, Ins Agts, cor Alabama and Whitehall.

JENNINGS, WILLIAM, Ins Agt, cor Alabama and Whitehall, res s s Fair, b Martin and Connally.

Jett, J Farmer, at w end of Magazine, near new corp line.

Johns, Geo W, plas, b Fair and Jones, opp Fair Ground.

JOHNSON, SNOW & CO, s s Marietta, b Whitehall and Broad.

Johnson, Mrs M J, s s Hunter, b Whitehall and Pryor.

JOHNSON, Mrs ELIZA, bdg h, e s Forsyth, b Mitchell and Peters.

JOHNSON & ECHOLS, (see p 178) Gro and Com Mer, w s Whitehall, b Hunter and Mitchell.

JOHNSON, GEORGE, (see p 196) Saloon, &c., basement of P O building, cor Alabama and Broad.

H. MARSHALL,

SURGEON DENTIST,

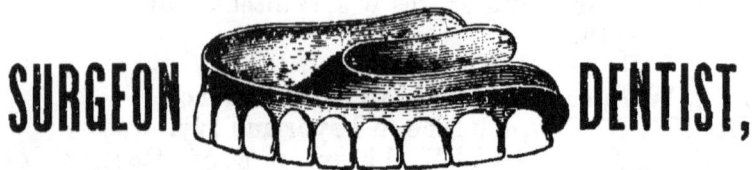

ATLANTA, GEORGIA,

Office, Corner Whitehall and Hunter Streets, Rawson's Building.
Office Hours from 9 o'clock, A. M., until 4 o'clock, P. M.

Dr. MARSHALL having been more than twenty years constantly engaged in the DENTAL PROFESSION before the late war, feels confident that he will be able to give entire satisfaction to all his patrons.

Every thing pertaining to the Profession attended to with neatness and dispatch.

Teeth extracted FREE OF CHARGE for *Widows* and *Orphans* who are unable to pay.

Special attention given to the management of CHILDREN'S TEETH, correcting irregularities and arresting decay.

Dr. MARSHALL has the pleasure of referring to the following citizens of Atlanta:

Rev. Dr. Brantly,	John G. Westmoreland, M. D.,
Rev. Dr. Hornady,	J. M. Johnson, M. D.,
Rev. Lewis Lawshe,	Thos. S. Powell, M. D.,
Rev. A. G. Haygood,	J. F. Alexander, M. D.,
E. E. Rawson,	Henry S. Orme, M. D.,
Chamberlain, Cole & Boynton,	Drs. Redwine & Fox,
Wm. Herring, Esq.,	Gen. A. Austell,
McNaught & Ormond,	Col. Robert Baugh,
Col. H. C. Barrow,	John J. Thrasher,
W. B. Lowe & Co.,	Judge Perino Brown,
S. A. Durand, Esq.,	Thos. G. Simms, P. M.,
Er Lawshe, Esq.,	Maj. J. R. Barrick.

Johnson, W C, clk Ga R R Depot, bds with J M C
Monday.

Johnson, W W, clk at Phillips & Flanders', bds with
W R Phillips.

Johnson, Marcus, com mer, e' s Frazer, s of Richardson.

JOHNSON, J M, M D, n e c Whitehall and Hunter, res
n e c Cooper and Rawson.

Johnson, J C P, emp Ga R R, bds with J M C Monday.

JOHNSON, Rev RICHARD, s s Fair, s w of City
Cemetery.

Johnson, J W, e s Butler, b Hunter and Fair.

Johnson, R J, carp, w s Whitehall, near old corp line.

Johnson, J L, bds Mr withs M J J.

Johnson, Wm B, bds with M J J.

Johnston, F M, (McNaught, Ormond & Co,) res e s
Washington, s of Fulton.

Joiner, H, mach, bds with Mrs L A King.

Jones, W A, clk, bds with A P Bell.

Jones, Mrs C, n s Rock, b Fowler and Mangum.

Jones, Joseph H, carp, w s W & A R R, n of Rock.

Jones, John T, carp, w s Martin, b Jones and Rawson.

Jones, W R, A M, Atlanta High School.

Jones, J H, n s Mitchell, b Forsyth and Thompson.

Jones, O H, keeps livery stable, res s w c Hunter and
Lloyd.

JONES, E L, Cashier Ga National Bank.

Jones, Edward H, bk k, Ga N Bank.

Jones, D G, Teller, Ga N Bank.

Jones, William, bk m, s w c Collins and Wheat.

Jones, W R, printer, "Int Office," s e c Peters and
Thompson.

Jones, Joseph, cooper, n s Ellis, b Ivy and Collins.

Jones, S H, carp, e s Crew, s of Fulton.

JONES, THOS M, Trans Agt, W & A R R, e s Crew,
s of Rawson.

Jones, W L, clk, bds with D H Day.

Jones, Mrs Celete A, s s Boothe's alley, b Peters and
Walker.

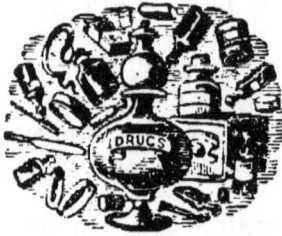

Jones, William, bds at Thos McFarland's.

Jordan, Wm, e s Race, s of Stonewall.

Jordan, J B, carp, s s Hunter, b Calhoun and Butler.

Jordan, John, clk, bds with Mrs Mary Bruckner.

Jordan, A, mer, bds at Planters' Hotel.

Jourdan, R T, with Dr W F Westmoreland.

JUDSON, D N, Dealer in Marble, res s s Walton, b Forsyth and Cone.

Judson, W N, med student, bds with D N J.

K

KANE, B, Fam Gro, s s Marietta, b Spring and Bartow.

KEAN, WM R, (Wade & K,) s w c Collins and Ellis.

Keely, John, clk, bds at Planters' Hotel.

KEHOE, Mrs E S, Mil and Fancy Goods, n s Walton, b Forsyth and Cone.

KEHOE, J, n s Walton, b Forsyth and Cone.

KEITH, J L, bk k, s c c Calhoun and Houston.

KELLY, JAMES G, Carp, Ga R R shop, n w c Hunter and Terry.'

Kelly, Mrs Johanna, n s Fair, b Terry and Martin.

Kelly, James P, carp, bds with Geo T Ogletree.

KELSEY, J, Mach, Ga R R shop, e s Crew, s of Rawson.

Keltner, G W, carp, s s Jones, b Martin and Connally.

Keltner, Wm, shoe mkr, s w c Whitehall and Mitchell, res s w c Haynes and Race.

Keltner, Thos W, bds with Wm K.

KELTNER, DANIEL E, Carp State shop, n w c Peters and Thompson.

KENDRICK, S S & CO, (see p 180) Carpts, &c, s c c Whitehall and Hunter.

KENDRICK, S S, (K, S S & Co,) n s Irwin, e of Houston.

KENNEDY, Miss MARY, Milliner, n s Whitehall, b Alabama and Hunter.

Kennedy, W A, boot mkr, cor Decatur and Bell.

Kennedy, A, (A R Mill and Min Co,) s s W & A R R, opp Rolling Mill.

Kennedy, Henry, fireman, W & A R R, s s Fair, b Frazer and Terry.

Kennedy, John, carp, bds with H Kennedy.

Kennedy, Simon, cor Lloyd and Fair.

Kennedy, Hugh, gardener, b Rhodes and Magazine, w of Haynes.

Kennedy, J W, n s Mitchell, b Lloyd and Washington.

KENNEDY, J E, bldr, n s Stephens, w of Walker.

Kennedy, Mrs Edward, e s McDonough, s of Rawson.

KENNEY, M E, at Chicago Ale House, s s Alabama, b Whitehall and Pryor.

KEARLY, JOHN, cab mkr, State shop, n s Rhodes, near R R.

Kerby, Tim, clk, bds with Wm Downing.

Kerlin, John R, emp W & A R R, with J W Richardson.

Kernodle, Mrs V, s s Ga R R, b Butler and Terry.

Kernodle, G M, cond, A & W P R R, bds with Mrs V K.

Kershaw, John, mach, s s Hunter, b Calhoun and Butler.

Kershaw, John, Jr, bds with John K.

Ketcham, Wm, (Shackelford & K,) n c c Pryor and Line.

KETCHAM, Rev R C, s s Hunter, b Calhoun and Butler.

Kicklighter, Mrs Mary A, s s Stephens, b Walker and Race.

KIDD, Mrs N N, bdg h, e s Pryor, s of Hunter.

KILBY, W J, Tailor, s e c Hunter and Broad.

Kile, James, at junction of Peters and Walker.

KILE, WM, w of Peters, near old corp line.

KILE, THOS, Mer, s e c Pryor and Houston.

Kile, Mrs C L, s e c Hunter and Pryor.

Kiley, John, miller, bds with C E Grenville.

Killen, Charles, clk, bds with Wm Solomon.

KING, Rev H K, manuf brick, n s Mechanic.

King, J C, carp, w s Walker, s of Boothe's alley.

KING, Mrs L A, bdg h, n w c Marietta and Forsyth.

King, James, on State road, bds with Mrs E McGibboney.

KING, J L & SON, Com Mer, e s Peachtree, n of Walton.

King, J L, (K, J L & Son) w s East-Peachtree, b Baker and Oslin.

KING, HARDEE & CO, (see p 186) Com Mer, w s Broad, n of R R.

King, Ralph B, J H, and C A, (K, Hardee & Co.)

Kingsey, Harry, mach, State shop, bds with Mrs A D Rhodes.

Kirkpatrick, W N, mer, e s Washington, b Jones and Rawson.

KIRKSEY, G W, Eng, Ga R R, n s Fair, e of Terry.

Kirksey, Elisha, n s Ellis, b Ivy and Collins.

Klassett, Andrew, boot mkr, s s Nelson, near Walker.

KNIGHT, G WALTON, (see p 182) Com College, s s Alabama, b Pryor and Lloyd.

Knight, Mrs Aaron B, e s Terry, b Hunter and Fair.

KNOX, WM G, Pressman, s w c Washington and Rawson.

KNOX, MRS WM G, (see 184) Mil and Fancy Goods, e s Whitehall, s of Alabama, up stairs.

KONTZ, CHRISTIAN, s s Marietta, b Forsyth and Spring.

Kontz, Henry, n s Mitchell, e of Mangum.

Krogg, Fred, carp, n s Decatur, b Randolph and Gartrell.

Krous, Harry, bds with Willis Peck.

Krenson, Henry, eng W & A R R, n s Mechanic.

KUHN, F, (see p 180) Photo Gallery, e s Whitehall, b Alabama and Hunter.

KUHRT, HENRY G, (Beermann & K,) s s Fair, b Cooper and Pryor.

L

Lacky, T F, fam gro, s s Marietta, near Gate City Foundry.

LADD, A C, (see p 210) Dealer in Lightning Rods, w s Whitehall, b R R and Alabama.

LAMB, B T, clk at John Ryan's.

Lamb, Merideth, carp, s s Rawson, b McDonough and Frazer.

Lambert, Joseph, and Alfonzo, gardeners and nurserymen, res n of Delay, w of Haynes.

LANDRUM & BRO, Gro, e s Whitehall, s of Alabama.

Landrum, L L, and W F, (Landrum & Bro.)

Landrum, John, clk, bds with A Gay.

LANDSBERG & HARRIS, Proprietors Phœnix Planing Mill, s e c Butler and Gilmer.

LANDSBERG, ——, (L & Harris,) bds at Bell Mansion.

Lane, R C, mail agt, bds at Bellevue House.

LANE, O R, (see p 190) Photo Gallery, s s Alabama, b Whitehall and Pryor, bds at Planters' Hotel.

Lang, Jeptha A, w s Martin, b Jones and Rawson.

Lang, E, w s Forsyth, s of Garnett.

Langford, W Y, s s Ga R R, b Terry and King.

LANGFORD, SEAY & McCRATH, s s Hunter, e of Whitehall.

Langford, L B, (L, Seay & McCrath,) w s Collins, b Cain and Harris.

LANGSTON, CRANE & HAMMOCK, (see p 194) Gro and Com Mer, e s Whitehall, b Hunter and Mitchell.

Langston, T L, (L, Crane & Hammock.)

Langston, James, carp, w s East-Peachtree, b Oslin and Currier.

Langston, Elijah W, carp, bds with James L.

Langston, D B, bds with O H Jones.

Langston, W J, eng w s East-Peachtree, b Oslin and Currier.

LANIER, WILLIS P, w s Thompson, b Mitchell and Peters.

Lanier, Lewis R, carp, cor M & W R R and Bartlett's alley.

LANIER, JAMES A, policeman, with W P Lanier.

LARENDON BROTHERS, Grocers, w s Whitehall, n of R R.

Larendon, G, n s Hunter, b Terry and King.

Lattimer, Maj Charles, s w c Washington and Fair.

Lattimer, H B, n s Marietta, near junction of Walton.

LAWSHE, ER, (see p 188) Jeweler, w s Whitehall, b Alabama and Hunter, res w s Peachtree, b Ellis and Cain.

LAWSHE, Rev LEWIS, at w end of Stephens, near new corp line.

LAWSHE, WM, bds with J G Trammel.

Lazenby, A, mer, s s Marietta, b Forsyth and Spring.

Leak, G G, clk, bds at American Hotel.

LEAK, HENRY F, clk, Talley, Brown & Co's, res cor Walker and Stonewall.

Lee, Wm, clk, bds with A Gay.

Lee, Thomas, M D, bds with Mrs G B Douglas.

LEE, SAUNDERS W., e s Rawson, b Cooper and Windsor.

Lee, Joel F, n s Rock, near Mangum.

Lee, J F, blk s, e s McDonough, b Jones and Rawson.

Lee, S W, Jr, bds with S W Lee, Sr.

Leitner & Fricker, jewelers, e s Whitehall, b Alabama and Hunter.

LEMMON, JOHN, s s Marietta, b Bartow and Foundry alley.

Lester, Mrs N H, s s Owens, near Forsyth.

Lester, Sylvester, printer, Int Office, with Mrs N H L.

LESTER, Mrs S A, s e c Spring and Luckie.

Lester, Miss M A, dress mkr, bds with Mrs S A L.

Letson, G H, cond, S Road, n s Fair, e of King.

Levy, Wm, bds at Bellevue House.

Lewis, E W, carp, bds with R W Smith.

LEYDEN, A, (Herring & L) w s Peachtree, b Ellis and Cain.

LEIBERMAN & BROTHER, Dry Goods, e s Whitehall, b Alabama and Hunter.

Lieberman, ——, (L & Bro,) w s Washington, b Hunter and Mitchell.

Light, Baily, bk m, on Green, w of Haynes.

Lin, Mrs Amanda, s s Decatur, e of Bell.

Lin, C B, clk, bds with Mrs Amanda L.

14

Lindsay, Frank, bk m, s w c Hunter and King.

Lipes, M, carp, bds with W H Barry.

Little, James, painter, s s Marietta, b Bartow and Foundry alley.

Lichtenstadt, Morlets, mach, s s Garnett, b Forsyth and Thompson.

LIVINGSTON, J H, Expressman, n s Stonewall, w of Race,

Loftis, J P, butcher, n s Wheat, b Ivy and Pryor.

Logan, J L, trader, s w c Foundry and Temple Vale.

Longley, B F, carp, bds with T A Morris.

Longley, Hugh, emp State Road, bds with Mrs E McGibboney.

Lother, Wm P, stone m, s c c Calhoun and Gilmer.

LOUGHMILLER, W C, Bakery, s s Marietta, b Forsyth and Spring.

Love, D G, carp, w s Martin, b Jones and Rawson.

LOVE, S B, Clk City Council, e s Crew, b Fair and Jones.

LOVEJGY, JOHN H, (see p 196) Wholesale Liquor Dealer, &c., e s Peachtree, opp Walton, res n e c Peachtree and Harris.

Lovejoy, Burton, with John H L.

LOWE, T B & CO, Fam Gro, s s Mitchell, w of Whitehall,

LOWE, Col THOS F, Com Mer, bds with A W Brown.

Lowery, R J & Co, com mer, s s Alabama, b Pryor and Lloyd.

Lowery, R J, (L, R J & Co,) bds with Wm Markham.

Lowery, W M, com broker, n e c Peachtree and Baker.

Lloyd, J H, e s McDonough, b Fair and Jones.

LLOYD, J W, s s Ga R R, e of King.

Lloyd, J M, clk, bds at Planters' Hotel.

LUCKIE, W D, bk k, bds with O H Jones.

Lumpkin, Jesse, blff, e s Peters, w of M & W R R.

Lyle, C B, and D R, s s Marietta, b Whitehall and Broad.

LYNCH, M & CO, (see p 194) Booksellers, w s Whitehall, b Alabama and R R.

LYNCH, M, (L, M & Co,) n e c Decatur and Calhoun.

LYNCH, PETER, Fam Gro, w s Whitehall, near Mitchell, res w s Mangum, near Markham.

LYNCH, JAMES, Gro Mer, n s Decatur, b Pryor and Ivy, res on Gilmer, b Ivy and Collins.

LYNCH, JEREMIAH, Tailor, n s Decatur, b Pryor and Ivy.

LYNCH, OWEN, Clk, W & A R R Depot, s w c Hunter and Butler.

Lynch, Wm S, eng W & A R R, bds with J J Adcock.

LYNCH, DANIEL, Bar k, bds at Planters' Hotel.

Lynch, Patrick, Sen, with James L.

LYNCH, PAT, Jr, Stone m, e s Peachtree, b Harris and Baker.

Lyon, Mrs Henrietta, s s Mitchell, b Whitehall and Forsyth.

Lyons, Mrs Mary, s s Ga R R, b Butler and Terry.

Lyons, J L, carp, e s Frazer, s of Henry alley.

M

McAffee, George, carp, bds with D H Teat.

McAffee, W W, s s Hunnicutt, w of Hayden.

McAllister, A J, bds with Mrs M L Harris.

McAllister, James, clk, bds at Covington House.

McARTHUR, THOS W, cor Peters and Pryor.

McBride, Dorsett & Co, crockery, n w c Whitehall and Hunter.

McBride, A J, (McB, Dorsett & Co,) bds with Mrs S H Coleman.

McCallister, John H, clk, bds with Mrs S H Coleman.

McCAMY & CO, (see p 200) Druggists, e s Whitehall, b Alabama and Hunter.

McCamy, C R, (McC & Co,) s s Wheat, b Pryor and Ivy.

McClellan, Archie, National Hotel.

McClelland, Joseph, e s Butler, b Hunter and Fair.

McCoin, A W, dairyman, w s Peters, s of old corp line.

McCONNELL, WM, Bldr, n s Alexander, e of Steam Tannery.

McCOOL, JAS A, cond W & A R R, bds at American
Hotel.

McCOWN, E P, Painter, State shop, s s Foundry, w of
Fowler.

McCown, Wm C, printer, at Franklin House, w s Frazer,
s of Rawson.

McCOWN, ROBT, Cab Mkr, n w c Peters and Boothe's
alley.

McCown, R W, cab mkr, n w c Luckie and Simpson.

McCoy, Hugh M, n e c Rock and Fowler.

McCoy, John, tailor, bds at Bellevue House.

McCrath, J W, (Langford, Seay & McC,) n s Hunter, e
of King.

McCrosky, R H, (see p 200) Grocer, s e c Whitehall and
Mitchell, res s s Mitchell, w of Whitehall.

McDade, Mrs Rebecca, e s Calhoun, b Wheat and Houston.

McDade, Robt, fireman Ga R R, bds with Mrs R McD.

McDade, David, fireman W & A R R, bds with Mrs R
McD.

McDade, Windsor C, eng, bds with A H McWaters.

McDANIEL, STRONG & CO, (see p 202) Cotton and
Com Mer, n w c Hunter and Pryor.

McDANIEL, P E, (McD, Strong & Co,) e s Pryor, b
Peters and Mitchell.

McDaniel, James, blk smith, bds at Mechanic House.

McDANIEL, IRA O, Com Mer, w s Whitehall, b
Mitchell and Peters, res n s Richardson, b Whitehall
and Windsor.

McDANIEL, J C, Tchr, Peters Street Male and Female
School.

McDANIEL, Miss VESTA, Tchr, Primary Dept, Peters
Street Male and Female School.

McDaniel, Jas, carp, e s McDonough, s of old corp line.

McDANIEL, W J, Tchr, w s Crew, b Fair and Jones,
bds with A B Forsyth.

McDonald, O V, carp, w s Forsyth, s of Garnett.

McDonald, A H, carp, s s Delay, w of R R.

McDougal, Wm J, painter, w s Calhoun, b Gilmer and Wheat.

McDuffee, Mrs Sarah, cor Haynes and Rock.

McElroy, John A, bk k, with Smith & Richmond.

McFARLAND, THOS, Eng, Ga R R, n e c Mitchell and Lloyd.

McGIBBONEY, Mrs ELIZABETH, n w c Forsyth and Hunter.

McGeacher, David, bds with Mrs E McGibboney.

McGinnis, Wm, w s Calhoun, b Wheat and Houston.

McGinnis, G A, bds with Wm McG.

McGinty, B F, with Means & Roberts.

McGinty, Manassah, bk m, s s Marietta, b Bartow and Foundry alley.

McGriff, J, s s Marietta, opp Rock.

McGuire, G M, b Marietta and Luckie, near Simpson.

McHAN, THOS G, Eng, n s Fair, opp Martin.

McKeel, James, mldr, s s Delay, w of W & A R R.

McLEAN, J, Tailor, s e c McDonough and Fair.

McLendon, J, carp, cor Decatur and Pratt.

McLendon, Nicholas E, mer, w s Washington, b Jones and Fair.

McLin, James G, Janitor Med Col, res s w c Ivy and Cain

McManus, John, n w c Luckie and Foundry alley.

McMillian, Oscar F, e s Collins, b Gilmer and Wheat.

McNAB, D A, Eng, Phœnix Planing Mill, res e s Calhoun, b Wheat and Houston.

McNAUGHT, ORMOND & CO, Hardware, e s Whitehall, b Hunter and Mitchell.

McNaught, Wm, (McN, Ormond & Co,) bds with W W Wallace.

McPherson, Nathaniel, butcher, c of Mangum, b Green and Rhodes.

McPherson, A P, boot and shoe mkr, n s Decatur, b Ivy and Collins.

McVay, John, carp, S shop, s of Delay, w of Mangum.

McWaters, Alex H, carp, e s Butler, b Hunter and Ga R R.

Mabry, Milus J, bar k, s s Ga R R, b Terry and King.

MACON & WESTERN RAILROAD FREIGHT DEPOT, n e c M & W R R and Mitchell street, R A Anderson, Agent.

MADDOX, Col ROBT F, Produce Broker, bds with E R Sasseen.

Maffitt, Mrs Carrie, e s Ivy, b Baker and Oslin.

Maher, Michael, bar k, w s Lloyd, b Hunter and Mitchell.

Mahoney, Michael, fam gro, n w c Decatur and Calhoun.

MAIER, JOHN, (Dill & M,) Artist.

Malloch, Martin, carp, s w c Fowler and Magazine.

MALONE, THOS J, blk k, Ga R R Depot, e s Lloyd, b Alabama and Hunter.

Mangum, Mrs Mary L, n e c Mitchell and Haynes.

Mangum, Calvin W, with Mrs M L M.

Mann, Mrs Elizabeth, e s Pryor, b Hunter and Mitchell.

Mann, Charles G, with Mrs E M.

Mann, W J, clk, bds with Mrs E M.

Mann, James, blk s, w s Pryor, b Hunter and Mitchell.

MANNING, J W, Clk Inferior Court.

Manning, A M, eng, W & A R R, e s Calhoun, b Decatur and Gilmer.

MANNING, WM H, Wagon Mkr, bds with J W Lloyd.

Mansfield, James, carp, bds with Mrs L A King.

Marburg, L and M, dry goods, mer, bds with E Lang.

Marion, Mrs Joe, e s Whitehall, near Garnett.

MARKET HOUSE No 1, n w c Ivy and Line, F T Ryan, Clerk.

MARKET HOUSE No 2, n w c Mitchell and Pryor, Theo. Harris, Clerk.

MARKHAM, WM, n w c Walton and Cone.

MARKHAM, M O, (Peck & M,) with Wm Markham.

Marsh, Ed W, (Moore & M,) e s Collins, b Wheat and Houston.

Marsh, John G, supt rolling mill, bds with J D Gray.

MARSHALL, II, (see p 198) Dentist, s e c Whitehall and Hunter, res cor Luckie and Hunnicutt.

Marshall, Wm II, with II M.

Martin, Ganaway, plasterer, n e c West-Peachtree and Mills.

Martin, Nevelton, w s Frazer, near old corp line.

MARTIN & MITCHELL, Fam Gro, n s Decatur, b Peachtree and Pryor.

MARTIN, JOHN G, (M & Mitchell,) w s Crew, b Jones and Rawson.

Martin, Thos, eng, A & W P R R, s s Rawson, b Crew and Washington.

Martin, John, clk at Garrett & Brother's.

MASONIC TEMPLE, n w c Marietta and Broad.

Mason, John, painter, w s Fowler, b Thurman and Rock.

Mason, Thos C, clk, w s Walker, s of Boothe's alley.

MASON, WM K, Ornamental Painter, n s Gilmer, b Calhoun and Butler.

MASSEY, SWANSON & CO, (see p 210) Druggists, s s Mitchell, near Whitehall.

MASSEY, DR R J, (M, Swanson & Co,) s w c Richardson and Windsor.

Mast, Nicholas, bar k, bds with A W Brown.

MAYS, JOHN P, Cond, W & A R R, res w s Fowler, b Thurman and Rock.

Mead, Mrs Sarah, s e c Ivy and Gilmer.

Mead, W T, with Mrs Sarah M.

MEADOR BROTHES, (see 204) Com mer and Tobacco Factors, s s Alabama, b Whitehall and Pryor.

MEADOR, N J, (M Bros,) s s Decatur, b Calhoun and Butler.

MEANS & ROBERTS, Lumber Yard, s e c Garnett and M & W R R.

Means, J W, (M & Roberts,) w s Thompson, near Garnett.

MECASLIN, JOHN H, City Flouring Mills, res s e c Butler and Jenkins.

MECHANIC HOUSE, T N Delany and W B Reavis, Pro's, e s Lloyd, b Alabama and Hunter.

Meeks, W M, printer, bds at Mechanic House.

Mell, Wm H, bk k, w s Calhoun, b Jenkins and Wheat.

Menko, Martin, mer, n s Peters, b Whitehall and Forsyth.

MERCER, ED, Trader, s e c Thurman and Fowler.

METHODIST EPISCOPAL CHURCH, Wesley Chapel, e s Peachtree, at junction of Broad, Rev W P Harrison, Pastor.

METHODIST EPISCOPAL CHURCH, Trinity Chapel, s s Mitchell, opp City Hall, Rev W M Crumley, Pastor.

MICHALI, REMOLDO, Painter, S shop, n s Rhodes, near W & A R R,

Mickler, Nicholas, n s Fair, opp jail.

MIDDLEBROOKS & BARNES, Fam Gro, w s Peters, w of M & W R R.

Middlebrooks, Wm M, (M & Barnes.)

Middleton, J A, s w c Frazer and Rawson.

Middleton, M J, bds with J A M.

Middleton, Green, gas fitter, bds with E C Downs.

Mihalovitch, L, (Franklin & M,) w s Forsyth, near Garnett.

MILLEDGE, JOHN, Jr, Atty, n s Peters, b Washington and Crew.

MILLER, J I, Supt Int Office, s e c Hunter and Lloyd.

Miller, John II, w s Ivy, n of Line.

Miller, Wm M, blk s, n s Magazine, near W & A R R.

Miller, Mrs Mary, with J R D Ozburn.

Miller, O F, bar k, e s Calhoun, b Decatur and Gilmer.

MILLS, F M, Clk Post Office, n s Marietta, n w of Gate City Foundry.

MILLS, J G W, (Gate City Foundry and Machine Co,) n s Marietta, b Alexander and Mills.

MIMMS, WM, Supv A & W P R R, (see General Office.)

Miner, Thos, carp, n s Terry, b Hunter and Fair.

MITCHELL, A W, e s Whitehall, b Mitchell and Peters.

MITCHELL, W A, e s Whitehall, b Mitchell and Peters.

MITCHELL & O'CONNOR,) Saddlers, in basement, c s Whitehall, b Alabama and Hunter.

Mitchell, W E, (M & O'Connor,) w s Spring, b Marietta and R R.

MITCHELL, W D, Eng, (Martin & M,) cor Butler and Ga R R.

Mitchell, Wm, bds with W D M.

MITCHELL, Rev ISAAC G, n s Garnett, b Forsyth and Thompson.

Mobley, E D L, bds with D N Judson.

Magill, W J, Ins Agt, s s Wheat, b Calhoun and Butler.

MONDAY, J M C, bdg h, e s Butler, b Ga R R and Hunter.

MOONEY, ROBERT A, Watchman at Gate City Foundry, s s Delay, w of R R.

Moore, Wm, clk, bds with A L Grant.

Moore, A C, blk s, bds with W H Berry.

MOORE, B F, (M R Bell & Co,) bds with Mrs G B Douglas.

Moore, W C, phys, n e c Marietta and Spring.

Moran, Leary, eng, s e c Foundry and Fowler.

MORGAN & CO, (see p 206) Furniture, e s Whitehall, b Alabama and Hunter.

Morgan, A E & W H, (M & Co.)

Morgan, J B, special agt, Ætna Ins Co, w s Peachtree, b Baker and Harris.

Morgan, J H, agt, hand loom, bds with Maj H Goode.

Morgan, J L, bds at American Hotel.

MORRIS & BROTHERS, Fam Gro, w s Peachtree, n of Walton.

MORRIS, W L, Fam Gro, s w c Peters and Boothe's alley.

MORRIS & TRIMBLE, Dry Goods and Groceries, s e c Peters and M & W R R.

Morris, John F, (M & Trimble.)

Morris, G L, carp, S shop, w s Butler, s of Hunter.

MORRIS, J S, Eng, S road, s e c Luckie and Simpson.

MORRISON & NEWMAN, Real Est Agts, w s Alabama, b Whitehall and R R.

Morrison, J J, (M & Newman.)

15

MORRISON, JOHN, (McNaught, Ormond & Co.)

Morrison, Mrs E, w s Fowler, b Thurman and Rock.

Morrison, J C, emp S road, cor Haynes and Rock.

Morrow, W H H, clk, with J C Rogers, bds with Dr J M Boring.

MOSES, B F, Cotton Broker, s w c Pryor and Garnett.

Mounce, John, s w c Decatur and Butler.

MUHLENBRINK, H, Saloon and Ten-Pin Alley, w s Whitehall, b Alabama and R R, res s c c Ivy and Ellis.

Mulligan, B, carp, c s Butler, b Hunter and Fair.

Mullins, Frank, bds with M H Bradley.

MUNDAY, ED W, (see p 208) Dry Goods, &c, w s Peachtree, near Marietta, res s e c Wheat and Pryor.

Murphy, Anthony, lumber dealer, n c c Luckie and Bartow.

MURPHY, E C, Deputy Marshal, n c c Marietta and Bartow.

Murphy, T E, 2nd Lieut Pol, n w c Decatur and Butler.

Murphy, Dan'l, clk W & A R R Depot, e s McDonough, s of Hunter.

Murphy, Michael, n s Hunter, b Terry and King.

Murphy, Jas, bds with Michael M.

Murphy, Dennis, bds with Michael M

Muse, E H, mer, res West End.

Muse, C C, clk, bds at Planters' Hotel.

Myers, John, carp, bds with Mrs L A King.

Mynatt, P L, (Hammond, M & Wellborn) n w c Ivy and Houston.

N

NANCE, J M, Fam Gro, s s Decatur, e of Bell.

NALL, J S, Clk P O, bds with Mrs A J Simms.

NATIONAL HOTEL, (see p 212) n w c R R and Whitehall, Pond and Corey, Pro's.

Nelson, J M, gro mer, c s Calhoun, b Wheat and Houston.

Newman, W T, (Morrison & N,) cor Pryor and Fair.

Newman, Will T, atty, n s Decatur, b Peachtree and Pryor.

New, James M, carp, with Joseph H Jones.

Newton, C S, Druggist, at McCamy & Co's.

Nichols, J S, Dancing master, e s Whitehall, b Alabama and Hunter.

Nichols, C W, carp, s s Hunter, e of King.

Nicholson, Mrs S A, pro Bell Mansion bdg h, s e c Collins and Wheat.

Nix, S H, mach, at Winship's, w s Broad, b Hunter and Mitchell.

NORMAN, J J, (Witt & N,) e s Ivy, b Gilmer and Wheat.

Norman, John B, brass mldr, e s Fowler, near Rhodes.

Nort, Chas, s s Marietta, b Bartow and Foundry alley.

North, Henry, blk s, w s Frazer, near old corp line.

NOTT, Rev R M, (S S Kendrick & Co,) e s Whitehall, s ef junction of Forsyth.

NOTT, BENJ, Eng Ga R R shop, e s Butler, b Hunter and Fair.

Nunally, Aaron, clk, n s Richardson, b Whitehall and Windsor.

O

OATMAN, S B, (see cover,) Agt, Marble Dealer, e s Bellevue House, Alabama st, near Washington.

O'Connor & McGuire, dry goods and gro, n s Marietta, w of Broad.

O'Connor & Hardage, mil and fancy goods, n s Marietta, w of Broad.

O'Connor, Pat, (O'C & McG,) w s College, b Wheat and Houston.

O'Connor, Miss K, milliner, n s Hunter, b Terry and King.

ODD FELLOWS' HALL, e s Peachtree, opp Walton.

O'DONNELLY, Rev JOHN, n w c Race and Davis.

OGLETREE, Mrs BERSHEBA, lives with J M Bookout.

OGLETREE, GEO T, Bldr, cor Crew and Jones.

O'HALLORAN, WM, Pro Planters' Hotel, s w c Alabama and Pryor.

O'Keefe, Edward, s s Marietta, b Bartow and Foundry.

O'KEEFE, D C, M D, w s McDonough, b Rawson and Clark.

Oliver, Wm, shoe mkr, with Wm Keltner.

OLIVER & WADDAIL, (see p 212) Gro and Com Mer, s e c Alabama and Forsyth.

Oliver, J S, (O & Waddail.)

O'Neal, J, mach, w s Lloyd, b Jones and Rawson.

O'NEILL, PATRICK H, Eng, n s Decatur, b Collins and Calhoun.

OPERA HOUSE, s w c Marietta and Forsyth.

O'REILLY, Rev THOS H, Pastor Catholic Church, "Immaculate Conception," s s Hunter, e of Lloyd.

Orme, Dr L H, bds with W W Clayton.

ORME & FARRAR, Gro and Com Mer, s s Marietta, b Whitehall and Broad.

Orme, A J, (O & Farrar,) bds at National Hotel.

ORME, HENRY S, M D, (Alexander & O,) bds at Planters' Hotel.

ORME, WM P, Treas, A & W R R, res n e c Calhoun and Harris.

ORME, F H, Hom Phys, n s Decatur, e of Peachtree, bds with Wm P Orme.

Ormond, Jas, (McNaught, O & Co,) w s Washington, near old corp line.

O'SHIELDS, HARVEY, Fam Gro, w s W & A R R, n of Delay.

O'Shields, Robert, s w c Mangum and Delay.

O'Shields, Wiley, s w c Mangum and Delay.

Overby, Mrs E E, n e c East-Peachtree and Currier.

Owen, Judge P, e s Terry, b Ga R R and Hunter.

Owens, B F, carp, s w c Forsyth and Peters.

Owens, Calvin, bk m, n s Hunter, w of Forsyth.

Owens, Mrs E R, n s Fulton, b Windsor and Pryor.

OZBURN, J R D, Cotton Broker, cor Haynes and Markham.

Ozburn, M N, fireman, A & W P R R, s e cor Jones and Frazer.

P

Pace, Charles, s s Gilmer, b Ivy and Collins.

Page, ——, bk k, A R Mill & Min Co, cor Marietta and Alexander.

PAIGE, FLEISHEL & CO, (see p 216) Dry Goods, w s Whitehall, b Alabama and Hunter.

PALMER, JOE A, Druggist, with Taylor & Davis, bds with E R Sasseen.

PAOLIELLO, G, Conf, w s Whitehall, s of and near Hunter.

Parish, J R, manuf Butter-Scotch Candy, n s Peters, b Whitehall and Forsyth.

PARKER, Dr A M, s e c Garnett and Thompson.

Parker, J R, s s Marietta, b Bartow and Foundry alley.

Parker, James, butcher, s s Mitchell, near corp line.

Parker, J H, bds with W C Loughmiller.

Parker, W L, blk s, s s Ga R R, b Butler and Terry.

Parker, T O, National Hotel.

Parks, Mrs Ann, e s McDonough, b Jones and Rawson.

PARROTT, GEORGE W, (Fains & P.)

PARSONS, RICHARD, Dairyman, n s Mitchell, near old corp line.

Parsons, Edward, bds at Bellevue House.

Paschall, Daniel, painter, s s Foundry, near W & A R R.

PATILLO, W P, (see p 216) Ins Agt, at Tommey & Stewart's, bds with Wm Herring.

Patterson, James, Blff, s e c Peachtree and Ellis.

Patterson, James L, carp, S shop, e s Fowler, b Foundry and Magazine,

PATTON, J M, bk k "Ladies Home" office, res n s Irwin, at old corp line.

PAYNE, COLUMBUS M, bds with C W Hunnicutt.

Payne, Ed, n s Marietta, b Mills and Hunnicutt.

Payne, Mrs Elizabeth, w s Monroe R R street.

Payne, R R, bds with Mrs E P.

Payne, Mrs, and McAllister, dress mkrs, w s Whitehall, b Hunter and Mitchell.

Payne, William, bds with Geo A Zachry.

Payne, Peyton T, carp, e s McDonough, near old corp line.

Payne, Dr Robert N, bds with Geo A Zachry.

Peacok, James T, n s Garnett, near Thompson.

PEASE, P P & Co, (see p 214) Gro and Com Mer, s s Alabama, b Pryor and Lloyd.

PEASE, P P, (P P Pease & Co,) s e c Whitehall and Cooper.

PECK & MARKHAM, Pro's Emp Steam Planing Mill, n s Decatur, e of Bell.

PECK, J C, (P & Markham,) n s Houston, b Peachtree and Ivy.

PECK, JOHN B, M Tr W & A R R, office in Ft Depot bldg, bds with Willis Peck.

Peck, Willis, plasterer, n w c Peachtree and Cain.

PECK, THOMPSON & CO, (see p 220) Dry Goods, s s Decatur, near Whitehall.

Peck, W F, (P, Thompson & CO,) bds with Willis P.

Peel, John, baker, n w c Spring and W & A R R.

Pegg, Dr W H, w s Forsyth, b Grenville and McLin.

PERDUE, Rev FRANCIS P, s s Hayden, b Baker and Simpson.

Perkins, Richard, painter, bds at Wm Downings.

Perry, Wm, carp, bds with Hardy Treadwell.

Perry, Frank, bds with Hardy Treadwell.

PETERS, RICHARD, s w c Forsyth and Mitchell.

PETERS, WM G, (Butler & P,) s w c Pryor and Mitchell.

PETERS STREET MALE AND FEMALE SCHOOL, n s Peters, b Whitehall and Forsyth, J C McDaniel, S M Ainsworth, Miss Vesta J McDaniel, Mrs S M Ainsworth and M'lle E Sterchi, Teachers.

PETERSON, J S, New Era office.

PETTUS, H H, Dealer in Lumber, n e c Rawson and Martin.

Pettus, Wm, n s Green, b Mangum and Haynes.

Petty, Anderson, e s McDonough, near old corp line.

Phillips, Joel, carp, s s Jones, b Martin and Connally.

PHILLIPS & FLANDERS, (see p 218) Dry Goods, &c, e s Whitehall, n of Mitchell.

PHILLIPS, L B, (P & Flanders,) bds with Wm R P.

PHILLIPS, WM R, res n e c Forsyth and Garnett.

Phillips, Henry, blk s, bds with H L Wilson.

PHILLIPS, H L, Local Ed Christian Index, bds with Mrs Mary Bruckner.

Phillips, Geo, fam gro, s s Marietta, e of Foundry.

PHŒNIX PLANING MILL, s e c Butler and Gilmer, Lansberg & Harris, Pro.

Pilgrim, G A, City Sexton, s e c Fair and Connally.

Pilgrim, Isaac B, printer, with G A P.

PINCKNEY, Dr CHARLES, s w c Pryor and Peters.

Pinion, Sanford, s w c Race and Trebursey.

PITTMAN, DAN, Atty, and Judge Court of Ordinary, e s Ivy, b Wheat and Houston.

Pittman, R A, Ex mess, bds with T J Boyd.

Pittman, J M, s s Baker, b Collins and Calhoun.

Pitts, Columbus A, (Joseph Winship & Co.)

PLANTERS' HOTEL, (see p 218) s w c Alabama and Pryor, Wm O'Halloran, Pro.

Plummer, Mrs Isabella, s s Peters, b Whitehall and Forsyth.

Plummer, E T, fireman, M & W R R, with Mrs Isabella Plummer.

Plunket, John, w s Terry, b Fair and Jones.

Pollard, Thos, clk, bds with A P Bell.

POMEROY, R S, Hom Phys, s e c Pryor and Mitchell.

POND & COREY, Pro's National Hotel, n w c R R and Whitehall.

Pond, E B, National Hotel.

Pond, S A, National Hotel.

Pool, Johnson, carp, s s McLin, near M & W R R.

Pool, Benj J, s s McLin, near M & W R R.

Pool, D N, n s Ellis, b Ivy and Collins.

POPE, JOHN D, (Brown & P,) e s East-Peachtree, near old corp line.

Porter, Raymond, mer, bds with A P Bell.

Porter, J T, w s McDonough, s of Richardson.

POST OFFICE, under Bell-Johnson Opera Hall, n e c Alabama and Broad.

Pound, John G, supt City magazine, n s Foundry, w of Haynes.

POWELL, T S, M D, office in Empire Block, e s Whitehall, b Hunter and Mitchell, res on Race st, w of M & W R R.

Powell, Dr Chapman, n w c Peachtree and Ellis.

Powell, Mrs Isabella, s e c Rawson and Martin.

Powell, C, Auc, e s Whitehall, b R R and Decatur.

Powers, George, bdg h, w s Whitehall, b Mitchell and Peters.

POWERS, W & SONS, Gro and Com Mer, s s Marietta, b Whitehall and Broad.

Powers, Wm, (P, W & Sons,) n w c West-Peachtree and Mills.

Powers, W E & R H, (P, W & Sons,) bds with Wm P.

Praither, John S, s s Ellis, b Collins and Calhoun.

Praither, Aug, carp, bds at Mechanic House.

PRATTE, EDWARDS & CO, Gro and Com Mer, w s Forsyth, b R R and Marietta.

Pratte, B A, (P, Edwards, & Co,) res on McDonough.

Pratte, S A, bds with B A P.

Pratt, Rush, National Hotel.

PRESBYTERIAN CHURCH, 1st, s s Marietta, w of Forsyth, Rev J S Wilson, D D, Pastor.

PRESBYTERIAN CHURCH, 2nd, w s Washington, opp City Hall, Rev Rufus K Porter, Pastor.

Purse, Isaiah, with Clayton & Adair, res s s Hunter, e of King.

Purtell, J H, mer tailor, s w c Peachtree and Cain.

Q

Quail, Pat, s e c McDonough and Jones.

Queen, J L, gro mer, e s Crew, b Jones and Rawson.

Queen, David, bds with J L Q.

Queen, F M, dealer in lumber, bds with T Kile.

R

RAAB, GEORGE, carp, S shop, n s Mechanic.

RAGAN, Maj A B, Manuf Brick, n s Rawson, b Cooper and Pryor.

Ramsey, Wm, emp State Road, bds with Mrs E McGibboney.

Ransford & McNulty, dry goods, w s Whitehall, b Alabama and Hunter.

Ransford, H, (R & McNulty,) bds with C P Cassin.

Randall, W H, bk k, with L C & T L Wells, res e s Walker, s of Nelson.

RANSOM, J H, Cond A & W P R R, n w c Collins and Baker.

RAWSON, E E, Pryor, b Rawson and Richardson.

Ray, A J, n s Trebursey, near Mitchell.

Ray, S S, carp, e s Mangum, b Rock and Delay.

Ray, T H, carp, e s Butler, b Wheat and Houston.

Ray, R P, carp, s s Alley b Thurman and Rock, w of Fowler.

Ray, E S, M D, s s Alabama, b Whitehall and Pryor, res s s Wheat, b Pryor and Ivy.

Redwine & Fox, druggists, s e c Whitehall and Alabama.

Redwine, C L, (R & Fox,) w s Pryor, b Peters and Garnett.

REED, HARVY, Tanner, e s Forsyth, s of Garnett.

Reed, J Y, cond, W & A R R, bds at Planters' Hotel.

Reed, Thos, blk s, n e c Foundry and Fowler.

Reed, Wm, mach, n s Magazine, e of Fowler.

Reeder, John M, clk, State Road Depot, bds with R B Campbell.

REEVE & CO, (see p 226) Clothing, w s Whitehall, b R R & Marietta.

Reeve, J C, (R & Co.) s e c Cone and Church.

Reeves, Jas A, s w c Forsyth and Peters.

REGISTER, O J, Gardener, s s Stephens, at old corp line.

Reid, P P, carp, s s Hunter, b Terry and King.

REINHARDT, CHRISTIAN, Day-Watch, State shop, n s Mechanic.

Reinhardt, A M, law student, bds at Mechanic House.

Reynolds, T S, job printer, e s Whitehall, b Alabama and R R, res n e c Mitchell and Mangum.

Reynolds, W P, carriage trimmer, s s Peters, b Forsyth and Thompson.

Reynolds, J W, bk m, e s Crew, s of Fulton.

Reynolds, J C, printer, Int Office, n e c Collins and Oslin.

RHODES, MRS A D, bdg h, s s Rhodes, near W & A R R.

RHODES, C, C, Supt Gas Works, e s Lloyd, b Alabama and Hunter.

RICE, F P, Dealer in Lumber, n w c Ivy and Ellis.

Rice, Green, bds with Thos McFarland.

Rice, Wm, carp, State shop, n s Rhodes, w of Haynes.

Rice, Wm H, stone m, w s Calhoun, b Cain and Harris.

RICHARDS, J J & S P, (see p 224) Booksellers, s s Alabama, e of Whitehall.

RICHARDS, J J, (R, J J & S P,) e s Washington, b Fair and Jones.

RICHARDS, S P, (R, J J & S P,) s s Peters, b Whitehall and Forsyth.

RICHARDS, Rev WM, bds with J J Richards.

Richards, H H, Agt Daily Int, bds with Samuel Grubb.

Richards, H P & W B B, fam gro, e s Peachtree, n of Walton.

RICH, WM & CO, (see p 226) Dry Goods, e s Whitehall, s of and near R R crossing.

RICHARDSON, F M, (see p 222) Stoves, Tin Ware, &c, e s Whitehall, b Hunter and Mitchell, res cor Washington and Richardson.

RICHARDSON, JOHN W, Asst Yard Master, State Road, s w c Rock and Mangum.

Richardson, D L, fireman, A & W P R R, bds with J M C Monday.

RICHARDSON, J A, A M, Prof Math, Atlanta High School.

RICHMOND, J L, (Smith & R,) Tobaconists and Com Mer, bds with Mrs A J Simms.

RILEY, T G, Soda Fount and Confectionary, w s Whitehall, b Hunter and Mitchell.

RIPLEY, THOS R, (see p 224) Crockery, &c, w s Whitehall, b R R & Alabama, res e s East-Peachtree, near
old corp line.

Rives, Mrs N H, n s Mitchell, b Forsyth and Thompson.

ROACH, Dr E J, City Phys, n e c Whitehall and Peters.

Roach, W H, blk s, w s Calhoun, b Gilmer and Wheat.

Roberts, G B, e s Whitehall, near Fair.

Roberts, Aug, bar k, bds with Lewis Coulter.

Roberts, W F, ptr, bds at Mechanic House.

Roberts, M L, s s Alabama, near M & W R R.

ROBERTS, THOS, Cond, Ga R R, n s College, b Calhoun and Butler.

Roberts, Mrs A J, n s Stonewall, w of Race.

Robertson, I P, carp, W & A R R shop, s w c Fowler
and Green.

ROBERTSON, P A, carp State shop, n s Rock, w of
Mangum.

Robertson, F A, carp, n s Decatur, b Moore and Pratte.

ROBERTSON & WILLIAMS, Grocers, e s Peachtree,
opp junction of Broad.

Robins, Mrs N E, w s Washington, s of Richardson.

Robins, Wiley, s s McDaniel, b Whitehall and Windsor.

Robinson, Jesse, bk m, e s Frazer, s of Richardson.

Robinson, Geo M, atty, bds with Mrs E Johnson.

Robinson, James, bk k, s e c Race and M & W R R.

Robinson, J D, pressman, Franklin Printing House, bds
at Bellevue House.

Robinson, James L, carp, e s Butler, opp Med College.

Robinson, J C, mach, s e c Washington and Fair.

Robinson, Jeff, eng, A & W P R R, s s Ga R R, b Butler and Terry.

Robinson, S C, carp, e s Peachtree, b Harris and Baker.

ROBSON, S B, n s Marietta, near Spring.

ROBSON, R C, Pres Castle Rock Coal Co, e s Whitehall, b Alabama and R R.

Roebuck, J Z, carp, bds with S A Verdery.

Rogan, Lawrence, watchman Ga Depot, cor Mangum and Mechanic.

Rogan, Daniel, with Lawrence R.

Rogan, Michael, cor Peters and M & W R R.

Rogan, William, watchman, W & A R R Depot, bds Lawrence R.

Rogers, John, mach, s s Marietta, e of Gate City Foundry.

Rogers, J J, clk, with Phillips & Flanders.

ROGERS, JOHN C, (see p 220) Fam Gro, w s Whitehall, n of and near Mitchell.

Rogers, Joseph, bds with Mrs E McGibboney.

Rooney, William, plasterer, bds with Mrs E Haney.

ROSENFELD & BRO, Clothiers, e s Whitehall, b Alabama and Hunter.

Rosenfeld, J, mer, bds at Planters Hotel.

Rosenfeld, Isaac, mer, s s Peters, b Forsyth and Thompson.

Ross, John, stone m, bds with Pat Lynch.

Rosser, Wm S, w s Mangum, n of Rock.

Rosser, Isaac, clk, with Thos S Scarbrough.

Rucker, J W, (Chapman & R,) w s Peachtree, b Harris and Baker.

Ruddell, H F, carp, bds at Bellevue House.

Rudy, F O, bds at American Hotel.

Rush, J A, carp, e s Pryor, s of Richardson.

RUSHTON, WM M, mach Ga R R shop, n w c McDonough and Jones.

RUSSELL, GEORGE H, with Phillips & Flanders.

Ryan, John, dry goods mer, w s Whitehall near Hunter, res c s Whitehall, s of Garnett.

Ryan, Frank T, Clk 2nd Market.

S

SAGE, B Y, Chief Eng Ga A L R R, bds at Bell Mansion.

Sage, Ira, Asst Eng Ga A L R R, bds at Bell Mansion.

SALMONS, L S & Co, Gro and Com Mer, n w c Whitehall and Alabama.

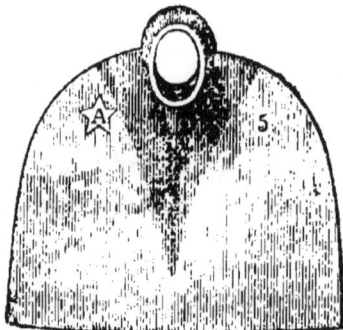

Salmons, Lewis S, (S, L S & Co,) w s McDonough, s of Rawson.

Samuels, J P, butcher, bds with J P Loftis.

Sanson, Thos, carp, bds with W J Dickey.

SASSEEN, E R, bdg h, s w c Broad and Luckie.

Sasseen, G W, with E R S.

SAWTELL, EPHRAIM, Cooper, bds with John S Chester.

Sawtell, H C, clk, with G L Anderson & Co, bds with George Powers.

Saye, Newton, carp, State shop, s s Mechanic.

SCARBROUGH, THOS, Fam Gro, n w c Forsyth and Peters.

Schenck, F H, mach, n s Decatur, e of Bell.

Schenck, J T, mach, Ga R R shop, n e c Ivy and Ellis.

SCHIKAN, JOHN, Fam Gro, s s Mitchell, w of M & W R R.

SCHNATZ, CHARLES, Plasterer, s w c Collins and Wheat.

SCHŒN, JACOB H, n s Mitchell, b Broad and Forsyth.

SCHRAMM, PHILIP, (Gross & S,) e s McDonough, b Fair and Jones.

SCHOFIELD, LEWIS, Real Est Agt, e s Peachtree, at junction of Pryor.

Scott, Mrs N J, cor Marietta and Hunnicutt.

SCOTT, Rev W J, (see p 234) Proprietor Scott's Monthly Magazine, res cor West-Peachtree and Mills.

Scott, H M, cor West-Peachtree and Mills.

SCOTT & FREEMAN, (see p 238) Dry Goods, s w c Peachtree and Walton.

Scott, J B C, & Charles P Freeman, (S & Freeman.)

Scrutchin, Thos, (McNaught, Ormond & Co,) s w c Mitchell and Mangum.

Scruggs, Wm L, journalist, w s Whitehall, s of Garnett.

SCUDDER, L B, (M R Bell & Co,) bds with A P Bell.

SEAGO, A K, (see p 240) Gro and Com Mer, res West End, near Green's Ferry Avenue.

Seay, J J, (Langford, S & McCrath,) w s Collins, b Cain and Harris.

Seay, M N, boot mkr, n s Line, b Pryor and Ivy.

Seay, Ransom, carp, n s Line, b Pryor and Ivy.

Self, B H, w s Haynes, n of Rock.

SELLS, Dr H, bds with Dr J N Simmons.

Seltzer, Henry, crockery mer, w s Peachtree, n of Walton, res n s Marietta, b Foundry and Duncan.

Seymore, Isaiah, mer, n s Simpson, w of Hayden.

SHACKELFORD & KETCHAM, Auc and Com Mer, e s Whitehall, b Alabama and Hunter.

Shackelford, S J, (S & Ketcham,) n s Decatur, b Butler and Pratt.

Shackelford, H P, bds with S J S.

Shackelford, R L, bds with S J S.

SHARP, GEORGE, Jr, (see p 228) Wines and Liquors, e s Peachtree, opp Walton.

SHAVER, Rev D, D D, Editor Christrian Index & Southwestern Baptist.

Shaw, Samuel H, printer, Era Office, s e c Ivy and Houston.

Shaw, George, printer, s e c Ivy and Houston.

Shearer, Wm, keeps saloon, n s Ga R R, b Calhoun and Butler.

SHEPHERD, MRS, & INGLES, Dress Mkrs, e s Whitehall, b Alabama and Hunter.

SHELDON & CONNOR, (see p 258) Book Sellers, e s Whitehall, b Alabama and Hunter.

Sheldon, A E, (S & Connor,) bds at Bell Mansion.

Shelpert, L, National Hotel.

Shelton, Wm, carp, State shop, s s Rock, w of Mangum.

Shelverton, Josiah, mach, s s W & A R R, opp Rolling Mill.

Sherburn, George, carp, bds at Bellevue House.

Sheridan, G W, eng W & A R R, n w c Collins and Ellis.

Sheridan, Thos, eng A & W P R R, bds with T C Murphy.

Shermanton, E, telgh opr, bds at Planters' Hotel.

Sherman, Miss M K, with O J Register.

Sherman, Mrs M I, with O J Register.

Sherrie, Thos, bk m, bds with John McManus.

SHERWOOD, S B, (see p 226) Contr and Bldr, n e c Decatur and Butler.

SHERWOOD, MRS C W, Dress Mkr, up stairs, e s Whitehall, b Alabama and Hunter.

Shield, Robert, painter, n s Hunter, e of King.

Shiver, Burrell, bds at Mechanic House.

SHURLEY, HENRY, mldr, n s Rhodes, near W & A R R.

Sigsford, William, National Hotel.

SILVEY & DOUGHERTY, (see p 232) Dry Goods, cor Decatur, Peachtree, and Line.

SILVEY, JOHN, (S & Dougherty,) s e c Marietta and Spring.

SIMMONS, J R, (Steadman & S,) bds at American Hotel.

SIMMONS, Dr J N, s s Marietta, b Forsyth and Spring.

SIMMS, THOS G, Post Master, w s Forsyth, b Walton and Luckie.

SIMMS, Mrs A J, bdg h, e s Forsyth, s of Hunter.

Simms, P B, mail agt A & W P R R, with Mrs A J S.

Simms, Julius, Asst Surv Ga A L R R, bds at Bell Mansion.

Sims, Calvin, e s Butler, b Hunter and Fair.

Simpson, W G, s s Marietta, opp Thurman.

SISSON, V P, Local Ed "Daily Int,' bds with W W Clayton.

SISSON, H M, bk k, with Talley, Brown & Co.

SITTON, P M, bk k, with Taylor & Davis.

SKINNER & Co, Fam Gro, e s Whitehall, s of Mitchell.

Slaughter, Miss Eliza, bds with W W Wallace.

Stemmons, James, mach, State shop, s e c Fowler and Mangum.

SMALL, W J, Ft Agt A & W P R R, n w c Ga R R and Pratte.

SMITH, B D, Judge County Court, w s Pryor, near Wheat.

Smith, C D, printer, Int Office.

Smith, Levi F, carp, n s Terry, b Hunter and Fair.
Smith, Ed, carp, n s Fair, b Terry and King.
Smith, J R, w s Fowler, b Green and Rhodes.
Smith, Mrs Susan, n w c Collins and Gilmer.
Smith, Jesse A, bds with Mrs Susan S.
Smith, R W, carp, n s Houston, b Calhoun and Butler.
Smith, Jacob H, clk, s s Luckie, b Bartow and Foundry.
SMITH, JAMES T, Cond Ga R R, bds with C W Berry.
SMITH, JESSE, mach, at Ga R R shop.
Smith, John W, w end of Mechanic.
SMITH, JOHN B, Ex, bds with Mrs Susan S.
SMITH, JONAS S, City Tax R and Col, s e c Whitehall
    and Peters.
Smith, Andrew, n w c Luckie and Bartow.
Smith, Zachariah, carp, with A S.
SMITH, R WINDSOR, Ex, w s Whitehall, n of
    McDaniel.
Smith, G B, carp, s s Marietta, opp Thurman.
Smith, W J, clk, bds at American Hotel.
SMITH & RICHMOND, (see p 230) Tobacconist and
    Com Mer, s s Alabama, b Whitehall and Pryor.
SMITH, W H, (S & Richmond.)
Smith, T T, bds with Mrs G B Douglass.
Smith, Levi J, bds with Mrs S H Coleman.
SMITH, J HENLY, with G W Adair, res n of Mitchell,
    near old corp line.
Smott, Amos, bds at Bell Mansion.
SNEED, WM H, Atty, bds with W W Wallace.
SNOOK, P H, Dry Goods, w s Whitehall, b R R and
    Marietta, bds with Geo P Frazer.
Snow, John, eng, A & W P R R.
Solomon, Wm, s w c Mitchell and Crew.
Somer, M, clothing, w s Whitehall, b Alabama and
    Hunter.
SOUTHERN EXPRESS COMPANY, (see 242) s s
    Alabama, b Pryor and Lloyd, V Dunning, Agt.
Sparks, Ludlow, cab mkr, bds with H Treadwell.
Sparks, Joseph, carp, bds with H Treadwell.

THE ATLANTA INTELLIGENCER,

PUBLISHED DAILY AND WEEKLY BY

JARED IRWIN WHITAKER,

AT

ATLANTA, GEORGIA.

THE OLDEST PAPER IN UPPER GEORGIA.

Subscription Rates.

Daily, per annum,..$10,000
Weekly, per annum,..3.00
Daily, per Month,...1,00

Advertising Rates.

For each square of ten lines or less, for the first insertion $1, and for each subsequent insertion, 50 cents.

Special Notices, 20 cents per line, first insertion, and 10 cents per line for each subsequent insertion.

Liberal contracts made with parties for large advertisements, by the month or year.

The Weekly Intelligencer

IS A POPULAR LEGAL ADVERTISING MEDIUM.

SPAULDING, V, Land Agt, e s McDonough, s of Rawson.

Spence, A, mail agt, bds at Covington House.

Spenceley, James, plasterer, with C E Earnest.

SPENCER, THOMAS, Mach, State shop, n s Race, w of Mangum.

Spiller, E N, (Porter, Butler & Co,) s of Fair Ground, near old corp line.

Spinks, Lewis B, car insp, W & A R R, n s Fair, at junction of Hunter.

Spivy, Jordan, eng, State road, n s Rock, near R R.

Sponcler, Jacob F, pattern mkr, n s Decatur, e of Bell.

SPRAYBERRY, H J, Atty, n s Decatur, b Peachtree and Pryor.

STACY, Dr R Q, w s Whitehall, b Hunter and Mitchell, bds with Dr N L Angier.

Stains, M, w s Spring, b Walton and Luckie.

Stanley, Elisha, bk m, e s Race, s of Stonewall.

Stancil, Levi, bk m, s e c Hull and Simpson.

Stallings, Mrs A, n s Rawson, b McDonough and Crew.

Stallings, David W, clk, bds with Mrs A S.

Stallings, Jeff J, bk m, w s Mangum, n of Rock.

STAPLER, R F, Cond, A & W P R R, bds at Covington House.

STEADMAN & SIMMONS, Gro and Com Mer, s s Marietta, near Whitehall.

STEEL, Maj JOHN H, Ed "Daily Int," res e s Calhoun, b Decatur and Gilmer.

Steenhann, J F, tin smith, bds with J M C Monday.

Stegall, W D M, mldr, bds with J M C Monday.

Steinheimer Brothers, clothiers, w s Whitehall, b Alabama and Hunter.

STEPHENS, D V, Cond, M & W R R, n s Mitchell, b Forsyth and Thompson.

Stephens, H J, carp, w s Peters, n of junction of Walker.

Stephens, Wm J, with H J S.

Stephens, John M, with H J S.

Stephens, George T, with H J S.

17

STEPHENS, C E, Master Carp, bds with Mrs Hayne.

STERCHI, J H, bk k, with R J Lowery & Co.

Sterling, Dr W L, e s Calhoun, b Decatur and Gilmer.

Stewart, Geo W, emp W & A R R, bds at Mechanic House.

Stewart, Fred, cont and bldr, n Marietta, opp Gate City Foundry.

Stewart, W F, bds with Robert Crawford.

STEWART, GEORGE, Overseer streets, res n s Boothe's alley.

STEWART, G B, mach, n s Boothe's alley.

Stewart, D W, with George S.

Stewart, A P, clk, with F M Richardson.

STEWART, JOSEPH S, (Tommey & S.)

Stinson, Mrs Julia, with J R D Ozburn.

STOCKIN & ROE, Notions, e s Forsyth, b Mitchell and Peters

Stocking, S, at National Hotel.

Stockton, Mrs Sarah A, n s Foundry, e of Mangum.

Stockton, J W, with Mrs Sarah A S.

Stokes, James, bds with J C Robinson.

STOVALL, Dr O, w s Race, at junction of Nelson.

Stowers, G L, carp, s s Stephens, w of Race.

Strauss, J, clk, bds at Bellevue House.

Street, F M, painter, bds with Mrs E McGibboney.

Stroup, Alexander W, carp, n s Foundry, e of Fowler.

STRONG, C H, (McDaniel, S & Co,) s w c Forsyth and Luckie.

Sullivan, Dennis, e s Ivy, b Decatur and Gilmer.

Swann, James, gro mer, bds with A Austell.

Swartz, Samuel, with Freedman & Loveman.

Sweat, Abner, w s Frazer, near old corp line.

T

TALLEY, BROWN & CO, (see p 236) Dry Goods, w s Whitehall, b Hunter and Mitchell.

TALLEY, A S, (T, Brown & Co,) bds at American Hotel.

Talley, J T, clk, s c c Calhoun and Harris.

Tanner, Wm J, clk, bds with G T Dodd.

Tarrance, Wm, carp, on Green, w of Haynes.

Tatum, T H R, w s East-Peachtree, b Oslin and Currier.

TAYLOR & DAVIS, (see p 244) Druggists, n w c R R and Whitehall.

TAYLOR, JAS A, (T & Davis,) w s Mangum, b Green and Rhodes.

Taylor, Wm H, dry goods mer, s e c Mitchell and Mangum.

Taylor, J H, Auditor, W & A R R, bds with H Goode.

Taylor, L F, bds with W C D Christian.

Teat, D H, shoe mkr, s c c Forsyth and Garnett.

TENNESSEE SALE & LIVERY STABLES, (see p 244) W J Wootten, Pro, n e c Alabama and Forsyth.

Tenant, Lewis, mach, bds with W L Calhoun.

Tenny, W A, carp, bds with W H Freeman.

Terham, James, mer, s w c West-Peachtree and Hunnicutt.

TERRY, GEORGE W, Mach, Ga R R shop, s s Hunter, b Terry and King.

THEME, A, Silver Smith, w s Whitehall, b R R and Alabama, res on Pryor, b Hunter and Mitchell.

Thaden, Henry, clk, bds with A W Brown.

THOMAS, Rev CHARLES W, Pastor St Philip's Episcopal Church, res West End, near Green's Ferry Avenue.

THOMAS, GEO S, Solicitor of County Court, office n s Decatur, b Pryor and Ivy.

THOMAS, JOHN, Dry Goods Mer, w s Whitehall, near Mitchell, res n s Hunter, b Broad and Forsyth.

THOMAS, L P, Sen, Chief Marshal, e s McDonough, s of Richardson.

THOMAS, L P, Jr, Gro Mer, res n s Trebursey, w of Race.

Thomas, Robt, tailor, e s Mangum, b Green and Rhodes.

Thomas, J A, carp, n s Houston, near old corp line.

Thomas, Mrs Eliza, s s Ga R R, opp Moore.

Thompson, Richard, carp, n w c Luckie and Bartow.

Thompson & Henderson, fam gro, s w c Thurman and R R.

Thompson, John R, (T & Henderson,) s s Peters, b Forsyth and Thompson.

Thompson, Dr W R D, phys, s s Peters, s of M & W R R.

Thompson, John T, n e s Mangum and Rock.

THOMPSON, Dr JOSEPH, s e c Pryor and Jones.

Thompson, Mrs A, w s Martin, b Jones and Rawson.

Thompson, J B, bds with Mrs A T.

Thompson, W W, bds with Mrs A T.

Thornton, M V, fam gro, w s Peters, w of M & W R R.

THRASHER, B H, Atty, s e c Luckie and Harris.

THROWER, J K, Printer, Int Office, n s Clark, b McDonough and Frazer.

Thrower, B, jail guard, s s Fair, b Washington and Crew.

Thrower, O A, bds with B T.

Thrower, Thomas L, eng, s s Mitchell, b Whitehall and Forsyth.

THURMAN, F D, M D, D D S, s e c Martin and Rawson.

Thurman, Mrs Nancy, e s Mangum, b Thurman and Rock.

Thurman, John C, with Mrs Nancy T.

Thurman, Henry, bk mldr, w of Haynes, n of Rock.

Thurman, David, n s Rock, near Mangum.

TIDWELL & HOLLIDAY, (R W T, & G H Holliday,) Fam Grocers, n s Mitchell, b Whitehall and Broad.

TIDWELL & FEARS, Attys, n s Decatur, b Pryor and Ivy.

Tiller, John, n s Peters, b Thompson and M & W R R.

Tinnon, T L, beer saloon, bds with Mrs N N Kidd.

TIPPIN, J B, (Van Epps & T,) bds with J M Calhoun.

TOMMEY & STEWART, (see p 248) Hardware, &c, e s Whitehall, b Hunter and Mitchell, (sign of the Game Cock and Mill Saw.)

TOMMEY, VINCENT R, (T & Stewart.)

Tommey, Albert P, with Tommey and Stewart.

Toney, Seaborn E, carp, cor Fair and Frazer.

TOY, JAMES M, Eng, A & W P R R, e s Calhoun, b Decatur and Gilmer.

TOON, J J, Prop Franklin Printing House, n s Alabama, b Whitehall and Pryor.

TRAMMEL, JOHN G, bdg h, e s Pryor, b Wheat and Houston.

Travis, Joseph, eng, W & A R R, bds with John J Adcock.

TREADWELL, HARDY, Carriage Mkr, n w c Ga R R and Butler.

Treslin, Walter, mach, Ga R R shop.

Trimble, P M, (Morris & T,) s s Peters, near M & W R R.

Trippe, Harvey, emp W & A R R, s s Marietta, opp Thurman.

Tubbeville, M M, carp, bds with Isaiah Seymore.

Tuck, Robt M, with J W Richardson.

Tucker, Wm, carp, w s Martin, b Jones and Rawson.

Tucker, J W, steward at Planters' Hotel.

TULLER, W H, Cash A N Bank, s s Marietta, b Forsyth and Spring.

TURNER, ARCHIBALD M, plas, s s Mitchell, near corp line.

Turner, John B, carp, s e c McDonough and Fair.

Turner, G W, fireman, W & A R R, s s Thurman, near R R.

Turner, Samuel T, emp W & A R R, s s Boothe's alley.

TURNER, WINGUIT H, bk k, at McNaught, Ormond & Co's.

Turnipseed, R W, e s Race, w of Haynes.

Turpin, Miles, clk, s s Wheat, b Collins and Butler.

Tuttle, J A, carp, n s Hunter, b Terry and King.

TYLER, CHARLES, Eng, W & A R R shop, s w c Fowler and Foundry.

U

Underwood, M, carp State shop, n s Rock, w of Mangum.

Upshaw, J M, supt bk yd, bds with Maj A B Ragan.

V

VALENTINO, MRS CATHERINE, c s Broad, b Alabama and Hunter.

Valentino, Louis, clk, with Mrs Catherine V.

VAN EPPS & TIPPIN, Grocers, s s Alabama, b Whitehall and Pryor.

Van Epps, A C, (Van E & Tippin,) bds with Dr J N Simmons.

Van Loan, A H, bldr, bds with J P Clotz.

VAN GOIDSNOVEN, Agt Nurseryman, w s Whitehall, b Alabama and Hunter.

Vaughan, James, carp, bds with A M Manning.

VENABLE, RICHARD, Clk Superior Court, office at City Hall.

VERDERY, S A, (Zimmerman & V,) cor Washington and Richardson.

Verhine, Mrs Matilda, s s Mechanic.

W

WADDAIL, B C, (Oliver & W.)

WADE & KEAN, (see p 262) Groceries, &c, e s Peachtree, opp Luckie.

WADE, P H, (W & Kean.)

Wade, John W, mach, Ga R R shop, s e c Gilmer and Pratt.

Wadsworth, H B, clk, A & W P R R Depot, n s Decatur, b Moore and Bell.

Waits, Mrs N E, with Mrs C Harden.

Waits, A M, carp, w s Washington, b Richardson and Fulton.

WALKER, E B, Supt, M & W R R, w s Ivy, b Wheat and Houston.

Walker, Thos E, clk W & A R R, with E B W.

WALL, W W & CO, Fam Gro, w s Peters, w of M & W R R.

Wall, W W, (W, W W & Co.)

WALL, R M, (J W Clayton & Co,) res s s Decatur, b Collins and Calhoun.

WALLACE, W W, bdg h, s e c Forsyth and Peters.

WALLACE, A M, Com Mer, w s Forsyth, next to Opera House.

WALLACE, JOHN R, office at P & G T Dodds, res s e c Peachtree and Oslin.

Wallace, Campbell, Supt W & A R R, office at Depot.

Walsh, Miss Jane, n e c Calhoun and Ga R R.

Ward, Frank, bds with John McManus.

Ware, Thos N, e s McDonough, near old corp line.

WARE, Dr J E II, M D, bds with Mrs S II Coleman.

Ware, Edwin A, n w c Houston and Calhoun.

Warner, Obediah, mach, State shop, with Jacob Weaver.

WARREN, J D, Fam Gro, n s Fair, e of Terry.

Warren, Dr T A, n s Hunter, e of King.

Warwick, John C, cond W & A R R, s s Foundry, near R R.

Warwick, Wm, clk, So Ex Co, s s Hunter, b Butler and Terry.

Warwick, E A, cond M & W R R, bds with Wm W.

WARWICK, T F, Gun Smith, bds with Wm W.

Waters, R S, n of Race, w of Haynes.

Waters, John, tin smith, bds with Mrs L A King.

Waters, J C, clk, W & A R R Depot, bds at Planters' Hotel.

WATKINS & FLOYD, Fam Gro, w s Whitehall, b Hunter and Mitchell.

Watkins, J C, (W & Floyd,) n s Garnett, b Whitehall and Forsyth.

WATKINS, WM, Judge Inferior Court, w s Fair, b McDonough and Crew.

WATSON, WM H, Rev Assessor, bds with C C Hammock.

WATSON, W A, s e c Hunter and Butler.

WATSON, A R, Loc Ed New Era.

WATTS, A B, cigar mkr, w s Martin, b Jones and Rawson.

Watts, G W, mldr, w s Martin, b Jones and Rawson.

Weaver, Jacob, blk s, State shop, n s Mechanic.

Weaver, J M, gro mcr, n s Walton, b Spring and Bartow.

Webb, Mrs Elizabeth C, n s Peters, b Whitehall and Forsyth.

Webb, John B, carp, w s Race, s of Stonewall.

Webb, Brice, fam gro, n s Walton, at junction with Marietta.

WEIL, S, (see p 254) Atty, w s Whitehall, b Alabama and Hunter.

Welch, George, blk s, n s Luckie, at junction with Cain.

WELLBORN, C B, (see cover,) Com Mer and Gen'l Ins Agt, office at L H Hope's, w s Whitehall, b Alabama and Hunter.

Wellborn, C M, (L H Hope & Co,) n s Wheat, b Ivy and Pryor.

Wellborn, Olin, (Hammond, Mynatt & W.)

Wellborn, J D, fireman, State shop, s s Rhodes, near R R.

Wells, A P, bk m, s e c Decatur and Moore.

WELLS, L C & T L, Grocers, w s Whitehall, b Hunter and Mitchell.

Wells, T L, (W, L C & T L,) bds with W H Randall.

Wells, Levi C, (W, L C & T L,) s cor Whitehall and McDaniel.

WELLS, CHARLES W, Printer, Int Office, w s and fronting M & W R R, s of Mitchell.

WERNER, E A, bk k, Int Office.

Wernwag, Joseph, fam gro, n s Houston, b Calhoun and Butler.

WEST, W D, Carp, State shop.

West, W H, emp W & A R R, s s Luckie, b Bartow and Foundry alley.

WEST, THOS W, Soda Water Factory, e s Whitehall, b Grenville's alley and Fair.

WEST & GUTHRIE, Grocers, e s Peachtree, near junction of Broad.

West, Henry, (W & Guthrie,) s e c Collins and Oslin.

Westbrook, Moses M, carp, n s Stonewall, w of Race.

Westwater, Thos, mldr, s s Thurman, b Foundry and R R.

WEST, W D, carp, State Shop.

WESTERN & ATLANTIC R R GENERAL OFFICE, in Freight Depot Building, Campbell Wallace, Supt, Jno B Peck, M Transportation,

WESTERN & ATLANTIC R R FREIGHT DEPOT, s w c Forsyth and W & A R R, Jno M Bridges, Agt.

WESTERN & ATLANTIC R R MACHINE SHOP, etc, w of Ft Depot. John Flynn Master of Machinery, Wm G Gramling, Supt Car Factory.

WESTMORELAND, H, MD., n w c Whitehall and Peters.

WESTMORELAND, JOHN G, Dean of A Med College, bds with W F W.

WESTMORELAND, WILLIS F, M D, n s Marietta, b Forsyth & Cone.

WHITAKER, JARED IRWIN, (see pp 256 and 266) pro Int Office, e s Washington b Fair and Jones.

WHITAKER, THOS E, pro Tattersalls Stables w s Pryor, n of Line

Whitcomb, J C, carp bds with Jas M Toy

White, M, n s Fair, b McDonough and Frazer.

White, Mrs E, pro Covington House, s s Decatur, b Lloyd and Collins.

White, J C, butcher, s e c Peachtree and Baker.

WHITE, J H & Co, (see p 254) Dry Goods, e s Whitehall, b Alabama and Hunter.

White, J H, w s Peachtree, b Oslin and Currier.

White G W, bds at American Hotel.

WHITE & WHITLOCK, pros American Hotel.

White, E T, (W & Whitlock.)

White, Wesley C, cond M & W R R, w s Old Monroe R R Street.

White, V M, (Gardner & W)

White, G E, Fam Gro w s Peters, s of M & W R R

Whitehead, C, Ins Agt, w s Cooper, b Jones and Rawson.

Whitehead, J T, bds with W J Gilleland.

Whitehead, G W M, bds with W J Gilleland.

Whitehill, I, clothing, w s Whitehall b Alabama and Hunter.

18

Whitice, W A, carp, s e c Frazer and Jones.

WHITLOCK, M G, (White & W,) American Hotel.

WHITMIRE, WM C, pressman, Int Office, bds at Mechanic House.

WHITNER, J C, (see cover,) Ins Agt, at McCamy & Co's Drug Store, res cor Cooper and Jones.

Whitney, Joshua, cor Calhoun & College.

Weimer, Conrad, cab mkr W & A R R shop, cor Haynes and Race.

WIGGINS, JESSE, cab mkr, n s Stonewall, w of Race.

Wight, Meador & Co, w s Whitehall, b Alabama and Hunter.

Wilby, John, mach, State shop, s s Foundry, e of Mangum.

Wilcox, Mrs M C, n w c Fair and Terry.

WILEY, W D Cl'k at American Hotel.

WILKIE, W G, Express Telgh Opr, bds at American Hotel.

Wilkins, Samuel, Clk, cor Peters and Booth's alley.

WILLIFORD, BENJ N, high sh'ff, w s Peters st and M & W R R.

Williford, J T bds with B N W

Williams, Joseph A, n s Mitchell, w of Haynes.

WILLIAMS, ENOS, Jeweler, cor Decatur and Whitehall—res e s McDonough, s of Rawson.

Williams, Amiziah, s s Ga R R, near Cemetery.

WILLIAMS, J E, e s Fort, opp Oslin.

Williams, M W S S, carp State shop.

Williams, H L, bk k, with Philips & Flanders ; s w c Gilmer and Collins.

Williams, J N, at office of Georgia State Lottery—res e s Ivy, b Baker and Oslin.

Williams, E H, Gro Mer, bds with D N Judson.

Williams, S S, car bldr, e s Luckie, near Hunnicutt.

Williams, Thos. law student, bds with W W Wallace.

Willingham, Riley M, carp, n s Decatur, b Calhoun and Butler.

WILLIS, J M & CO., brokers, office in basement of James's Banking House, n e c Whitehall and Alabama.

WILLIS, J M, (W, J M & Co,) cor Calhoun and College.

Wilkinson, T C, printer, at Franklin House, bds at Bellevue House.

Wilson, J J W, carp s w c Jones & Connelly.

Wilson, H A, mldr, bds with J J W W.

Wilson, J A, mlder bds with J J W W.

WILSON, Dr H L, w s Broad n of R R Bridge—res s e c Ivy and Wheat.

Wilson, Mrs Jane, Mil and Fancy Goods, n s Decatur, b Pryor and Ivy.

WILSON, Rev J S, D D, Pastor 1st Pres Church; res n s Walton, b Spring and Bartow.

Wilson, Monroe, carp, cor Butler and Jenkins.

Wilson, T B, carp, e s Mangum, n of Rock.

WILSON, Samuel, bk k, W & R R Shp, bds with Rev J S W.

WILSON, HENRY, carp, bds with Mrs Mary H Atkinson.

Wilson, M M, mach, Phœ Planing Mill.

WING, H L, cond M & W R R, e s Butler, b Ga R R and Hunter.

Wing, J M, cond A & W P R R, e s Butler b Hunter and Fair.

WINHAM, E L, printer at Franklin House, s w c Irwin and Randolph.

WINN, Dr E E, (see p 272) Dry Goods Mer, e s Whitehall, b Mitchell and Peters; res e s Whitehall, b Mitchell and Peters.

WINSHIP, JOSEPH & CO., Foundry and Machine Works, n w c Foundry and W & A R R.

Winship, Joseph, (J W & Co), n e c Walton and Bartow.

Winship, George, (J W & Co,) e s Ivy, b Cain and Harris.

Winship, Robt, (J W & Co,) n e c Ivy and Cain.

WITHERS, E A, mldr, at Winships's n s Hunter, e of King.

WITT & NORMAN, (see p 252) gro & com mer, n e c Decatur and Ivy.

Witter, Henry, cab mkr, at Phœnix Planing Mills.

WOOD, T S, Jeweler, e s Whitehall, b Alabama and Hunter; res cor Mitchell and Forsyth

WOOD, J C, Jeweler, bds with T S W.

Wood, Wm M, bds with T S W.

Wood, T W, Tinsmith, bds with J D Warren.

Wood, J W, bk m, bds with Mrs N N Kidd.

Wood, A P, bk m, n s Decatur, near Pratte.

Wood, T G, cor Marietta and Hunnicutt.

Wood, Coleman F, e s Crew, b Jones and Rawson.

WOODBERRY, Dr JOSEPH F, n e c Ivy and Harris.

Wooding, J W, carp, e s Butler, b Wheat and Houston.

Wooding, H W, tchr, bds with J W W.

Woods, Abram, mach, at Atlanta Rolling Mill.

Woods, J S, at State shop, n e c Fowler and Thurman.

WOODS, WM F, eng A & W P R R, n s Rawson, b Crew and McDonough.

Woodside, B F, cab mkr n s Simpson, b Hayden and Hull.

Woodruff, J W, clk, bds with D N Judson.

Woodruff, C R, Expressman.

WOOTTEN, CHAS F, Trader, s s Alabama, b Forsyth and Thompson.

WOOTTEN, W J, proprietor Tennessee Sale and Livery Stables, n e c, Alabama and Forsyth.

WORD, Dr ROBT C, w s Whitehall, b Hunter and Mitchell—res n s Mitchell, w of M & W R R.

Wreden, W H, carp, bds at Mechanic House.

WRIGHT, J A, (Glenn W & Carr,) n s Oslin b Collins and Calhoun.

Wright, Hinton, with Chamberlin, Cole & Boynton.

Wright, A G, gunsmith, etc., s s Garnett, near Peters.

Wright, Thos M, mldr, s s Thurman, b Fowler and R R.

Wright, Wm D, works at State shop.

Wright, C T, asst sawyer Empire Planing Mills.

Wright, C T, sawyer, Emp Planing Mill.

Wright, Mrs L B, Tchr, n s Peters, b Washington and Lloyd.

Wyatt, Wm, bar k, n s Hunter b Butler and Terry.

Wyly & Carroll, Grocers, w s Broad, b Hunter and Mitchell.

Wyly, Capt B F, (W & Carroll,) n w c Houston and Ivy.

Wyley, J M, carp, State shop, e s Ivy, b Wheat and Houston.

WYLIE, JOHNSON & Co, (see p 262) cor Peachtree and Wheat, wholesale Grocers, etc.

WYLIE, J R, (W, Johnson & Co,) s s Harris, b Calhoun and Butler.

Wylie, Mrs N H, n s Fair, b King and Terry.

WYNN, ALSTON &, attys, w s Broad, b Marietta and R R.

Y

YAHNKE, CHARLES, bar k, n s Alabama, near M & W R R.

Yarbrough, Amon, w s Peters, n of junction of Walker.

Yarbrough, Joseph, e s Walker, s of Stephens.

YARBROUGH, JOEL S, Fam Gro w s Peachtree, near Marietta.

Young, Robert, mach, W & A R R shop.

Young, Dr David, Druggist, e s McDonough, opp Mitchell.

YOUNG, JOHN, carp, at State shop, res n s Mitchell, w of M & W R R.

Young, R C, stone m, s s Jones, b Crew and McDonough.

Youngblood, Matthew A, carp, State shop; with Elias Black.

Z

Zachry, Bertrand, Fur Dealer; res at w end Rhodes st, near new corp line.

Zachry, James, Gro Mer; res at w end Magazine, near new corp line.

Zachry, Geo A, Mer, n s Houston, b Ivy and Collins.

Zachry, Dr J L, n s Hunter, e of King.

ZIMMERMAN & VERDERY, (see p 270) Gro and Com Mer, n c Marietta and Broad.

ZIMMERMAN R P, (Z and Verdery) e s Washington, b Clark a Fulton.

APPENDIX.

ADDITIONS AND CORRECTIONS.

Alexander, Thos G, with J H White & Co.

Adair, Aug C, (Clayton & A.)

Asher, Dr W C, w s Whitehall, b R R and Marietta.

Alston & Winn, Attys, w s Broad, n of R R bridge.

Ayer. L W, Supt yd Emp Steam P Mill.

Adamson, W R, carp, State shop.

Arcnz, C H, blk s Ga R R Shop.

Barnes, R M, fam gro, w s Whitehall, b Peters and Mitchell.

Bryson, T M, lumber dealer, e s Washington, near old corp line.

Berman, Joe, saloon, s s Ala, b Pryor and Lloyd.

Boyd, W W, Jr, at office of Ga State Lottery.

Brown, Sam S, So Ex Mess.

Boroughs, Jas M, with A K Seago.

Boyd, J L, rec and del clk M & W R R depot.

Buchanan, R C, eng, W & A R R.

Bridges, J, mach, at Winship's Foundry.

Buchanan, J J, mach, State shop.

Brady, M H, carp, State shop.

Brady, Thos E, mach, Ga R R shop.

Bishop, J V, blr mkr, Ga R R shop.

Berry, Wilson, eng on Ga R R.

Bacon, R A, chf clk Ft Dept, W & A R R.

Bowyer, C E, tel opr, W & A R R Depot.

Brocius, G W, pass cond, W & A R R.

Bell, S L, day pass cond, W & A R R.

Blair, A J, lt cond, W & A R R.

Bone, J C, ex ft cond, W & A R R.

Bell, N J, ex ft cond, W & A R R.

Boyd, T J, ex ft cond, W & A R R.

Boston, J H, ex ft cond, W & A R R.
Bessenger, A, carp, W & A R R shop.
Buchanan, J, blr mkr at Gullatt's Mach Shop.
Butler, R H, (Porter & B.)
Bleckley, L E, Atty, s s Alabama, b Pryor and Lloyd.
Bell, Marcus A, Atty, Granite Block, Broad St, b Marietta and R R.
Boyd & Walls, cor Peters and Forsyth.
W S Bradbury, painter, s s Hunter, w of Whitehall.
Chapman, W H, with E E Winn.
Cox, Huwald & Co., painters, s s Mitchell, e of Whitehall.
Connor, Geo C, (Sheldon & C.)
Chisolm, W P, broker, e s Whitehall near R R.
Connelly, Henry, with P Lynch.
Clayton, W H, So Ex Mess.
Culberson, J H, foreman Phœnix Planing Mill.
Culberson, A C, mach Phœnix Planing Mill.
Callaway, Joshua, mach Emp Planing Mill.
Church, Joseph, eng at Winship's Foundry.
Churchill, A R, mach at Atlanta Rolling Mill.
Crawford, M B, blk s, State shop.
Cunningham, W A, turner, State shop.
Crane, J E, carp, State shop.
Chandler, D B, carp, State shop.
Chapman, Henry, clk, W & A R R Depot.
Campbell, V M, checker, W & A R R Depot.
Clarke, Marshall J, Atty, s s Alabama, b Whitehall and Pryor.
Calhoun, J M & Son, Attys, s s Alabama, near Washington.
Cawhern & Co., e s Peachtree opp Luckie.
Crawford, Geo G, M D, w s Whitehall, near Mitchell.
Dewberry, W T, gro e s Whitehall, b Hunter and Mitchell.
Dobbins, M G & Co, Com brokers, cor Alabama and Whitehall.
Douglass, J M, turner, Phœnix Planing Mill.

Durden, A J, carp, Emp Steam Planing Mill.
Durden, G W, carp, Emp Steam Planing Mill.
Dewberry, Thos, mldr, at Winship's Foundry.
Dudley, Geo R, eng, at Atlanta Rolling Mill.
Dickson, Wm E, carp, State shop.
Donald, J, carp, State shop.
Dunn, I J, ex tt cond, W & A R R.
Dunn, Andrew, Sec'y Ga. Loom and Manuf. Co., e s
    Broad, next to P O; res corner Peachtree and Harris.
Daniel, James, mach, at Gullatt's Foundry.
Daniel, Jas E, clk, at Post Office.
Edwards, J L, carp, State shop.
Edwards, George, pat mkr, at Atlanta Rolling Mill.
Evans, B E, carp, State shop.
Evans, Wm H, mach, with Porter & Butler.
Eaton, Geo W, mldr, with Porter & Butler.
Ergenzinger, A, upholster and dealer in Furniture, n s
    Hunter, east of Whitehall.
Farrar, R M, Agt A & W P R R.
Franklin, Jas H, with E E Winn.
Freck & Eisenhut, boot mkrs, c s Whitehall, b Ala and
    R R.
Ferguson, L, with John Thomas.
Ferguson, D W, with Orme & Farrar.
Fleming, Richard, yd master Ga R R.
Flanders, James, eng, M & W R R.
Flynn, F W, cab mkr, Phœnix Planing Mill.
Frazer, C W, eng, W & A R R.
Ferrill, Sam, eng, at Winship's Foundry.
Fitts, J, blk s, State shop.
Fight, L, blk s, State shop.
Fifer, W H, mach, Ga R R shop.
Fouche, M, way ft cond, W & A R R.
Fuller, J W, bgge master, W & A R R.
Godfrey, J E, notions, e s Whitehall, b Ala and Hunter.
Gilbert, T, jeweler, s w c Ala and Whitehall.
Gilbert, J, phys, e s Whitehall, b Ala and R R

Glenn, Wright & Carr, gro and com mer, cor Forsyth St and W & A R R.

Glen, John C, trans clk Ga R R Depot.

Goodwin, Henry C, So Ex Mess.

Gentry, Sam, cond, M & W R R.

Gammage, T M, eng, W & A R R.

Gramling, J H, eng, W & A R R.

Gideon, John W, carp, Emp Steam Planing Mill.

Gramling, W E, turner, State shop.

Gray, R L, ptr, State shop.

Golden, Frank, checker, W & A R R Depot.

Garrett, Thos W, day pass cond, W & A R R.

Garrett, S, mach, W & R R shop.

Grady, Thos, mach, W & A R R shop.

Gartrell & Jackson, Attys, w s Whitehall b R R and Alabama.

Granberry & Pease, Restaurant, s s Alabama near Whitehall.

Hightower, T J, (Ford & H.)

Huwald, G A, (Cox, H & Co.)

Hill & Candler, Attys, e s Whitehall, b Ala and R R.

Harris, J R, M D, w s Whitehall, b Ala and Hunter.

Howell, A & Co, cor Whitehall and Marietta.

Howell, Clarke, clk, with A H & Co.

Hoyle, Wm E, trans clk, Ga R R Depot.

Hancock, John G, eng, M & W R R.

Henderson, A A, tel opr, M & W R R Depot.

Husketh, David, eng, M & W R R.

Harris, B, carp, State shop.

Hill, J A, carp, State shop.

Henderson, B, carp, State shop.

Harris, J H, carp, State shop.

Hudson, W J, eng, Ga R R shop.

Holland, M B, carp, W & A R R shop.

Hunnicutt & Buice, gro, e s Peachtree opp Walton.

Irby, D J, carp State shop.

Jones, T M, bdg h, w s Whitehall, b Ala and R R.

Johnson, M A, with Johnson & Echols.

Johnson, C W, So Ex Mess.
Johnson, W A, eng, W & A R R.
Jones, G L, M D, n w c Line and Ivy.
Knott, Dr E F, Drug, w s Whitehall, b Mitchell and
Peters.
Kilby, W J, tailor, with Herring & Leyden.
Kirby, Timothy, with Peter Lynch.
Kicklighter, Spencer C, with A K Seago.
Knight, James, eng, M & W R R.
Kile, C, eng, W & A R R.
Killen, N P, mach, W & A R R shop.
Kicklighter, Chas J, clk, with A K Seago.
Lowe & Stanton, successors to B T L & Co.
Lichtenstadt, M, sewing machines, e s Whitehall, b Ala
and Hunter.
Laws, E R, com and pawn broker, e of Whitehall St.
fronting R R.
Lester, B D, seedsman, at Johnson & Echols' store.
Lyons, J L, turner, Emp Steam Planing Mill.
Logan, Samuel, ptr, State shop.
Milledge, John, Jr, Atty, s s Ala, b Whitehall and Pryor.
McPherson, A P & Co, boot mkrs, w s Broad, n of R R.
Mitchell, E S, clk, at Southern Ex Office.
Mitchell, I S, with I G M.
Mitchell, Dr W D, w s Walker, near Peters.
McNabb, David, eng, Phœnix Planing Mills.
McGuire, John, carp, Phœnix Planing Mills.
Morris, T A, eng, W & A R R; res s e c King and Ga
R R.
Martin, Thos, eng, W & A R R.
Marsh, John, eng, W & A R R.
Manning, A A, clk, at Post-Office.
McAllister, G C, turner, State shop.
Milligan, P H, carp, State shop.
Martin, Silas, eng on A & W P R R.
Morse, L E, way ft cond, W & A R R.
Moore, J C ex ft cond, W & A R R.
Moreton, F. mach, W & A R R shop.

McClellan, Wm, pat mkr, W & R R shop.
Mell, E S, clk, W & A R R Car Factory.
Middleton, G, mach, at Gullatt s Foundry.
Municipal Government—Re-organization :

ALDERMEN.

1st Ward.—W T Castleberry, *Richard Peters.
2d Ward.—*E E Rawson, A W Mitchell.
3d Ward.—Geo W Terry, W C Anderson.
4th Ward.—J E Gullatt, W B Cox.
5th Ward.—*J A Hayden, A P Bell.

* *Elected February* 19.

STANDING COMMITTEES.

On Finance.—Peters, Mitchell, and Bell.
On Ordinances.—Mitchell, Hayden, Peters.
On Streets and Side-Walks.—Gullatt, Rawson, Hayden.
Wells, Pumps, and Cisterns.—Cox, Anderson, Castleberry.
Lamps and Gas.—Hayden, Terry, Peters.
Relief.—Rawson, Castleberry, Terry, Gullatt, Bell.
On Market.—Hayden, Gullatt, Castleberry.
On Fire Dept.—Bell, Gullatt, Cox.
On Police.—Rawson, Cox, Anderson.
On Cemetery.—Terry, Mitchell, Rawson.
On Public Buildings and Grounds.—Anderson, Terry, Peters.
On Tax.—Mitchell, Bell, Cox.
On Salaries.—Cox, Mitchell, Rawson.

OTHER CORRECTIONS.

E Hall, pol, instead of Jas. Campbell.
J A Hinton, policeman.
Woodliff, (A P) pol, should read O P Woodliff.
Roach, (R J) City Phys, should read E J Roach.

The above embodies all the changes from the original organization, published on pages 53, 54. and 55, up to March 10th.

Nelson, J M, fam gro, n s Mitchell, b Whitehall and For-
   syth.
Neely, C R, carp, Phœnix Planing Mill.
O'Keefe, D C, M D, e s Whitehall, near Hunter.
Owings, J D, clk, with Herring & Leyden.
Orr, John, eng, M & W R R.
Pegg, S G & Co, n s Mitchell, b Broad and Forsyth.
Paoliello G, conf, e s Whitehall, b Ala and Hunter.
Parr, J S & C W, painters, Phœnix Planing Mill.
Pate, Jas A, yd master, W & A R R.
Pearsall, A, blr makr, W & A R R shop.
Porter & Butler, proprietors Atlanta Machine Works,
   s w c King and Ga R R.
Porter, Jas H, (P & Butler.)
Price, Dr J W, pro Bellevue Hotel.
Pangle, H L, gro, s s Marietta, near Whitehall.
Quigley, Anoch, blr mkr, Ga R R shop.
Rutledge, Joseph I, Scalesman, Ga R R Depot.
Rusk, Wm, eng, M & W R R.
Renard, J F, eng, W & A R R.
Reid, Thos, blk s, at Winship's Foundry.
Robert, A J & Co, gro cor Broad St. and M & W R R.
Smith, Levi J, clk, with Ford & Hightower.
Salbide, M, with B Garcia.
Sells, Dr. H, Prest Ga Loom and Manufacturing Co, e s
   Broad, next P O.
Stewart, J A B, mon clk, So Ex Office.
Smith, Jesse, mon del clk, So Ex Co.
Slater, John J, So Ex Mess.
Stark, Jas H, So Ex Mess.
Shields, Robert, (Cox, Huwald & Co.)
Sparks, L, cab mkr, Phœnix Planing Mills.
Smith, M W, clk, Post Office.
Smith, Frank, pat mkr, at Atlanta Rolling Mill.
Schenck, E E, mach, Ga R R shop.
Shearer, W C, boiler mkr, Ga R R shop.
Strong, B R, receiving clk, W & A R R.
Shumate, A V W P, watchman, at Porter & Butler's.

Standard, Geo, mldr, with Porter & Butler.

Trimble, P M, gro, n w c Whitehall and Mitchell.

"The Daily Opinion," Granite Block, west s Broad St, n of R R ; W L Scruggs, editor and proprietor.

TALLULAH FIRE COMPANY, No. 3—

OFFICERS ELECTED FEBRUARY 22, 1867.

S W Grubb, Prest; E A Center, Vice Prest; W C Shearer, 1st Director; Geo Thompson, 2d Director; J J Rogers, Hose Director; John D Clarke, Sec'y; L H Clarke, Treas; John A Hill and A Thieme, Axemen ; W R Biggers, Del Fire Dept ; H S Orme, M D, Surgeon.

"The Ladies' Home," w s Broad, n of R R bridge; John S Prather editor and proprietor.

Tyler, C, eng, W & A R R Car Factory.

Thompson, B W, carp, State shop.

Tomlinson, H, Dalton ft cond, W & A R R.

Thompson, J R, switch cond, W & A R R.

Van Goidsnoven, E, conf and nurseryman, w s Whitehall, b Ala and Hunter.

Van Epps, Geo C, So Ex Mess.

Verdery, George, cond on Ga R R.

Watkins, J C, fam gro, Decatur St, opp A & W P R R.

Walker, Mathew T, Drug, with A Howell & Co.

Walker, James, So Ex Mess.

Welborn, C R, carp, Phœnix Planing Mill.

Waters, J C, turner, State shop.

Wallace, C B, Gen'l Agt W & A R R.

Webster, W R, chf clk pass dept, W & A R R.

Wilson, Hugh, mldr, at Gullatt's Foundry.

Wilson, Jas T, mldr, with Porter & Butler.

West, T W, Agt, soda water, w s Lloyd, b Alabama and Hunter.